Y0-EAE-088

The Christian Case for Virtue Ethics

Moral Traditions & Moral Arguments
A SERIES EDITED BY JAMES F. KEENAN, S.J.

The Evolution of Altruism and the Ordering of Love
  STEPHEN J. POPE

Love, Human and Divine: The Heart of Christian Ethics
  EDWARD COLLINS VACEK, S.J.

Bridging the Sacred and the Secular:
Selected Writings of John Courtney Murray, S.J.
  J. LEON HOOPER, S.J., editor

The Context of Casuistry
  Edited by
  JAMES F. KEENAN, S.J. and THOMAS A. SHANNON

Aquinas and Empowerment:
Classical Ethics for Ordinary Lives
  Edited by
  G. SIMON HARAK, S.J.

The Christian Case for Virtue Ethics

Joseph J. Kotva, Jr.

Georgetown University Press / Washington, D.C.

Georgetown University Press, Washington, D.C.
© 1996 by Georgetown University Press. All rights reserved.
Printed in the United States of America

10   9   8   7   6   5   4   3   2   1   1996

THIS VOLUME IS PRINTED ON ACID-FREE OFFSET BOOK PAPER

Library of Congress Cataloging-in-Publication Data

Kotva, Joseph J.
    The Christian case for virtue ethics / Joseph J. Kotva, Jr.
      p.   cm.—(Moral traditions & moral arguments)
    Includes bibliographical references and index.
    1. Christian ethics. 2. Virtue. 3. Virtues. 4. Ethics.
  I. Title. II. Series.
BJ1231.K67 1996
241'.4—dc20   96-11856
ISBN 0-87840-620-4

For my parents,
Joseph and Marjorie Kotva

Contents

Acknowledgments ix

Introduction: Christian Morality and Virtue Ethics 1
    NOTES 3

1
The Return to Virtue Ethics 5
    A SOCIETY IN CRISIS 6
    THE RISE OF HISTORICAL CONSCIOUSNESS 8
    THE INCOMPLETENESS OF MODERN THEORIES 10
    SUMMARY 12
    NOTES 13

2
What Is Virtue Ethics 16
    A TELEOLOGICAL ETHIC 17
    NATURE OF THE VIRTUES 23
    HUMAN AGENCY AND MORAL EDUCATION 26
    MORAL LUCK 29
    THE PRIORITY OF BEING 30
    DISCERNMENT AND THE PLACE OF RULES AND
       CONSEQUENCES 31
    A KIND OF PERFECTIONISM 37
    SUMMARY 38
    NOTES 39

3
Needed: A Christian Case for Virtue Ethics 48
    ON NOT RECOGNIZING THE NEED 50
    JUSTIFICATIONS FOR NEGLECT 51
    EPISTEMOLOGICAL ISSUES AND TRUTH CLAIMS 57

TOWARD AN ECUMENICAL CHRISTIAN VIRTUE ETHIC 59
NOTES 61

4
Theological Links 69

SANCTIFICATION AND PERSONAL ESCHATOLOGY 71
CHRISTOLOGY 78
CHRISTIAN ANTHROPOLOGY 90
CONCLUSION 93
NOTES 93

5
Biblical Connections 103

THE GOSPEL OF MATTHEW 104
THE LETTERS OF PAUL 119
CONCLUSION 130
NOTES 134

6
Theological and Biblical Objections 143

NARCISSISM 143
ARISTOCRATIC TENDENCIES 147
SECTARIAN 151
OTHER ETHICAL THEORIES 155
CONCLUSION 159
NOTES 159

7
Conclusion: An Appeal for a Christian Virtue Ethic 167

ADDITIONAL BENEFITS OF VIRTUE THEORY 170
CONCLUSION 176
NOTES 176

Index 179

Acknowledgments

Someone recently suggested to me that the scholarly life is a solitary life. I have not found this to be true. Indeed, had it not been for many colleagues and good friends, this book would not exist.

To James F. Keenan I owe much, including this book's genesis. It was Keenan who, in 1989, saw the potential for this project in a paper I wrote for a class in virtue theory. During my years as a student at Fordham University, Keenan was a better mentor than I could justifiably have hoped for. I continue to benefit from his keen scholarly eye and, even more, from his friendship.

I am also deeply grateful to Richard J. Dillon and Richard R. Viladesau, whose extensive comments on my Ph.D. dissertation have made this a better book; and to Richard M. Gula, who helped me see how the work might be restructured in moving it from a dissertation to a book. Likewise, the people at Georgetown University Press, especially the director, John Samples, have made the production of this book an almost painless process.

My good friend Mary Jo Iozzio deserves special mention. She has frequently listened patiently on the phone while I read long sections of the book with which I was struggling. Her ability to offer constructive comments at such times continues to amaze me. Dr. Iozzio also read drafts of several chapters. Her suggestions, both substantive and editorial, were invaluable.

A portion of chapter six is a shortened and reworked form of "Christian Virtue Ethics and the 'Sectarian Temptation'," *Heythrop Journal* 35(1) (1994): 35–52. I thank Blackwell Publishers for kindly permitting the use of that material here.

Another kind of debt is owed my congregation, the First Mennonite Church, Allentown, Pennsylvania. The idea of a scholar-pastor is rare in the Mennonite church. Yet this congregation has granted its pastor the freedom and space to pursue his academic interests, assuming, of course, that his research will serve the larger church. I hope and pray that their assumption is correct.

Finally, the deepest debt and the greatest gratitude are owed my family. My parents and sister have always loved and supported me. It is they who taught me to love God, to serve the church, and to seek the truth. My wife, Carol, has contributed to this book in several ways: tolerating the demands of my vocation, reading innumerable drafts of each chapter, and providing living proof of the virtues of generosity, hospitality, compassion, and charity. Our sons, Joseph and Matthew, continually remind me that playing with them is, in the scheme of eternity, more important than writing books. They fill my life with moments of such joy, they must be right about play.

*The Christian Case for
Virtue Ethics*

Introduction:
Christian Morality and Virtue Ethics

St. Thomas Aquinas does not play a direct or major role in this book. Yet, a plausible summary of the book's argument is that Thomas was right all along: Aristotle's ethics are notably well-suited to the Christian moral life. Without sacrificing what is fundamental to the Christian tradition, Thomas ingeniously merged Christian theology and Scripture with Aristotle's ethics.[1] Although St. Thomas was not right in every detail, his basic intuition that Christian moral reflection profits from the adaptation of an Aristotelian framework was correct. Thus, while Thomas is seldom mentioned, this book can be reasonably described as arguing for the resumption of Thomas's basic project.

This book is also an entry into the current debate about the merits of virtue theory. I will argue for the Christian adoption of a neo-Aristotelian virtue framework by showing that it is compatible with, readily amended to, and useful in expressing Christian convictions and modes of moral reasoning. I will contend that, when evaluated in light of Christian theology and Scripture, virtue theory emerges as a particularly promising way of understanding the moral life.

Some will view this contention as an unremarkable thesis. After all, several eminent Christian moral theologians, both Protestant and Roman Catholic, are reclaiming a virtue framework for Christian ethics—for example, Stanley Hauerwas, L. Gregory Jones, James F. Keenan, Gilbert Meilaender, Jean Porter, and Paul Wadell.[2] Why then do we need yet another book extolling the merits of virtue theory?

Despite a significant return over the last two decades by philosophers and theologians to theories of virtue, surprisingly little has been said about why Christians in particular should adopt a virtue framework. Proponents of virtue theory have done little to suggest why Christians as Christians might find the theory attractive. Are there reasons for supposing that Christians have a stake in virtue ethics? Is virtue theory compatible with a thoroughly Christian morality? Are nonvirtue theories as good as virtue theory at giving expression to

Christian moral insight? Theologians advocating virtue theory have generally failed to answer such questions. They have failed to provide an explicitly Christian case for virtue ethics.

In this book, I hope to rectify that failure by arguing that virtue theory offers an ethical framework notably well-suited to Christian convictions. I show that virtue theory is both compatible with and helpful in giving voice to Christian convictions about how we are to live the moral life. I argue, more specifically, that the ethical theory emerging in certain camps of neo-Aristotelian philosophy (e.g., in Alasdair MacIntyre, Martha C. Nussbaum, Nancy Sherman) promises an especially fitting framework for expressing the rich and textured moral vision that arises from Christian systematic theology and Scripture.[3]

The argument develops in seven chapters that are ecumenical Christian throughout. Chapter 1 reviews some cultural, historical, and philosophical developments that have led theologians and philosophers to a renewed interest in virtue theory. Virtue theory's basic elements and structure are then outlined in chapter 2. Because authors often differ in what they mean by "virtue ethics," chapter 2 also sketches the basic contours of virtue theory as I see it emerging among some neo-Aristotelian moral philosophers. The result is a teleological virtue ethic focused on the movement from who we are to who we can be.

Chapter 3 develops the need for a specifically Christian case for virtue ethics and explores the current lack of literature on why Christian ethics should be virtue ethics. It argues that we should not merely presume a fit between virtue theory and Christian convictions. Rather, we should demonstrate virtue theory's suitability to the Christian life.

The fourth chapter critically correlates virtue theory with contemporary Protestant and Roman Catholic theology. This correlation highlights potential links and parallels between virtue ethics and Christian systematic theology, focusing on basic features of sanctification, Christology, and theological anthropology. Thus, for instance, both sanctification and virtue theory stress lifelong, goal-oriented moral growth and the transformation of character.

Chapter 5 continues the process of critical correlation but shifts the focus from systematic theology to the New Testament. Matthew's gospel and the Pauline letters suggest numerous possible connections with virtue ethics; things like their concern with dispositions and attitudes, Matthew's use of rules, and Paul's language of moral discernment find striking parallels in virtue theory.

Chapters 4 and 5 also contend that a virtue framework is readily adapted to Christian convictions even when obvious parallels with virtue theory are missing. That virtue theory is easily altered to be fully Christian and can give fitting expression to Christian convictions about grace, forgiveness, life after death, and the centrality of Jesus, is apparent in chapter 4's discussion of Christology, for example. Jesus' normative humanity is not only compatible with, but is better expressed in a teleological virtue ethic than in other ethical theories.

Chapter 6 addresses several common criticisms of a Christian virtue ethic that result from misreading virtue theory. The chapter also argues that current nonvirtue theories are ill-suited to the variety and complexity of Christian convictions. While the objections to virtue ethics can be answered, nonvirtue accounts are inadequate for the rich moral vision suggested by theology and Scripture.

Chapter 7 provides the book's summary statement. It draws together the preceding chapters' arguments and claims that virtue theory and Christian convictions are complementary. On the one hand, Christian ethical reflection benefits from virtue theory's multifaceted account of the moral life and its exploration of themes not treated in Scripture or theology. On the other hand, Christian theology and Scripture offer vital resources for correcting, refining, and developing a virtue framework.

There is, I believe, a strong case for the Christian appropriation of a virtue framework. The following chapters begin to make that case. Over the course of those chapters, the reader will be persuaded, I hope, that Christian moral reflection benefits from a virtue framework. Since this book links virtue theory to Christian theology and Scripture, its chapters should also furnish a sense of what an explicitly Christian virtue ethic would look like.

NOTES

1. Preeminently in the *Summa Theologiae, Secunda Pars*.
2. See Stanley Hauerwas, *A Community of Character: Toward a Constructive Christian Social Ethic* (Notre Dame: University of Notre Dame Press, 1981); L. Gregory Jones, *Transformed Judgment: Toward a Trinitarian Account of the Moral Life* (Notre Dame: University of Notre Dame Press, 1990); James F. Keenan, *Goodness and Rightness in Thomas Aquinas's Summa Theologiae* (Washington, D.C.: Georgetown University Press, 1992); Gilbert C. Meilaender, *The Theory and Practice of Virtue* (Notre Dame: University of Notre Dame Press, 1984); Jean Porter, *The Recovery of Virtue: The Relevance of Aquinas for Christian Ethics* (Louisville: Westminster/John Knox Press, 1990); Paul J. Wadell, *Friendship and the Moral Life* (Notre Dame: University of Notre Dame Press, 1989).

3. See Alasdair MacIntyre, *After Virtue,* 2nd ed. (Notre Dame: University of Notre Dame Press, 1984); Martha C. Nussbaum, *The Fragility of Goodness: Luck and Ethics in Greek Tragedy and Philosophy* (Cambridge: Cambridge University Press, 1986); Nancy Sherman, *The Fabric of Character: Aristotle's Theory of Virtue* (Oxford: Clarendon Press, 1989).

1

The Return to Virtue Ethics

Today's resurgence of interest in virtue and character can hardly go unnoticed. Calls for a return to virtue are coming from many directions and range from careful philosophical treatments to best-selling books.[1] Indeed, the return to "virtue" has even made the cover of *Newsweek*.[2]

As recently as the early 1980s, theories of virtue occupied only a few Anglo-American moral theologians and philosophers. That has changed. The number of books on virtue ethics is growing rapidly and professional journals increasingly publish articles written from a virtue perspective. Although it is difficult to know how much of this output is simply the latest fad in ethical theory, "virtue" does now occupy a significant (if still minority) place on the academic landscape.[3]

But what is virtue ethics? And why this renewed interest in theories of virtue? Chapter 2 will outline the basic elements and structure of the kind of neo-Aristotelian virtue theory that I think Christians should adopt.[4] We can generalize here, however, and say that virtue ethics involves a shift in the focal point of ethical reflection.

Since the eighteenth century, ethical theory has usually focused on rules, principles, goods, and step-by-step decision making procedures for resolving moral quandaries. Modern ethical theory has thus concentrated on developing rules, principles, and exact methods for determining the moral status of specific acts. In contrast, virtue ethics is more agent-centered and less concerned with the analysis of problematic actions. Virtue ethics moves the focus away from specific acts to "background" issues such as character traits, personal commitments, community traditions, and the conditions necessary for human excellence and flourishing. Virtue ethics thus involves a radical shift in the focus of ethical reflection.[5]

It is easier to point to this shift than to explain the renewed interest in virtue ethics, which comes from several directions and reflects various concerns. Although I can only offer rough generalizations, identifying some of these concerns may clarify what is "new" and promising in the very old approach of virtue ethics. Three factors in particular have helped renew interest in virtue ethics: (1) the widespread perception that our society is in moral crisis, (2) the rise of historical consciousness, and (3) the failure of modern ethical theories to provide a complete picture of human moral experience.

A SOCIETY IN CRISIS

One factor encouraging a return to virtue ethics, or at least to the rhetoric of virtue, is the widespread perception that our society is in moral crisis. Many people view contemporary Western society as verging on moral bankruptcy and view our institutions as failing to inculcate good character. A recent *Newsweek* poll, for example, found that 76 percent of adult Americans think that "the United States is in a moral and spiritual decline."[6] That sense of moral decline is frequently echoed at PTA meetings, on op-ed pages and daily radio programs, and in Sunday school classes. That sense also stands behind calls for school prayer, character education, stronger criminal punishment, and the regulation of television violence.

Although these concerns and debates do not reflect full-blown or coherent theories of virtue, the current concern about the Western world's moral decline is often phrased in virtue terms and frequently invites virtue reasoning. Consider, for example, current speeches about the breakdown of the "traditional" family and violence on television. Some debates about the family tacitly recognize that children are less likely to become healthy, well-balanced moral agents if they lack loving parental guidance and appropriate role models. Similarly, concerns about television stem in part from the recognition that people emulate their heroes and that television's heroes are too often violent, even vicious.

These concerns about family and television find direct parallels in virtue ethics. Aristotelian virtue theory denies that virtuous character can be taught from a book or be quickly acquired. Instead, we learn the virtues through practice and in the company of others. We learn the virtues by imitating worthy role models, listening to the advice of virtuous friends and teachers, hearing the stories of virtuous people, and following rules of virtuous behavior.[7] Thus, concerns about family and television are directly related to virtue ethics—both recognize that worthy companions and role models are vital to the development of virtuous character.

The point here is that concern about society's moral impoverishment can occasion, even invite, comparison with and renewed interest in virtue ethics. The kinds of issues raised in debates about family, television, and education, find important connections in virtue ethics. Indeed, theories of virtue help us understand why these issues are so important. When we shift our attention from isolated acts to agents and their contexts, we begin to realize the moral significance of worthy companions and role models. We similarly begin to understand that violent television programming may not be innocuous after all.[8]

This movement from concern over society's moral bankruptcy to renewed interest in virtue ethics is not limited to its haphazard appearance in public discourse. The return to virtue ethics among theologians and philosophers seems to be explained in part by the perceived moral disorder of contemporary society.

Derek Phillips, for example, suggests that our age has made being "authentic" and "in touch with one's feelings" the ideal. But such an ideal is socially intolerable. We cannot accept or sustain a society in which many people are "authentic" and thus free to give themselves over to undisciplined urges and felt needs. If we are to secure a decent society, we need a population that internalizes moral principles and develops various virtues. In other words, a good society depends on a virtuous citizenry. Lacking such a citizenry, "life will become more and more like a jungle and the barbarians in our midst will devour the rest of us."[9]

The moral bankruptcy of modern Western civilization also provides the starting point for Alasdair MacIntyre's *After Virtue*. The force of MacIntyre's argument depends largely on his opening contention that we are in trouble—in particular, that public moral debate has been reduced to mere rhetoric and that our moral paradigms (the persons we aspire to emulate) are all manipulators of other persons.[10] MacIntyre's indictment of Western moral consciousness thus sets the stage for his invitation to reconsider the Aristotelian tradition of the virtues. MacIntyre sees virtue ethics as providing a very attractive alternative to contemporary moral disorder.[11]

But why virtue ethics? Even if one agrees with MacIntyre's indictment of contemporary morality, why not reassert some form of Kantian or utilitarian moral philosophy? The short answer is that MacIntyre views contemporary moral disorder as providing strong evidence of the failure of modern ethical theory. Indeed, MacIntyre not only claims that modern ethical theories have failed as remedies to our moral crises, he also contends that those theories are intertwined with the social and intellectual transformations that led to the current situation. In other words, modern ethical theories are part of the problem, not the solution.

In short, the common perception that we are involved in a widespread moral crisis is encouraging a return to virtue ethics. Some, like Phillips, begin to move toward virtue considerations as a corrective to current social ideals. Others, like MacIntyre, see our current situation as proof of the failure of modern ethical theories. In both cases, the Aristotelian virtue tradition is seen as offering the most promising way out of this predicament.[12]

THE RISE OF HISTORICAL CONSCIOUSNESS

Another factor helping to renew interest in virtue ethics is the growth in the second half of the twentieth century of what might loosely be called "historical consciousness."[13] Moral theologians and philosophers have increasingly recognized the relevance of our historical nature. We are historical creatures, situated in specific historical and cultural contexts with particular beliefs, practices, and commitments. All knowledge, including moral knowledge, is historically grounded and at some level informed by the setting from within which it is known.

The growing realization of history's relevance is altering ethical theory in at least two general ways: (1) limiting the role and status of rules, and (2) increasing the attention given to one's context. First, history's relevance challenges the status of moral rules. It is now almost impossible to view moral rules as purely objective and unchanging. Indeed, we can show that many norms and rules reflect development and the influence of the historical contexts in which they were formulated. Thus, for example, Catholic rules governing contraception and Mennonite norms concerning head coverings have undergone considerable change. Similarly, general Christian prohibitions against usury have been so altered that many church institutions now apply for and grant loans with interest.[14]

Historical consciousness has thus pushed ethical theory to rethink and qualify the place of norms and rules. Ethics can no longer simply elaborate lists of rules; instead it must also discuss their relative value and the historical situations in which they are applicable.

This thought brings us to a second, related consequence of historical consciousness: current ethical theory must pay considerable attention to the historically particular situation. The more aware we become of the fluid and changing nature of history, the more our moral judgments must attend to the details of the concrete situation. If nature and society are basically unchanging, then general principles are fine and we simply do whatever those before us did. But if nature and society change and develop, then we must attend to contextual variety and situational specificity. In other words, an awareness of history forces attention on the details and specific features of the situations in which moral decisions are made. The continuities of human life are no doubt important, but historical consciousness pushes ethical theory to acknowledge the potential uniqueness of each moment.

Christian ethics has an assortment of responses to the rise of historical consciousness. Various forms of "situational ethics," "proportionalism," and "liberation theology" arose in part as answers to historical consciousness.[15] Each of these approaches declines to view ethics as the deductive application of objective, unchanging moral rules. Each insists on contextual specificity and an openness to every situation's potential uniqueness. Each tries to take historical alteration and change seriously.

These same concerns are now prompting some moralists and theologians to reexplore virtue ethics.[16] Virtue ethics moves the focus from rules and acts to agents and their contexts. This move fits well with a concern for the dynamics of history. A focus on agents and their settings readily acknowledges our need to respond to each situation's specific features. In fact, most virtue accounts talk about a central virtue or perceptive capacity (usually called prudence or practical wisdom) for recognizing the distinctive features of each situation.

Theories of virtue are also open to the dynamics of history in other ways. For instance, virtue theories generally view us as developing character traits or virtues over time and within specific social contexts. The acquisition of virtue is thus a temporal or historical reality. Moreover, most virtue theories contend that it is precisely in the acquisition of certain virtues that we gain the skills necessary for dealing well with historically changing circumstances. In other words, we need certain virtues because situations and contexts change. Virtues such as courage, honesty, and prudence strengthen and direct us in those changing contexts. Virtue ethics is thus about the temporal acquisition of "the virtues necessary to transverse the dangers and opportunities of our existence—dangers and opportunities that are intrinsic to the timeful character of our existence."[17]

Theories of virtue provide a promising avenue for taking historical change and development seriously. Virtue ethics reduces the role of rules and recognizes the potentially distinctive features of each situation. Yet virtue ethics also recognizes that we need to develop certain enduring character traits if we are to deal well with the historical nature of our existence.[18]

THE INCOMPLETENESS OF MODERN THEORIES

A third factor encouraging a return to virtue ethics is the incomplete or partial picture of moral experience in most modern ethical theories. An increasing number of authors, especially those engaged in feminist ethics, view modern ethical theories as ignoring important aspects of human moral experience. These authors point, for example, to modern theories' slight attention to friendships and emotions.[19]

The problem with this inattention is twofold. First, our understanding of human morality is distorted by the neglect of central human realities like friendship and emotion. When these and other important features of human existence are ignored, the resulting ethical theories offer only impoverished pictures of the moral life. Such theories are also deceptive because they imply that moral decision makers can safely ignore these features of human experience. Even if such theories are basically correct, they are also somewhat misleading in what they fail to say.

Second, modern ethical theories not only neglect things like friendship and emotion, these theories are in some respects incompatible with and undermine those realities. For example, when modern theories focus on rational action, the affective side of life is viewed as misleading and dangerous or at least subordinate to rationally calculated action. Yet there is something terribly wrong with this view. Passions are praise or blameworthy. It is right to rejoice at a friend's success and wrong to be unmoved by the plight of others. Our emotions display the kind of people we have become, and our desires help determine our actions. There is, in other words, something very wrong with theories that devalue emotion.

Similarly, imagine what would happen to friendship should we follow the common deontological recommendation to always act from a sense of duty. Michael Stocker's simple illustration shows the inadequacy of such an approach:

> Suppose you are in a hospital, recovering from a long illness. You are very bored ... and at loose ends when Smith comes in once

again. You are now convinced more than ever that he is a fine fellow and a real friend—taking so much time to cheer you up, traveling all the way across town, and so on. You are so effusive with your praise and thanks that he protests that he always tries to do what he thinks is his duty, what he thinks will be best. You at first think he is engaging in a polite form of self-deprecation. ... But the more you two speak, the more clear it becomes that he is telling the literal truth: that it is not essentially because of you that he came to see you, not because you are friends, but because he thought it his duty.[20]

We must, I think, agree with Stocker that something is lacking here. What is lacking is commitment to the specific person. Friendship requires that the other person—with his or her particular needs, wants, commitments, experiences and idiosyncrasies—be an essential part of what is valued. My visiting you because I prize what you bring to our friendship and am concerned about your well-being is very different from my visiting you solely out of a sense of duty. Life without the former would be life without true friendship; yet modern ethical theories commend only the latter.

The point here is that modern ethical theories tend to ignore and even undermine important human realities like close friendships and powerful emotions. I suggest that the return to virtue ethics stems in part from growing frustration with this inadequate treatment of central human realities. In contrast to modern theories, virtue ethics seems to offer a fuller, more comprehensive picture of the moral life.

Most virtue theories stress, for example, the mutual moral tutoring that takes place between good friends. Friends provide a kind of moral mirror of shared values and commitments. It is also among friends that we are most likely to expose our judgments to others and to open ourselves to another's moral perspectives and experiences. Many virtue theories also claim that a good or happy life, the kind of life toward which we aim, is one that includes friendship. That is, virtue ethics views friendship as not only important for moral growth but also as part of what makes life worth living.[21]

Virtue ethics provides a similarly rich understanding of the moral significance of emotions and desires. Certain virtues like courage and compassion necessarily include affective dimensions. Emotions are also important because they reflect the kind of character we have developed. It is a good sign if we are angered when someone is raped and a bad sign if we do not care. Such emotional responses tell a lot about the kind of people we have become. Our emotions and desires are also important because they help determine what actions we pursue and which we avoid. Put most simply, since we often pursue what we desire, the content of our desires is terribly important. Virtue ethics thus sees emotions and desires as ethically central: emotions are intrinsic to certain virtues, and, combined with desires, they witness to the quality of one's character and help direct one's actions.[22]

The return to virtue ethics is partly explained as a reaction to theories that neglect central aspects of human moral experience. As the examples of friendship and emotion suggest, virtue ethics offers a fuller, more comprehensive picture of the moral life.[23] John Mahoney argues that the last twenty years of moral theology offer "so many manifestations of what may be considered a reaction against overfragmentation of the human moral enterprise in the past and, more positively, a drive towards totality."[24] What Mahoney says generally of moral theology is, I suggest, especially true of the return to virtue ethics.[25]

SUMMARY

Calls for a return to virtue are coming from many sides, and increasing numbers of moral theologians and philosophers are working from virtue perspectives.

This fresh attention to virtue involves a shift in focus. Instead of concentrating on principles and problematic actions, virtue ethics focuses on agents and their contexts. Instead of beginning with exacting procedures for decision making, virtue ethics starts by discussing character traits, personal commitments, community traditions, and so on.

Some explanation for this shift in focus is found in the general sense that our society is in moral crisis. The debates about this crisis often invite virtue considerations and some authors are turning to virtue ethics as the prescription for our society's perceived moral ills. Another catalyst for this return to virtue ethics is the rise of historical consciousness. Theories of virtue recognize historical change and development and recognize that each situation is potentially distinct. Yet virtue theories also realize that we become equipped to deal with historical change only by developing certain enduring character traits.

A third factor encouraging a turn to virtue ethics is the growing frustration with modern theories' inattention to various aspects of human experience. Virtually all advocates of virtue ethics view their enterprise as providing a more comprehensive or multidimensional understanding of human morality. Of course, none of these comments prove that the turn to virtue points us in the right direction. What they do suggest is that virtue ethics is a "hot" or timely topic with much promise.

NOTES

1. Alasdair MacIntyre's *After Virtue*, 2nd ed. (Notre Dame: University of Notre Dame Press, 1984) is probably the most widely read philosophical text of the last decade. By comparison, William J. Bennett's best seller, *The Book of Virtues: A Treasury of Great Moral Stories* (New York: Simon and Schuster, 1993), is much less philosophically rigorous and envisions a more general readership.

2. "The Politics of Virtue: The Crusade Against America's Moral Decline," *Newsweek*, June 13, 1994.

3. Gregory Trianosky, "What Is Virtue Ethics all About?" *American Philosophical Quarterly* 27 (October 1990): 335, 343–44; Lee H. Yearley, "Recent Work on Virtue," *Religious Studies Review* 16 (January 1990): 1, 8–9; Robert B. Kruschwitz and Robert C. Roberts, eds., *The Virtues: Contemporary Essays on Moral Character* (Belmont: Wadsworth, 1987), pp. 2–3, 17, 237–63.

4. "Neo-Aristotelian" is shorthand to refer to a broadly identifiable approach within contemporary moral philosophy. The reference is not meant to imply an exclusive focus on Aristotle but to suggest a style of ethics that receives its inspiration and direction from renewed attention to those who, like Aristotle and Thomas Aquinas, see virtues and vices as the heart of the moral life.

5. James F. Keenan, "Virtue Ethics: Making a Case as It Comes of Age," *Thought* 67 (June 1992): 116, and "Theological Trends: Christian Ethics: The Last Ten Years," *The Way* 32 (1992): 219; Robert B. Louden, "Virtue Ethics and Anti-Theory," *Philosophia* (July 1990): 94–97, 103–4; William Spohn, "The Return of Virtue Ethics," *Theological Studies* 53 (March 1992): 60–61; Kruschwitz and Roberts, *The Virtues*, p. 22; Rose Mary Volbrect, "Friendship: Mutual Apprenticeship in Moral Development," *Journal of Value Inquiry* 24 (October 1990): 301–2.

6. For this and what follows, see Howard Fineman, "The Virtuecrats," *Newsweek*, June 13, 1994, pp. 31–36; and Kenneth L. Woodward, "What Is Virtue?" ibid., pp. 38–39.

7. For example, Alasdair MacIntyre, *Three Rival Versions of Moral Enquiry: Encyclopaedia, Genealogy, and Tradition* (Notre Dame: University of Notre Dame Press, 1990), pp. 60–66; Julius M. Moravcsik, "The Role of Virtue in Alternatives to Kantian and Utilitarian Ethics," *Philosophia* (July 1990): 37; Martha C. Nussbaum, *The Fragility of Goodness: Luck and Ethics in Greek Tragedy and*

Philosophy (Cambridge: Cambridge University Press, 1986), pp. 248–50, 345–49; Volbrect, "Friendship," pp. 308–10.

8. "NAEYC Position Statement on Media Violence in Children's Lives," (Adopted April 1990) *Young Children* 45 (July 1990): 18–22 provides an entry into the debate about television violence and its effect on our children.

9. Derek L. Phillips, "Authenticity or Morality?" in Kruschwitz and Roberts, *The Virtues*, p. 34; see also, pp. 23–35.

10. MacIntyre, *After Virtue*, pp. 1–35.

11. Of course, not everyone agrees that things are as bad as MacIntyre and others suggest. See, for example, Jeffrey Stout, *Ethics After Babel: The Languages of Morals and Their Discontents* (Boston: Beacon Press, 1988), pp. 191–219; James Davison Hunter, *Culture Wars: The Struggle to Define America* (New York: Basic Books, 1991), pp. 314–17. Note, however, that neither Stout nor Hunter suggest that things are fine, and Stout clearly recognizes the public importance of cultivating virtue.

12. This claim is a significant part of MacIntyre's argument in *After Virtue*, pp. 36–120.

13. In developing the following discussion, I especially benefited from James M. Gustafson, *Protestant and Roman Catholic Ethics: Prospects for Rapprochement* (Chicago: University of Chicago Press, 1978), pp. 57–84; and John Mahoney, *The Making of Moral Theology: A Study in Roman Catholic Tradition* (Oxford: Clarendon Press, 1987), pp. 202–10, 220–21, 321–37.

I here use "historical consciousness" as an umbrella concept. A more careful and detailed discussion would involve accounts of diverse phenomena including the collapse of certain social institutions following World War II, the influence of existentialist philosophy on moral theory, and the role of the electronic media in our recognition of cultural and moral diversity.

Michael J. Himes, in "The Human Person in Contemporary Theology" (*Introduction to Christian Ethics: A Reader*, ed. Ronald P. Hamel and Kenneth R. Himes [New York: Paulist Press, 1989], pp. 49–63), argues that the roots of historical consciousness go back to the end of the seventeenth century. He may be right, but Himes also acknowledges (pp. 53ff) that historical consciousness has come to the fore of moral theology since the middle of the twentieth century.

14. See *The Westminster Dictionary of Christian Ethics*, 1986, s.vv. "Contraception," by John T. Noonan, Jr. and "Usury and Interest," by John Sleeman; and *The Mennonite Encyclopedia: A Comprehensive Reference Work on the Anabaptist-Mennonite Movement*, 1990, s.vv. "Headcoverings," V:364–65.

15. See, for example, John A. Gallagher, *Time Past, Time Future: An Historical Study of Catholic Moral Theology* (New York: Paulist Press, 1990), pp. 223–64; Mahoney, *The Making of Moral Theology*, pp. 321–37.

16. See Mahoney, *The Making of Moral Theology*, pp. 220–21; Gustafson, *Protestant and Roman Catholic Ethics*, pp. 81–82.

17. Stanley Hauerwas, "On Being Temporally Happy," *Asbury Theological Journal* 45(1) (1990): 14, and see also, p. 16.

18. See Gustafson, *Protestant and Roman Catholic Ethics*, pp. 77, 152, 156–57; Edward LeRoy Long, Jr., *A Survey of Recent Christian Ethics* (New York: Oxford University Press, 1982), pp. 105–8; Stanley Hauerwas, "The Virtues of

Happiness," *Asbury Theological Journal* 45(1): 21–33; Keenan, "Making the Case," pp. 119–21, 123.

19. In developing the following discussion, I especially benefited from Marilyn Friedman, "Friendship and Moral Growth," *Journal of Value Inquiry* 23 (March 1989): 3–13; Glenn A. Hartz, "Desire and Emotion in the Virtue Tradition," *Philosophia* (July 1990): 145–65; Daniel Putman, "Relational Ethics and Virtue Theory," *Metaphilosophy* 22 (July 1991): 231–38; Michael Stocker, "The Schizophrenia of Modern Ethical Theories," in Kruschwitz and Roberts, *The Virtues*, pp. 36–45; Volbrecht, "Friendship," pp. 301–14.

20. Stocker, "The Schizophrenia of Modern Ethical Theories," p. 42.

21. See, for example, Stanley Hauerwas, "Companions on the Way: The Necessity of Friendship," *Asbury Theological Journal* 45(1): 35–48; Nussbaum, *Fragility of Goodness*, pp. 362–66; Nancy Sherman, *The Fabric of Character: Aristotle's Theory of Virtue* (Oxford: Clarendon Press, 1989), pp. 118–56; Paul J. Wadell, *Friendship and the Moral Life* (Notre Dame: University of Notre Dame Press, 1989).

22. For example, Lawrence Blum, "Compassion," in Kruschwitz and Roberts, *The Virtues*, pp. 229–36; Robert C. Roberts, "Aristotle on Virtues and Emotions," *Philosophical Studies* 56 (July 1989): 293–306; and "Emotions among the Virtues of the Christian Life," *Journal of Religious Ethics* 20 (Spring 1992): 37–68; G. Simon Harak, *Virtuous Passions: The Formation of Christian Character* (New York: Paulist Press, 1993); Hartz, "Desire and Emotion."

23. See Spohn, "The Return of Virtue Ethics," pp. 60, 72–75.

24. Mohoney, *The Making of Moral Theology*, p. 320; See also, pp. 309–21.

25. See Keenan, "Theological Trends," p. 219.

2

What Is Virtue Ethics

This book's principal argument is that a virtue framework is especially well-suited for voicing Christian convictions about the moral life. But one cannot argue for the Christian adoption of an ethical scheme without first indicating the nature of that scheme. The necessity of this explanation is compounded by the large degree of confusion in contemporary theology and philosophy concerning "virtue." As Sarah Conly has noted, "one's first impression on reviewing contemporary literature on virtue is that here, more than most places in philosophy, anything goes."[1] In contemporary theology and philosophy almost any theory that mentions virtues or human dispositions can be called "virtue ethics."[2]

This chapter will cut through that confusion by outlining the basic structure and elements of the neo-Aristotelian ethical theory now being developed in certain circles of contemporary philosophy. Our concern is not to summarize everything being said about virtue but to sketch the basic contours of the virtue theory emerging in some camps of neo-Aristotelian philosophy. It is this specific framework that I will later argue that Christians should adopt.

I cannot, however, simply explicate a representative author's account of virtue theory. No single author develops adequately all the elements of virtue theory contained in the relevant segments of neo-Aristotelian philosophy. Even when all the elements and structures are present in a given work, they are often not the author's focus but a presupposition or subtheme. Thus, the account that follows will provide a synthesis of contemporary authors who are attempting to reclaim Aristotelian and Thomistic notions of ethics and virtue.[3] By focusing on how their works complement each other, rather than on a specific author's point of view, it casts new light on some major assumptions and related themes.

A TELEOLOGICAL ETHIC

Teleological Structure of Virtue Ethics

The first thing to note about the kind of virtue theory advocated here is its teleological character. It is an ethic premised on the notion of a true human nature with a determinate human good or end or *telos*.[4]

As MacIntyre notes, within this "teleological scheme there is a fundamental contrast between man-as-he-happens-to-be and man-as-he-could-be-if-he-realized-his-essential-nature." The latter hyphenated concept is that of the human *telos*, and this concept is central to virtue ethics' rationale. Virtue theory focuses on both the contrast or tension between what-we-happen-to-be and what-we-could-be and on how we "make the transition from the former state to the latter."[5]

Virtue ethics has then a tripartite structure: (1) human-nature-as-it-exists; (2) human-nature-as-it-could-be; and (3) those habits, capacities, interests, inclinations, precepts, injunctions, and prohibitions that will move us from point one to point two. Thus, within a teleological virtue ethic certain kinds of actions, habits, capacities and inclinations are discouraged because they direct us away from our true nature. Other kinds of actions, habits, capacities, and inclinations are encouraged because they lead us toward our true end. Virtue theory deals with the transition from who we are to who we could be. A concern with this transition requires that we also try to discover or uncover our true nature or *telos* and ascertain our present state or nature.[6]

To understand better the notion of a human *telos*, it is helpful to note the way many concepts, particularly functional and role concepts, yield evaluative criteria and judgments.[7] Concepts such as "watch," "knife," "farmer," and "father" yield such criteria and judgments. If we want to know what a "good farmer" is, we look to the point, purpose, role, or function of a farmer—maximizing crop yield without devastating the land, for example. A good farmer is one who well fulfills the function, role, or purpose of a farmer. A bad or poor farmer is one who does not fulfill well the same function, role, or purpose.[8]

Concepts like watch and farmer not only yield criteria based on their function, the concepts are themselves dependent on their function, point, or role. We would have no notion of a farmer if we could not appeal to crop yield and care of the land. We would have no concept of a watch without reference to time-keeping ability. Thus, in addition to providing evaluative criteria based on their function, the concepts themselves are tied to their function, purpose, or role.[9]

It follows that these concepts cannot be defined independently of evaluative criteria. For example, "the concept of a watch cannot be defined independently of the concept of a good watch nor the concept of a farmer independently of that of a good farmer."[10] Instead, these concepts stand in a relationship such that to understand X, we must understand what a good X would be—a good X defined as performing well whatever function or purpose or role is characteristic of X. Said differently, to understand "farmer" is to understand a farmer's function or role, and to understand that function or role is to have a criterion by which to test the degree someone is a "good farmer."

A teleological virtue ethic suggests that the concept "human" is similar to these other functional or role concepts. That is, humans should be "understood as having an essential nature and an essential purpose or function." Thus, " 'man' stands to 'good man' as 'watch' stands to 'good watch' or 'farmer' to 'good farmer'."[11]

In a way similar to evaluating a particular watch according to the function and purpose of watches, we can evaluate our current human nature and activity according to the true function or purpose or role of humans. That is, we can evaluate who we are and what we do against our true nature or *telos*, against the excellent performance of the functions or purposes characteristic of humans.

The craft or skill analogy can help clarify and expand this notion of evaluating our current human nature. For instance, to understand what it is to be a good shoemaker, we must understand what a shoemaker's functions are. This immediately provides some criteria. As Martha Nussbaum notes,

> It could not, logically, turn out that the function of the good shoemaker was to play the lyre: good functioning for any craft practitioner must remain within the boundaries of what that activity, in its nature, *is*. In the same way, it could not, logically, turn out that the best life for a human being was the good living of a life characteristic of ants.[12]

Thus, certain forms of life and activity are ruled out by knowing the craft's function or purpose. Moreover, the more fully we understand the craft's purpose or function, the more criteria we have for judging the employment of the craft. Since a central purpose of a shoemaker is to make usable shoes, one who only makes attractive but unwearable shoe-like objects is not a good shoemaker.

The craft analogy can take us further. With a craft we need to know not only the point or purpose of that activity, but the sort of capacities, traits, interests, or skills that allow one to pursue the craft intelligently and successfully.[13]

Consider the "craft" of a jazz musician. To know the point and purpose of the craft—in this case, the making and enjoying of excellent music—provides some criteria. The function or purpose of a jazz musician qua jazz musician is not to prize fight or make omelets; it is to make and enjoy a certain kind of music. It does not stop here, however. If we understand the characteristic functioning of the craft, then we can determine the kind of capacities or traits that are essential to performing that activity well. A jazz musician needs finger dexterity, a degree of spontaneity, and an "ear" or sense of tone, pitch, and rhythm. A jazz musician is also aided by an ability to read music and by an understanding of the musical tradition. Thus, a thorough understanding of the craft provides extensive criteria for judging the employment of the craft and provides criteria for determining how suited one is to the craft's activity. One is more or less suited for the craft's activity depending on things like finger dexterity and music-reading ability. One's progress toward engaging in the craft depends on one's development in the requisite capacities.

We thus see in the craft analogy the full tripartite structure of a teleological virtue ethic. Parallel to humans-as-we-could-be-if-we-realized-our-true-nature is the end or *telos* of the craft. The end or *telos* or good of a shoemaker is to do well what shoemakers do: make and repair shoes that are functional, warm, and stylish. Similarly, the end or *telos* or good of a jazz musician is the excellent performance of what jazz musicians do. To understand the point, purpose, or function of shoemaking or jazz playing is to understand its end or *telos* or good.

Parallel to humans-as-we-happen-to-be is the actual state of one's performance in the craft. When compared to one's actual performance in making shoes or jazz, the *telos* may provide extensive tension or contrast. There may be a larger or smaller gulf between one's actual engagement in the craft and what one could realize if one realized the true nature of the craft. I can make noise on a saxophone, but that is not the end or *telos* of jazz.

Recommendations can be made concerning the transition from one's current ability to a fuller realization of the craft. One versed in a craft can encourage or discourage actions, habits, capacities, and inclinations because they advance or detract from one's ability to perform the craft well. For instance, one could suggest working on scales to develop finger dexterity or repeated listening to specific recordings to develop a sense of rhythm. A teleological virtue ethic similarly encourages or discourages certain kinds of actions, habits, capacities, and inclinations because they direct us toward or away from our true nature or end.

In summary, the kind of virtue theory advocated here is teleological and has a threefold structure: (1) who we are, (2) who we could be, (3) the transition from point one to point two. Attention to functional or role concepts and to the craft analogy helps us understand the notion of a human good or *telos*. It also helps us understand how the human good or *telos* can provide evaluative criteria and provide guidance in acquiring capacities, interests, and habits.

The Content of the Human Telos

Although agreement is not widespread among authors concerning the precise content or quality of the human *telos*, consensus has been reached on a few points. First, the human good is largely constituted by the practice or exercise of various virtues. That is, the human good or *telos* requires activity, especially activity that exemplifies the virtues. The *telos* is not a static state or something one obtains and then clings to. Rather, the human good consists largely of a certain way of living, of a certain kind of activity: activity enabled by and consistent with the various virtues.[14]

A second, closely related point is that the virtues that lead us to the *telos* are also components of it, of the best kind of human life. The virtues are instruments or means to the human good, but they are never simply means. The virtues are constituent elements and essential components of the human good. Said differently, virtues like justice or courage or generosity are not solely external to the human good. They are not "means" in the sense of a path to some clearly distinct and separate end or destination. The virtues and their coinciding activity largely constitute the *telos*.

This point needs to be emphazied. Some authors reject the label "teleological," not because they reject virtue theory's need for a conception of the human good, but because "teleological" suggests to them an end external to, and ultimately independent of, the virtues. Similarly, the central role of the virtues in defining the *telos* must be emphasized in contrast to utilitarian understandings of virtue—where the virtues are merely means, no matter how indispensable, to an external end.[15] The teleological virtue theory advanced here views the virtues as both leading to and constituting the human *telos*.

The notion of a human good or *telos* includes the notion of becoming a certain sort of person: one who embodies and exemplifies such virtues as justice, courage, and temperance. Virtues are means to an end, for we could not reach the goal of becoming that sort of person without acquiring the virtues. But they are not mere means, for they are a central element of the goal itself.

A third point of agreement on the human good is its nature as both individual and corporate. Concern for the individual should be obvious from what has already been said. The individual's task and hope is to move toward the *telos*, toward realizing his or her true nature. Virtue ethics is not, however, concerned solely with individual improvement. Relationships and corporate activity are also central to the human good.[16]

There are different levels to this. At the most basic and instrumental level, the moral education of an individual requires the presence of others. Moral improvement is unlikely to begin, let alone progress, outside the instruction and guidance of parents, role models, and friends. This truth is most clearly seen with children, but it is not limited to children. We need others for our moral growth.

On a second and deeper level, relationships are central and essential to the human good itself. The human *telos* is found in common projects, shared activities, and intimate relationships. Things like friendship, filial relationships, and larger political affiliations are part of and essential to the human good. They are ends and activities we seek for their own sake. Such relationships have an intrinsic worth, and from a virtue perspective it is absurd to think of the human good apart from such interconnections. Social connections are valued for their instrumental benefits. But their worth is much deeper and more pervasive than instrumental gain: they provide the very form and mode in which the human good is realized.

The solitary life, one lacking the company of others, lacks elements essential to the *telos*. Things as simple as game playing, conversation, and love become impossible. Moreover, many virtues lose their point and purpose if deprived of social connections. For instance, courage, justice, and generosity lose something essential if we lack concern for another's well-being. The solitary life may be the *telos* of other beings (e.g., insects or gods), but the best life for human beings is social.

This insistence on our social or interrelational nature in no way denies that individuals retain their separateness, their distinct identities. Rather, virtue theory views us as creatures who fully flourish as individuals in relationships. The human *telos*, the best kind of life for humans, is one in which we become fully individuated in the midst of various kinds of intrinsically worthwhile relationships.[17]

In summary, while there is not agreement on the specifics of the human *telos*, there is agreement on three essential points: (1) the human good consists largely of activities enabled by and consistent with the virtues; (2) the virtues are both means to and constituent elements of the human *telos*; and (3) the *telos* includes both individual and social dimensions.

Determinate Telos and Multiple Forms of Life

Some who object to a teleological virtue ethic misconstrue the proposal. In particular, they often assume that the *telos* imposes a single, fixed, fully detailed notion that needlessly restricts the kind of ends and activities people pursue.[18]

There is, however, no reason to understand a teleological virtue ethic in this way. Most of those advocating a teleological virtue ethic are not proposing a narrowly defined, exact, and restrictive understanding of the human good or *telos*. They are suggesting that we need a broad, complex, comprehensive, and inclusive understanding of the human good. Such an understanding would allow for a variety of configurations of the virtues, a variety of forms of life, and differing ways of embodying social roles. The *telos* needs to be specific enough to provide guidance for acquiring the virtues, but it need not be so definite that it eliminates all but a few ways of living.[19]

Consider the analogy of game playing. Many games (e.g., chess or basketball) have clearly defined goals or ends that are compatible with various forms of play. Some kinds of activity are ruled out by the nature of the game. One does not punch opponents in basketball or move the pieces arbitrarily in chess. There is, however, an almost infinite spectrum of ways to play these games and achieve their ends. One need watch only a few basketball games or chess matches to realize that each has goals or ends congruent with various styles and forms of play. This is even truer of a teleological virtue ethic and the human good. A determinate notion of the human *telos* leaves open and almost infinite number of ways of realizing that end.[20]

Assume, for example, that the human good includes long-term trusting friendships and the virtues of justice and generosity. Such an understanding would call us to develop certain character traits and kinds of relationships. It would also exclude traits and behaviors opposed to justice and generosity and work against relationships that are based on fear and threats of violence. But saying this does not diminish the incalculable number of ways we still have in which to realize the goods of friendship, justice, and generosity. The sun-loving weight lifter is presumably as capable as the jazz-loving Mennonite pastor of realizing these goods, though how they manifest them will be quite different: they will have different friends, different occasions and expressions of justice and generosity, different emphases on when and how their character traits should be developed, and so on. Yet the weight lifter and pastor can be equally guided by a broad, shared vision of the human good.

In short, the kind of virtue theory advanced here does not have an overly narrow and restrictive understanding of the human good. Many forms of life and ways of embodying the virtues are compatible with the human *telos*. The human good can be realized in many different jobs, social roles, cultures, and interests.

NATURE OF THE VIRTUES

I can now say a little more concerning the nature of the virtues. Although there is little agreement on the exact nature or content of the virtues, I want to offer five generalizations that I believe are widely accepted among the relevant authors.

First, the virtues must be understood in relation to the human good or *telos*. The *telos* underlies our notion of what counts as a virtue and how virtues should be understood. The *telos* helps in this way: when we picture the best kind of life for humans to live, we also see the traits, dispositions, and capacities that contribute to or detract from that kind of life. The virtues are those states of character that enable or contribute to the realization of the human good. The vices are those that detract or hinder the realization of the good.[21]

The second generalization is that the various virtues include both the intellectual or rational part of the self and the affective or desiring part of the self. Sometimes a specific virtue is both intellectual and affective. More often, specific virtues deal primarily with the intellectual or affective part of the self. The important point is that reference to the virtues includes the whole range of human feeling, desiring, thinking, and reacting. The sum of the virtues encompass the fields of both intellect and will (the components of the self that go into choice and action).[22]

Third, the virtues, as a group, include tendencies, dispositions, and capacities. This generalization is similar to the second in scope. The virtues include tendencies to react in characteristic ways in similar and related settings. That is, a certain continuity marks one's reactions and concerns in comparable or similar settings. The virtues also include dispositions to seek certain ends and acts in settings that are appropriate to those dispositions. For instance, in settings where the distribution of goods is at issue, a just person will seek to give each his or her due. The virtues also include certain capacities or abilities. For example, the virtues include the ability to reason about means and ends.[23]

Terminology is not the essential point. One could as well speak about inclinations, skills, habits, and human excellences or perfections.[24] The essential point is the scope of the virtues. They include all those states of character or character traits that influence how we act and choose. The virtues include states of character that provide for continuity in one's actions and concerns, for consideration of appropriate issues in relevant situations, and for the abilities befitting the human good.

Fourth, the virtues are not a matter of whim or caprice, but of stability; they are relatively stable aspects of one's character. We do not lose or gain virtues overnight or in a single act. One occasionally acts "out of character" or in discontinuity with his or her character. In general, however, one acts in accord with one's virtues and vices, and character changes are seldom made with ease. One does not suddenly gain or lose the virtues. Instead, it is a matter of moral education and growth, of continual practice or neglect, of incremental advancement or decline. One most often develops character in steps. The steps may be uneven, but once one has made significant progress in a virtue, he or she is unlikely suddenly to cease being virtuous in the relevant respect.[25]

The stability of the virtues is implied in the notion that virtues provide for continuity in one's actions. The point here is to highlight that continuity or stability and link it to moral education or development. The virtues are states of character usually acquired through time and work, and character developed through time and work seldom evaporates quickly.[26]

Fifth, and finally, genuinely virtuous actions—that is, actions that express or are informed by the virtues—may be pursued "instrumentally" but must be done "for their own sake." Just and courageous actions can, for example, be performed because of the goods or ends they cause, such as survival, self-respect, and the respect of others. But for those acts to be truly virtuous, they must also be performed for their own sake—that is, performed simply because they are just or courageous actions. They must be ends in themselves. They must be the kinds of actions that would be valued even if they failed to achieve their goals or led to unexpected ill consequences. Actions truly expressive of the virtues are actions in which the means are prized at least as much as the extrinsic ends to which they are directed. Indeed, there are times when virtuous activity will lack all instrumental value but must still be done because it is in conformity with the virtues and part of the human good.[27]

This idea must be clarified. The notion of acts done for their own sake is not strange or foreign to us. Rather, it draws attention to activities we value and pursue even when they lack instrumental value—that is, even when the activity results in nothing beyond itself. We engage in, and value, many activities that do not, for instance, produce commodities, increase our possessions, lengthen our lives, or bolster our social standing. Indeed, as Robert Adams notes, all human societies and cultures "develop activities of play, conversation, ritual, and art that are carried on largely, if not solely, for their own sake."[28] We pursue all kinds of activities simply because we recognize their value. Such activities enrich our lives in ways that are hard to specify, but we know we would be less as people without them.[29]

Further, to say that just, courageous, or generous acts are done for their own sake does not deny that they are also done for the sake of the *telos*. There is no contradiction in saying that actions in conformity with the virtues are done both for themselves and for the human good. The *telos*, the best life for human beings to live, is an inclusive end constituted in large part by virtuous activity. A just act is done because it is a just act and because the human good is composed of such acts. It makes sense to enjoy music for its own sake and because it is an important part of one's life. Similarly, it makes sense for one to perform virtuous acts for themselves and as part of the agent's *telos*.[30]

Virtue theory affirms the satisfaction or enjoyment that often accompanies activity that is done "for its own sake." Indeed, the virtuous person will generally find enjoyment or satisfaction in activity conforming to the virtues. This affirmation does not mean, however, that the notion of "enjoyment" or "satisfaction" is a more basic or fundamental criterion than the appeal to the human *telos* with its constituent virtues and activities. According to virtue theory, "enjoyment" or "satisfaction" is not a single thing that adheres to different activities and so provides a criterion for judging between them. The enjoyment of drinking good coffee, for example, is not equivalent or comparable to the enjoyment of swimming or playing with a child. In other words, enjoyments or pleasures are heterogeneous and as different as the activities to which they adhere.[31]

Moreover, what one finds enjoyable will depend in large measure on the sort of person one is. But if it is true that different people find different activities enjoyable, then the appeal to "enjoyment" does not tell us what we should enjoy—that is, what activities belong to human excellence—but merely what we currently enjoy. The problem becomes apparent when we consider that not all forms of enjoyment are praiseworthy. Some people find enjoyment in activities that are corrupt or vicious and cruel.

Further, the claim that we perform some activities for their own sake implicitly denies that the primary end of those activities is enjoyment. Indeed, virtue theory claims that there are some activities that we would choose even if they brought no enjoyment. The plausibility of this assertion is evident when we recall people who have chosen "to sacrifice life itself, and therefore all possibility of present and future pleasure, for the sake of acting well or helping a friend."[32] In short, according to virtue theory, the enjoyment or satisfaction that supervenes on successful activity cannot replace an appeal to the human *telos* and its constituent activities.

In sum, the virtues simply are those states of character acquired over time that contribute to the realization of the human good.[33] The virtues involve both the intellect and the will, the rational and affective parts of the self. They also involve tendencies, dispositions, and capabilities. In addition, although virtuous activity often has external goals and is accompanied by satisfaction or enjoyment, it is ultimately done for its own sake, simply because it is virtuous.

HUMAN AGENCY AND MORAL EDUCATION

Virtue ethics works with an understanding of the self as a self-forming and determining agent. This understanding of agency falls somewhere between behaviorism and voluntarism. It acknowledges that we choose and act without being completely determined. Yet an explanation of our choices and actions must refer to our desires, states of character, and personal history. In other words, virtue theory assumes that we are embodied creatures whose choices and actions are neither completely determined nor completely free.[34]

For a sense of what is at stake, consider the following remark by Nussbaum:

> When Aristotle arrives on the philosophical scene, he is . . . confronted, on the one hand, by a model of explanation whose *aitia* [explanation] is so "common" that it assimilates all intentional actions both to one another and to other cases of response to an external physical stimulus; on the other, with a model that is not "common" enough to do justice to our beliefs about what we share with "the other animals," and about what links together different elements in our own behavior.[35]

According to Nussbaum, Aristotle confronted a choice between behaviorism on the one hand and voluntarism or intellectualism on the other. Behaviorism reduces all human action to forces external to the person, or at least outside the person's control. Voluntarism disregards our embodied nature (including what we share with other animals) and overlooks the importance of beliefs, perceptions, and prior actions for explaining our current activity.[36]

Needed was an account midway between these two. For actions to be morally meaningful, they cannot be reducible to external causes. But to reflect adequately our embodied and historical nature, Aristotle could not be content with an account that places the self behind or above its actions—as if untouched by its body, history, or beliefs.

The issue confronting Aristotle remains. Contemporary virtue theory needs, or at least presupposes, an account of human agency that falls between behaviorism and voluntarism. Today's virtue ethics cannot, any more than Aristotle, be content with reducing all human actions to external causes or to a self free from body, history, and beliefs.[37]

Other ethical theories may also require an account of human agency, but virtue ethics has a particular stake in such an account. A major reason for this is virtue theory's concern for moral education or development. Virtue theory needs an account of agency to coincide with its understanding of the acquisition of the virtues. Virtues involve feelings and intellect, tendencies, dispositions, and capacities. However, it makes no sense to talk about developing the virtues unless we also understand human agency as a means of shaping character. Moreover, it makes no sense to talk about the virtues unless conditions of character are important components of decision and action. In other words, an ethical theory concerned with virtue is unintelligible unless we participate in the formation of our tendencies, dispositions, and capacities. Conversely, conditions of character are irrelevant unless they are involved in the process of choosing and acting.

Put simply, a concern with the acquisition of the virtues is premised on understanding ourselves as self-forming and determining agents. In virtue ethics, we acquire the virtues in or through our actions and choices, by habituation and training, and through the praise or blame, censure or encouragement of others. The acquisition is often a gradual process in which both our and others' choices and actions overflow and return to us. Choosing and acting justly or generously now makes it more likely that we will choose and act justly in the future. The instruction or encouragement of a teacher or friend can help us develop the right kind of tendencies or dispositions. In short, we shape ourselves and each other toward or away from the virtues by our choices, actions, and interaction.[38]

Neither a behaviorist nor voluntarist account can explain how we acquire the virtues. The former reduces everything to mindless behavioral manipulation. The latter does not consider the way our actions influence who we become: it projects a self standing behind or above its acts that is not altered by those acts. The latter is also unconcerned with the virtues because they play no role in choice and action. In the former, we do not participate in the formation of our character. In the latter, our character is largely irrelevant.

According to virtue theory, by contrast, we develop and help form our tendencies and dispositions through our choices and actions. But those tendencies and dispositions also inform and direct our choices and actions. We are not, as the behaviorist account suggests, simply at the mercy of forces outside our control; we help form our own and each other's character. We also are not, contrary to the voluntarist account, free from the constraints of character. Past choices and actions influence the kind of persons we become, and the kind of persons we become informs our choices and actions.

We choose and act, and our choices and actions play a central role in the development of character—our own and others'. But, in turn, our character helps inform and direct our choices and actions. This is a circle, but not a vicious circle. One can change, but the change often requires time and work.

MORAL LUCK

Virtue theory's concern with "moral luck" is closely related to its understanding of human agency. The idea of moral luck is that people face events, influences, and circumstances that are not under their control but are morally significant. Such events, influences, and circumstances can affect the acquisition, exercise, and maintenance of the virtues. Thus, one's ability to acquire the virtues and live the best human life is not entirely under the individual's control.[39]

A person who grows up lacking social relationships that exhibit the virtues is unlikely to exhibit many virtues as an adult. This outcome has little to do with the child's efforts. Deprived of parents, peers, and teachers who display and encourage the virtues, the child is unlikely to develop many virtues. This is a case of moral luck. The circumstances are morally relevant but not under the individual's control.[40]

Another example of moral luck is that of one who confronts extreme tragedy. For instance, a kind or courageous person can meet tragedy so great that he or she breaks: that person becomes vicious or cowardly and regains the virtues only through work and good fortune. Consider World War II and the Holocaust. Many people found a way to act well in terrible circumstances. Many others, people who could only be viewed as well-ordered and virtuous, were broken and driven to become unkind, cowardly, and vicious. Many never became fully whole again. This is also a case of moral luck.[41]

According to many authors, virtue theory's ability to acknowledge the reality of moral luck is one of its merits. Nussbaum in particular views its ability to acknowledge risk and contingency as morally relevant—as an asset. She is not alone. Many authors on virtue contend that any adequate moral theory must allow for the moral importance of risk and contingency, of events, influences, and circumstances outside the agent's control.

I cannot say much more on moral luck. While it is clear and straightforward as an idea, its further significance or implications are not yet obvious. Authors call attention to moral luck but say little beyond this. Little is said, for example, about whether certain virtues are more vulnerable than others to luck, nor is there any visible consensus on which virtues are most important for dealing with the dynamics of luck or fortune.[42]

The generalization to be made here is that attempting to live the best human life contains elements of risk. An adequate account of virtue includes the realization that the moral life involves events, influences, and circumstances outside the agent's control. Perhaps philosophers will delve further into the significance or implications of "moral luck." The important thing for us is that virtue ethics recognizes the importance of luck and contingency in the moral life.

THE PRIORITY OF BEING

The shift in focus that accompanies a renewed interest in virtue ethics (see Chapter 1) can be further clarified by noting virtue theory's understanding of the relationship between "being" and "doing." In simplest terms, "being" precedes "doing," but "doing" shapes "being." That is, who we have become, including our states of character, precedes and informs our choices and actions. But our choices and actions help shape who we are and thus our future choices and actions.[43]

We act out of who we are. One who has a just orientation and character will generally treat others fairly. One who has a cowardly orientation and character will often make decisions based on fear and run from danger at inappropriate times. Cowardly choices and actions also tend to reinforce a cowardly character or weaken a courageous character. Similarly, choices and actions that are more or less just tend to strengthen or weaken a just character.

When this is understood, virtue ethics' concern with virtues and vices is not viewed as lack of concern for right action. It is, rather, the realization that right action, right judgment, and rightly ordered character are intimately linked. Indeed, the ability to determine and do the right is premised on one's having the requisite states of character.[44]

There is, however, a certain priority or primacy of character, a special concern for the kind of people we become. Lacking the appropriate tendencies, dispositions, and capacities, the chances of perceiving or doing the right are greatly reduced.[45] Thus, before we can concern ourselves with analyzing particular actions, we need to concern ourselves with becoming the right sort.

If this sounds overstated, consider the following examples. (1) Most of us do not go to just anyone when we seek moral advice. We do not ask moral advice from young children or persons known for their dishonesty. Rather, we seek people who are trustworthy, honest, courageous, and wise. In so doing we acknowledge the importance of the virtues. We seek people of moral maturity because we know they are the best suited for giving moral advice. They are, for example, the most likely to identify the issues correctly and be honest with us. Thus, states of character are important in identifying and communicating the right.[46]

(2) Many women confronting unwanted pregnancies never consider abortion, even though our society treats abortion as a matter of personal choice. These women carry the fetuses to term then either care for the children themselves or put the babies up for adoption. Their view of themselves and their vision of the world precludes the question of abortion. Thus, their characters not only delineate how moral questions are handled, but what they confront as moral questions.[47] For these women, abortion is not a moral question or matter of choice.

(3) Most of us have a few glaring character faults or at least know someone with such limits. One may have a compulsive personality, a short temper, or a problem with fidelity. Often the difficulty here is not with knowing the right, but doing it. People lacking in temperance, patience, or fidelity often know how they should act but find themselves unable. Thus, their states of character greatly influence their ability to do the right.

Of course, people lacking discipline, forbearance, loyalty or other virtues may not correctly identify the right. Cowardly people frequently view their flight as morally justified. People having affairs sometimes see nothing wrong in their actions, and people lacking moderation do not see their actions as obsessive but as the dutiful response to some cause, ideal, or desire. Thus, perceiving the morally right course of action can depend on one's virtues, or lack of them.

These examples help clarify how and why states of character have a certain priority over concern with specific acts. The virtues give one the wisdom to find the right (1 and 3), help one know which issues are morally relevant (2), and strengthen one to do the right (3).

DISCERNMENT AND THE PLACE OF RULES AND CONSEQUENCES

Given what was said about the priority of being, What about action-guiding? What about deliberating on moral questions? Does virtue ethics provide any guidance for action and choice? Or does virtue ethics leave us stranded when it comes to actual decisions and dilemmas?[48]

The short answer to these questions is yes and no. Much can be said within virtue theory on moral deliberation; however, a full-blown, systematic theory of deliberation with precise, math-like, calculations for action is not and will not be developed.

I shall deal with the latter point first. The consensus is that virtue ethics cannot provide a thoroughly systematic account of moral deliberation to guide us in every detail. Indeed, virtue ethics should not aspire to such an account. Nancy Sherman, for example, suggests that we recall

> Aristotle's repeated methodological warnings against transforming ethical theory into a practical *science* (*episteme*, e.g., 1084b13-27, 1098a25ff). While the philosophical temperament may aspire to make more precise and systematic the data of moral life, theory is ultimately misguided if it seeks the sort of precision that characterizes practical reason and judgment. The best that theory can do is to give a general specification of the kinds of good that should be included within the best life.[49]

The reasoning here and in similar statements by others is straightforward: the deliberation and practical wisdom appropriate to the moral life eludes formulation. A sketch can be given. The remainder must be filled in by experience, practice, and the acquisition of the virtues. Theory cannot reflect the complexity, specificity, and decisiveness of good moral reasoning. Nor can theory substitute for experience and practice in practical reasoning. Theory can provide an outline. The picture must be drawn in experience.[50]

This limit does not apply only to theories of virtue. According to authors developing neo-Aristotelian virtue ethics, no form of ethical theory that promises a type of moral calculus delivers the goods. Whether deontological or consequentialist, no theory can provide algorithmic moral principles. No theory can completely capture the elements of surprise, complexity, contextual variety, and situational specificity relevant to good moral deliberation. Any theory that claims to account for everything (or claims these elements are morally irrelevant) is worse for its excessive claims and myopic vision.[51]

Still, there is much that virtue ethics can say about moral deliberation. First, good moral judgment requires a kind of perceptive ability: an ability to recognize and respond to the specific and contextual features of often complex situations. Such perception is not a deductive or inferential ability. It is a sensitivity to the concrete particulars of life. It is the flexibility to give attention to the particular features, relationships, and issues relevant to a specific situation.[52]

Second, the tendencies and dispositions (including feelings and desires) identified by specific virtues are a component of choosing and acting well. For example, one who has internalized a concern for justice or friendship will be guided by a concern for justice or friendship in relevant situations. These virtues help one perceive when a situation involves issues of justice or friendship. People who have developed these virtues will tend to notice issues surrounding the distribution of property or the causing of offense, for instance. Moreover, when one realizes that justice or friendship is at stake, he or she will seek actions appropriate to the realization of those virtues or ends. Thus, tendencies and dispositions can both sensitize one to relevant features of the situation and provide the ends for which one acts.[53]

Third, a teleological virtue ethic is not consequentialist or deontological, though it does have a place for both rules and consequences. It is a mistake to view virtue ethics as a form of consequentialism. In virtue ethics, the *telos* concerns the exercise of the virtues and participation in virtuous relationships. Consequentialism seldom, if ever, makes these ends central.[54] Consequentialism takes one thing or a list of things as good—for example, happiness, pleasure, economic well-being—and evaluates action according to whether and how much of that thing will result.

The problem with consequentialism is that the end being sought is not human excellence. Another problem with consequentialism is that in theory any action is justifiable if it results in the right end. But in virtue ethics some actions must be prohibited as absolutely incompatible with the pursuit of the virtuous life and virtuous relationships.[55]

Yet another difference from consequentialism is seen in the observation that the enjoyments or pleasures that accompany successful activity are as divergent as the activities to which they adhere. This understanding of pleasures as heterogeneous is in striking contrast to many consequentialist or utilitarian theories that view pleasure as a common value or good by which all activities can be measured. Virtue theory, however, denies that there is a common value (pleasure or otherwise) that renders the various goods of life commensurable. We certainly weigh and balance the activities, goods, and ends of life. But according to virtue theory, we do so in light of a complex understanding or picture of the human good—a good that includes numerous virtues and relationships that are "ends in themselves" and thus diverse and not strictly commensurable.[56] This virtue claim is clearly at odds with many consequentialist and utilitarian accounts.

Still, virtue ethics is concerned with consequences. A person concerned with justice, generosity, or friendship must take account of results and consequences. What kind of friend am I if I do not care that my actions have dire consequences for you? Or how could I claim concern for justice and yet be indifferent to the unjust consequences of my acts? Virtue ethics is not consequentialist, but good moral deliberation often involves weighing effects.[57]

It is also a mistake to view virtue ethics as a deontological theory. Deontological theories tend to focus on a set of predetermined rules or principles or on a rule-governed procedure for decision making. The most obvious difference from virtue ethics is the focal point. Deontological theories focus on rules or principles; virtue theory focuses on becoming a certain kind of person.[58] Similarly, most deontological theories judge an action's propriety according to rules or principles that are themselves established antecedent to any discussion of human virtues or the human good. In a teleological virtue ethic, an action's propriety depends on its conformity to the *telos* and its constituent virtues.[59]

Moreover, as we have already noted, virtue ethics asserts that "practical choices cannot, even in principle, be adequately and completely captured in a system of universal rules."[60] Good moral judgment must take account of things like previously unencountered events and circumstances, subtle differences in human interaction (including changes in one's tone or touch), and personal commitments to causes, people, or issues.[61] Thus, virtue ethics should not be viewed as a deontological theory since the former denies the latter's ability to encompass good moral judgment.

Still, virtue ethics is concerned with rules at many levels. To begin with, virtue theory admits that communities and societies must set minimal rules or laws.[62] This admission makes sense based on the communal nature of the *telos*. We seek not only to become virtuous individuals, but also to become a certain kind of community. However, any community seeking a common good must stipulate when someone's actions have placed him or her outside the common pursuit. That is, a group seeking a common end must identify the kinds of behavior that excludes one from the group precisely because it impairs the group's movement toward the end. Actions such as theft and murder immediately come to mind as incompatible with a community seeking a common good. Thus, communities will develop rules or laws concerning behavior the group cannot tolerate.

The societal need for rules is widely acknowledged in neo-Aristotelian circles. However, rules may also function at several additional levels within a virtue framework. Although often developed by only one or two virtue theorists, these additional functions are complementary, not idiosyncratic developments. For example, Nussbaum suggests several ways in which rules can function within a neo-Aristotelian framework. She suggests that rules and principles can be

> summaries of particular decisions, useful for purposes of economy and aids in identifying the salient features of the particular case.... Principles are perspicuous descriptive summaries of good judgments, valid only to the extent to which they correctly describe such judgments.[63]

Thus, rules work as summaries of previous wise decisions. They can be overridden or revised according to the particulars of the case, but they provide a reference point of previous good judgments.[64]

Nussbaum also suggests that rules can have an educative function. Rules "are guidelines in moral development: for people not yet possessed of practical wisdom and insight need to follow rules that summarize the wise judgments of others."[65] To see how rules might work in moral development, consider a parent's use of rules. Parents use rules to help train their children. Often the rules concern mundane matters like crossing the street, brushing one's teeth, or knowing when to study. The intent is not that the child should follow the same rules throughout life. The hope is that the child will develop certain habits, abilities, and concerns—in part by following the rules.

Thus, a parent sets rules hoping that the child will develop a sense of street safety, personal hygiene, and studiousness. The rules act as guides in shaping the child's character. And as Nussbaum notes, we should not assume that the educative function of rules is applicable only to children. Adults also need guidelines for their further moral development.[66]

Nussbaum also suggests that rules are helpful when time is limited or when bias and passion threaten to exert undue influence.[67] One can often rely on a rule or principle rather than make a hasty judgment, and rules can sometimes counterbalance our biases and frenzy. Rules here are not the norm or center of moral judgment but important resources when time, bias, or emotional frenzy threaten good judgment.

There is an additional way rules might function within a virtue framework: as depicting or calling one to the virtues. For instance, Pincoffs suggests that rules "do not tell us exactly what to do so much as they indicate what we should struggle toward in our own way."[68] Only a few authors have taken up this thought, and they only hint at it.[69] Still, it may be an important role for rules or principles in virtue ethics. Whether it's a general rule like "be kind and generous," or something more specific like "always be willing to share your cookies," the rule can function as a call to become a certain kind of person. Such injunctions do not provide exact guidance but suggest where we should be headed.

Whether or not we accept all of these uses, virtue ethics clearly has a place for rules. The important point is that the rules serve the virtues; the virtues do not serve the rules. Rules and principles assist in the acquisition and execution of the virtues. The virtues are not subservient to the rules.[70]

A fourth general point of agreement on practical reasoning concerns community. Specifically, the emphasis on social relationships in a teleological virtue ethic makes it clear that moral deliberation is not, on the whole, an individual matter. Individuals certainly make decisions as individuals. But attention to the importance of friendships, mentors, and role models shows that the moral life is not primarily about individuals making isolated decisions. Rather, individuals make decisions in the context of relationships that include moral guidance, censure, and encouragement.[71]

Individuals engaged in deliberation are not without communal resources. Friends can challenge our biases and help us see dimensions or aspects of the situation we have overlooked. Children have parents to guide them through hard decisions and to help them develop morally.

Many adults also have mentors or persons we regard as wise, persons who can help us with difficult choices and decisions. We can also follow role models, examples, and "experts." That is, we can learn from persons of practical wisdom even if they are not present. By observing how others have handled situations similar or analogous to our own, we gain insight into how our situation should be judged. Even when attention to moral role models and examples cannot give concrete guidance, they can challenge us toward the *telos*, toward fuller embodiment of the virtues. In short, our communities, both small and large, provide a most important resource for moral deliberation.[72]

Virtue theory cannot offer a thoroughly systematic account of moral deliberation that would guide us in every detail. Indeed, according to virtue ethics, no theory can offer such an account. Still, it should now be clear that concern with virtue does not leave us voiceless when it comes to moral deliberation and good practical judgment.

A KIND OF PERFECTIONISM

If it is not already obvious, it should be noted that a teleological virtue ethic espouses a type of perfectionism. It is perfectionist in two senses: (1) every voluntary human act is considered morally relevant, and (2) one is encouraged to improve continually all aspects of his or her character.[73]

As David Norton observes, many modern ethical theories consider things like vocational choice, the cultivation of friendships, and one's selection of books to be morally irrelevant. In virtue ethics these choices "are moral choices.... because choices of vocation, of avocations, of friends to cultivate and books to read . . . have a direct bearing on the development of moral character."[74] In fact, almost nothing in human experience and choice is morally meaningless. Even "trivial desires, choices, and acts" have moral significance because all such things "have some effect—no matter how small—on the person we are in the process of becoming."[75]

In short, because virtue theory focuses on the movement toward the human *telos*, toward the best life for human beings to live, no aspect of choice or action is exempt from moral concern. Because our choices influence the kind of people we become, every voluntary human act is morally relevant and susceptible to moral scrutiny. Indeed, the range of morally relevant concerns is even greater than this. Every institution and every human practice affects the kind of people we become. So even institutions and practices invite moral attention.[76]

The parallel to this point is the call for continual growth in all aspects of one's character. We are to work continually to become more just, more courageous, more generous, more discerning. Obviously we cannot always be at work on every aspect of our character, and sometimes the development of one aspect means neglecting another. But we can always take a step, no matter how large or small, toward moral growth, toward our *telos*.[77]

Note, however, that virtue theory is not a form of "brittle perfectionism" where the ideal must be realized for one to receive positive evaluation.[78] The *telos*, as an ideal of human excellence and perfection, can never be fully actualized. That is the nature of ideals. The *telos* is always in front of us, always calling us forward to a fuller realization of the human good. But the human good need not be fully realized before one's person and acts are valuable. Virtue ethics is not perfectionist in the sense of mandating an impossible ideal. It is perfectionist in the sense of viewing all aspects of life as morally relevant and in calling everyone to continual growth in every area of life.

SUMMARY

From this outline of virtue theory's basic structure and elements, a brief summary is now possible.

The virtue theory advanced here is teleological and has a tripartite structure; it moves from who we are to who we could be. The human good or *telos* involves activity enabled by and consistent with the virtues. This activity is performed both for its own sake and as part of the human good. Further, the *telos* or human good encompasses both individual and social dimensions. The *telos* is, in short, the best kind of life for humans to live.

A partially determinate notion of the human good is necessary for this kind of virtue ethics, but the *telos* need not be narrowly or restrictively defined. The human good can be understood in a way that allows for many forms of life and ways of embodying the virtues.

Virtues are those states of character or character traits acquired over time that contribute to the human good. The virtues involve both the intellect and the will, both the rational and affective parts of the self. They also are the tendencies, dispositions and capabilities necessary to the human good, to the best kind of human life.

A teleological virtue ethic understands the self as a self-forming or determining agent. One plays a role in the formation of his or her character. In turn, one's character helps to shape one's choices and actions. Said differently, one's "being" is formed in and through "doing," through choices and actions. But one's "being" also informs choices and actions. This involves a circle, but not a vicious one. We can be formed toward our *telos* through time, work, and social interaction.

This assertion does not mean that the moral life is wholly under the agent's control. According to virtue theory, the moral life also depends in significant degree on appropriate forms of social interaction and is vulnerable to various hazards and contingencies. We must, in other words, acknowledge and struggle with the role of luck in the moral life.

In matters of discernment, virtue ethics emphasizes or gives priority to character over particular actions or issues. We need to be equipped to encounter, determine, and carry out the morally right before we focus on specific issues or actions. Virtue ethics also maintains that theory cannot fully capture good moral reasoning. No formula or calculus will direct us in every instance. An outline or helps and hints can be offered, but the rest must be filled out in experience and practice.

Allowing for the limits of theory, good moral judgment involves many elements. It includes an ability to recognize and respond to the specific and contextual features of the situation, reference to the tendencies and dispositions named by the virtues, the use of rules and consequences, and an openness to important relationships (especially those of friends, mentors, and role models).

A teleological virtue ethic also involves a kind of perfectionism. It is perfectionist in the sense of viewing all aspects of life as morally relevant and in calling everyone to growth in every area of life. It is not perfectionist in the sense of mandating an impossible ideal. Instead, the *telos* is always before us, always calling us toward a fuller realization of the best life for humans to live.

There are unquestionably other generalizations that could be made concerning the relevant authors and a teleological virtue ethic. We can expect over the next few decades to see many developments, more nuance, greater content, and more disagreements. Still, enough has been said to provide the basic meaning of "virtue ethics." Unless otherwise indicated, phrases like "virtue ethics," "virtue theory," "a teleological virtue ethic," "a virtue ethic," and "virtue framework" henceforth refer to the theory that has been outlined in this chapter.

NOTES

1. Sarah Conly, "Flourishing and the Ethics of Virtue," in *Midwest Studies in Philosophy XIII Ethical Theory: Character and Virtue*, ed. Peter A. French, Theodore E. Uehling, Jr., and Howard K. Wettstein (Notre Dame: University of Notre Dame Press, 1988), p. 84 (cited hereafter as *Midwest Studies XIII*.)

2. For examples of the range of concerns that are sometimes referred to as "virtue ethics," see John W. Crossin, *What Are They Saying About Virtue?* (New York: Paulist Press, 1985); Edward Leroy Long, Jr., *A Survey of Recent Christian Ethics* (New York: Oxford University Press, 1982), pp. 101–38; Alasdair MacIntyre, *After Virtue* 2nd ed. (Notre Dame: University of Notre Dame Press, 1984), pp. 181–85; David Solomon, "Internal Objections to Virtue Ethics," in *Midwest Studies XIII*, pp. 428–29; Gregory Trianosky, "What Is Virtue Ethics all About?" *American Philosophical Quarterly* 27 (October 1990): 335–44.

3. To facilitate this integrated account, this chapter focuses most often on the following works: *Midwest Studies XIII;* MacIntyre, *After Virtue* and *Whose Justice? Which Rationality?* (Notre Dame: University of Notre Dame Press, 1988); Martha C. Nussbaum, *The Fragility of Goodness: Luck and Ethics in Greek Tragedy and Philosophy* (Cambridge: Cambridge University Press, 1986); Daniel Mark Nelson, *The Priority of Prudence: Virtue and Natural Law in Thomas Aquinas and the Implications for Modern Ethics* (University Park: The Pennsylvania State University Press, 1992); Nancy Sherman, *The Fabric of Character: Aristotle's Theory of Virtue* (Oxford: Clarendon Press, 1989). Frequent reference also will be made to Edmund L. Pincoffs, *Quandaries and Virtues: Against Reductivism in Ethics* (Lawrence: University Press of Kansas, 1986).

A focus on these works (especially those of MacIntyre, Nussbaum, Nelson, and Sherman) broadly indicates the kind of neo-Aristotelian "virtue ethics" advocated here. This is not to deny that the authors often hold different and incompatible views. There will be occasion below to mention some of these. What is essential, however, is that these authors agree on the basic structure and elements of a teleological virtue ethic and their studies often complement or supplement each other.

4. For example, James F. Keenan, "Virtue Ethics: Making a Case as It Comes of Age," *Thought* 67 (June 1992): 120–21, 123; Nelson, *Priority of Prudence,* pp. 32–33, 83; Daniel A. Putman, "Virtue and the Practice of Modern Medicine," *Journal of Medicine and Philosophy* 13 (November 1988): 441. This book uses the terms "human good," "end," and *"telos"* as essentially synonymous, except that "end" may also refer to something more proximate than the full human good.

5. MacIntyre, *After Virtue,* p. 52.

6. Ibid., pp. 53–55. See also: Solomon, "Internal Objections," pp. 429–32. Cf. David L. Norton, "Moral Minimalism and the Development of Moral Character," in *Midwest Studies XIII*, pp. 181–82.

7. This section is primarily dependent on MacIntyre, *After Virtue,* pp. 57–59, but also Conly, "Flourishing," p. 86; Philippa Foot, *Virtue and Vices and Other Essays in Moral Philosophy* (Berkeley: University of California Press, 1978), pp. 133–40; Stanley Hauerwas, "On Being Temporally Happy," *Asbury Theological Journal* 45(1): 11–12; Nelson, *Priority of Prudence,* p. 33.

8. Admittedly, words like "watch" and "farmer" may have become too expansive in our society to be true functional or role concepts—for example, a "watch" can be a timepiece or a piece of jewelry worn for its aesthetic value. Correct functional or role concepts may be more restricted terms like "stopwatch" and "subsistence farmer."

9. Of course, one can begin to use functional or role concepts like "farmer" or "watch" even though he or she lacks an understanding of their

function. A child who lacks the notion of cultivating land might still correctly identify Joe as a farmer because Joe rides a tractor and wears overalls. However, the child's identification of farmer Joe (1) is based on a thin concept of "farmer"—that is, farmers do many things besides ride tractors and tractor riding is not essential to the notion of farming, (2) could be a misidentification and an erroneous use of the word "farmer"—that is, not everyone who rides a tractor is a farmer and not all farmers ride tractors, (3) ultimately depends on the essential tie between the notion "farmer" and the role of cultivating land—that is, we associate farmers with tractors because tractors are frequently used to raise and harvest crops.

10. MacIntyre, *After Virtue,* p. 58.
11. Ibid.
12. Nussbaum, *Fragility of Goodness,* p. 293.
13. James D. Wallace, "Ethics and the Craft Analogy," in *Midwest Studies XIII,* p. 223.
14. For this and the following point, see Robert Merrihew Adams, "Common Projects and Moral Virtue," in *Midwest Studies XIII,* pp. 299–300; Hauerwas, "On Being Temporally Happy," pp. 11–13, 17n.4, and "The Virtues of Happiness," *Asbury Theological Journal* 45(1): 21–22; Robert B. Kruschwitz and Robert C. Roberts, eds., *The Virtues: Contemporary Essays on Moral Character* (Belmont: Wadsworth, 1987), p. 10; MacIntyre, *After Virtue,* pp. 148–49, and *Whose Justice?,* p. 109–13, 132; Nelson, *Priority of Prudence,* pp. 36–38, 71; Nussbaum, *Fragility of Goodness,* pp. 296–97, 322–24, 329, 332–36, 341; Sherman, *Fabric of Character,* p. 77.
15. Cf. Trianosky, pp. 338–39, 343n.2; Pamela Hall, "The Mysteriousness of the Good: Iris Murdoch and Virtue-Ethics," *American Philosophical Quarterly* 27 (October 1990): 314–15.
16. For this and what follows, see Adams, "Common Projects," pp. 300–301; G. Simon Harak, *Virtuous Passions: The Formation of Christian Character* (New York: Paulist Press, 1993), pp. 58–59; MacIntyre, *After Virtue,* pp. 174, 178, 220, 223, 229, 258, 263, and *Whose Justice?,* pp. 121–123, 132–136; Nelson, *Priority of Prudence,* pp. 37–38; Nussbaum, *Fragility of Goodness,* pp. 344–66; Sherman, *Fabric of Character,* pp. 77, 109–11, 124–33, 151–54; David B. Wong, "On Flourishing and Finding One's Identity in Community," in *Midwest Studies XIII,* pp. 325–35. Nussbaum and Sherman are particularly helpful here.
17. This aspect of the *telos* is seen, for example, in good friendships. We value certain friends precisely because of who they are. True friends are not generic, easily interchangeable people, but individuals we have come to appreciate and value in their particularity. Similarly, true friendships do not preempt our agency and sense of separateness. True friends do not demand that we be exactly like them and they do not make all our decisions for us. True friends will have many things in common, but they will also differ; and it is because friends recognize this mixture of commonality and difference that they can develop a shared pursuit of the human good and individual self-knowledge. See, for example, Stanley Hauerwas, "Companions on the Way: The Necessity of Friendship," *Asbury Theological Journal* 45(1): 36, 39, 40; Sherman, *Fabric of Character,* pp. 137–51; William Spohn, "The Return of Virtue Ethics," *Theological Studies* 53 (March 1992): 73, 75; Rose Mary Volbrect, "Friend-

42 What Is Virtue Ethics

ship: Mutual Apprenticeship in Moral Development," *Journal of Value Inquiry* 24 (October 1990): 304–9.

18. For example, Pincoffs, *Quandaries and Virtues*, pp. 6–7, 96–97, 107–11; Conly, "Flourishing," pp. 84, 86–89; Wallace, "Ethics and the Craft," pp. 226–31; cf. Volbrecht, "Friendship," pp. 310–11.

19. For a sense of this see Robert M. Adams, "Saints," in Kruschwitz and Roberts, *The Virtues*, pp. 153–60; MacIntyre, *After Virtue*, pp. 161–63, 219, and *Three Rival Versions of Moral Enquiry* (Notre Dame: University of Notre Dame Press, 1990), pp. 62–66; David L. Norton, "Moral Minimalism and the Development of Moral Character," in *Midwest Studies XIII*, pp. 184–85, 191–92; Nussbaum, *Fragility of Goodness*, pp. 297, 303–6, and "Non-Relative Virtues: An Aristotelian Approach," in *Midwest Studies XIII*, p. 44; Sherman, *Fabric of Character*, pp. 76–80, 85–94, especially pp. 102–5, 119, 133, 141–43. See also L. Gregory Jones, *Transformed Judgment: Toward a Trinitarian Account of the Moral Life* (Notre Dame: University of Notre Dame Press, 1990), pp. 39–40, 167nn. 43–44.

20. Similarly, although the kind of virtue theory advanced here requires a starting, partially determinate notion of the *telos*, our understanding of the virtues and the *telos* is open to change and development. See, for example, MacIntyre, *After Virtue*, p. 219; Nussbaum, "Non-Relative Virtues," p. 45; Sherman, *Fabric of Character*, pp. 43–44, 89, 94.

21. See Conly, "Flourishing and the Ethics of Virtue," p. 86; MacIntyre, "Sophrosune," p. 7; Solomon, "Internal Objections," p. 429; cf. MacIntyre, *After Virtue*, pp. 202–3. Although Conly rejects a teleological virtue ethic, she correctly understands its structure.

22. For example, Harak, *Virtuous Passions*, pp. 66–68, 88–98; MacIntyre, *After Virtue*, pp. 149, 154, 161–62, and *Whose Justice?*, pp. 109, 128, 130; Nussbaum, *Fragility of Goodness*, pp. 307–8, 383–84, and "Non-Relative Virtues," p. 37; Sherman, *Fabric of Character*, pp. 2, 27, 38, 45–49, 63–64, 119–24, 166–71. See also Foot, *Virtues and Vices*, pp. 5–8; R.B. Brandt, "The Structure of Virtue," in *Midwest Studies XIII*, pp. 64–68; Pincoffs, *Quandaries and Virtues*, p. 81. Cf. Robert C. Roberts, "Aristotle on Virtues and Emotions," *Philosophical Studies* 56 (July 1989): 293–306, and "Will power and the Virtues," in Kruschwitz and Roberts, *The Virtues*, p. 124.

23. For example, Foot, *Virtues and Vices*, pp. 8–11; Pincoffs, *Quandaries and Virtues*, pp. 77–80, 88, 152; Solomon, "Internal Objections," p. 429; James D. Wallace, *Virtues and Vices* (Ithaca: Cornell University Press, 1978), p. 36–51.

24. James F. Keenan, *Goodness and Rightness in Thomas Aquinas's Summa Theologiae* (Washington: Georgetown University Press, 1992), pp. 93–99; MacIntyre, *After Virtue*, pp. 122, 148–49, 154, 191, 219, and *Whose Justice?*, pp. 109–16; Nelson, *Priority of Prudence*, pp. 73–76; Nussbaum, *Fragility of Goodness*, pp. 296–97, 329, 332–33, 375–76; Roberts, "Aristotle on Virtues and Emotions," p. 293; Amelie O. Rorty, "Virtues and Their Vicissitudes," in *Midwest Studies XIII*, p. 136.

25. For example, Nelson, *Priority of Prudence*, pp. 73, 76; Sherman, *Fabric of Character*, p. 1; cf. Servais Pinckaers, "Virtue Is Not a Habit," *Cross Currents* 12 (1962): 65–82. Pinckaers makes the important point that the stability of a virtue is not a "habit" in the ordinary meaning of the term. "Habits" can be automated actions devoid of reflection and decision, devoid of human reasoning and will. Virtues, however, are those states of character that ensure that practical reason and will can perform well. That is, virtues involve the engagement of human reason and will and thus are not "habits" in the ordinary sense. On this point, see also Sherman, ibid., pp. 157–60, 177–79.

26. Brandt, "Structure of Virtue," pp. 64ff; Nelson, *Priority of Prudence*, pp. 99, 101, 143; Nussbaum, *Fragility of Goodness*, pp. 332–39, 346–47, 362–64; Sherman, *Fabric of Character*, pp. 39, 43, 191–98; cf. Harak, *Virtuous Passions*, pp. 16, 31, 36, 39, 117. Often the stability of the virtues and the tie to moral development is more implicit than explicit. For example, see MacIntyre, *After Virtue*, pp. 154, 191, 203, 219, and *Three Rival Versions*, pp. 60–63; Norton, "Moral Minimalism," pp. 187–92.

27. For example, MacIntyre, *Whose Justice?*, pp. 111, 113, 132; Nussbaum, *Fragility of Goodness*, pp. 341, 349; A. Chadwick Ray, "A Fact About the Virtues," *Thomist* 54 (July 1990): 438; Sherman, *Fabric of Character*, pp. 51, 114–16, 176.

28. Adams, "Common Projects," p. 300.

29. Classical music provides a possible example. We find satisfaction in the activity of hearing or playing music. We care about the quality of the activity itself: the way a piece is performed and our perception of subtle changes in tone. Often there is little or no instrumental value to this activity; yet, we know our lives would be diminished without it.

30. MacIntyre, *Whose Justice?*, pp. 109, 111; Nussbaum, *Fragility of Goodness*, p. 297.

31. For this and the next two paragraphs, see Glenn A. Hartz, "Desire and Emotion in the Virtue Tradition," *Philosophia* (July 1990): 147–49; MacIntyre, *After Virtue*, pp. 60–64, 160; Nussbaum, *Fragility of Goodness*, pp. 294–97; Sherman, *Fabric of Character*, pp. 77, 85–86, 114–16.

32. Nussbaum, ibid., p. 297.

33. It should be noted that I never offer a comprehensive list of the virtues. Nor do MacIntyre, Nussbaum, or Sherman provide what they consider exhaustive lists. Moreover, MacIntyre *("Sophrosune")*, Robert C. Roberts ("Virtues and Rules," *Philosophy and Phenomenological Research* 51 [June 1991]: pp. 336–37, 340) and Rorty ("Virtues and Their Vicissitudes," p. 145) argue that what counts as a virtue is at least partially conditioned historically and socially. Rorty (ibid., pp. 140) also suggests that terms like prudence do not identify a single disposition or capacity, but are umbrella concepts "for a wide range of independent traits." Pincoffs (*Quandaries and Virtues*, p. 85) lists sixty-five virtues and is not entirely clear on whether this list is comprehensive. Finally, Wallace ("Ethics and the Craft Analogy," pp. 229–31) seems to suggest the number of virtues is large, diverse, and at least partially role and interest dependent.

34. For this and what follows, see especially Nussbaum, *Fragility of Goodness*, pp. 264–89. MacIntyre, *After Virtue*, pp. 154, 160–62, 204–20 and Sherman, *Fabric of Character*, pp. 63–64, 157–99 (particularly pp. 176–83) are also helpful. See also MacIntyre, *Whose Justice?*, pp. 118, 124–30, 136–40; and Nelson, *Priority of Prudence*, pp. 48–54, 62–68, 73–76, 99. Foot, *Virtues and Vices*, pp. 62–73,

148–52, can be read as working at similar issues. Although Pincoffs does not develop an account of agency, some such account is clearly presumed in his discussion of moral education (*Quandaries and Virtues,* pp. 133–74). The best places to start on these questions remain Aristotle, *Nicomachean Ethics* 1110a-1115a, and St. Thomas Aquinas, *Summa Theologiae* I-II, 6–21.

35. Nussbaum, Fragility of Goodness, p. 273.
36. Ibid., pp. 269–70.
37. Although the need for some account of human agency is evident in the philosophical literature (see n. 34), I first became aware of this need from Stanley Hauerwas, *Character and the Christian Life: A Study in Theological Ethics* with new introduction (San Antonio: Trinity University Press, 1985), pp. 25–29, 35–67, 83–113.
38. In addition to the sources listed in n. 34, see also Crossin, *What Are They Saying about Virtue?,* p. 8; Harak, *Virtuous Passions,* 46–48; Keenan, "Virtue Ethics: Making a Case," pp. 116, 119; Hartz, "Desire and Emotion," p. 160; cf. Pinckaers, "Virtue Is Not a Habit," 72–81.
39. For this and the following, see MacIntyre, *After Virtue,* pp. 128–29; Nelson, *Priority of Prudence,* p. 37; Nussbaum, *Fragility of Goodness,* pp. 318–72, especially pp. 319, 340–41; Sherman, *Fabric of Character,* pp. 51, 130; Solomon, "Internal Objections," pp. 433, 439–41; Margaret Urban Walker, "Moral Luck and the Virtues of Impure Agency," *Metaphilosophy* 22 (January/April 1991): 14–27. See also Bernard Williams, *Moral Luck: Philosophical Papers 1973–1980* (Cambridge: Cambridge University Press, 1981), pp. 20–39. The notion of luck or fortune is at the center of Nussbaum's book.
40. Cf. MacIntyre, ibid., p. 258, and *Whose Justice?,* pp. 121–23, 132–36; Sherman, ibid., pp. 153–56.
41. Nussbaum uses Euripides' *Hecuba* to make similar points (*Fragility of Goodness,* pp. 397–421).
42. For two provocative but different answers to what we need most for dealing with luck, see Hauerwas, "On Being Temporally Happy," p. 16; Walker, "Moral Luck," pp. 19–21.
43. Most of this and the following is the logical outgrowth of what has already been said. For additional texts, see Joel Kupperman, "Character and Ethical Theory," in *Midwest Studies XIII,* pp. 115–25; Pincoffs, *Quandaries and Virtues,* pp. 4–5, 16, 30, 62, 65, 81–82, 145, 147, 169. Cf. Nussbaum, *Fragility of Goodness,* pp. 248–50, 306; Solomon, "Internal Objections," p. 437. Kupperman is not developing a neo-Aristotelian virtue ethic, but his treatment of the priority of character is useful and accords with virtue theory.
44. Cf. James F. Keenan, "Die erworbenen Tugenden als richtige (nicht gute) Lebensführung: Ein genauerer Ausdruck ethischer Beschreibung," in *Ethische Theorie Praktisch,* ed. Franz Furger (Münster: Aschendorff, 1991), pp. 19–35.
45. For example, Nelson, *Priority of Prudence,* pp. 44, 48, 82; Sherman, *Fabric of Character,* pp. 3–5, 13, 29.
46. Cf. Harold Alderman, "By Virtue of a Virtue," in Kruschwitz and Roberts, *The Virtues,* p. 61; Nussbaum, ibid., pp. 290, 300. These examples are mine, but they highlight the kinds of issues important to the authors cited in nn. 34, 38, and 43–45.

47. Cf. Harak, *Virtuous Passions,* pp. 34–35.

48. Robert B. Louden ("On Some Vices of Virtue Ethics," in Kruschwitz and Roberts, *The Virtues,* p. 70) argued that virtue theory is unable to offer guidance on specific actions and choices, but he has recently reversed his position ("Virtue Ethics and Anti-Theory," *Philosophia* [July 1990]: 101). See also Solomon, "Internal Objections," p. 432; Trianosky, "What Is Virtue Ethics All About," p. 341.

49. "Common Sense and Uncommon Virtue," in *Midwest Studies XIII,* p. 108.

50. For example, Nussbaum, *Fragility of Goodness,* pp. 294–95, 312; Sherman, *Fabric of Character,* pp. 13, 39, 43, 191–98; Solomon, "Internal Objections," pp. 437–39.

51. See, for example, Louden, "Virtue Ethics and Anti-Theory," pp. 95–97, 101–5; Nussbaum, ibid., pp. 302–4; Spohn, "The Return of Virtue Ethics," 66, 74; Solomon, ibid. See also Pincoffs, *Quandaries and Virtues,* pp. 14–36. Cf. Sherman, *Fabric of Character,* pp. 13–28, 85–86.

52. For example, Nussbaum, *Fragility of Goodness,* p. 305, and "Non-Relative Virtues," p. 44; Sherman, "Common Sense," pp. 100, 107; MacIntyre, *After Virtue,* p. 154; Nelson, *Priority of Prudence,* pp. 55, 57, 79–80, 82, 132–33.

The relevant features of a situation may differ from instance to instance and from individual to individual. One has to consider, for example, not only whether justice, courage, generosity, or all three are at stake, but the specific nature and content of relevant relationships and the moral development of the actors involved. See also MacIntyre, *Whose Justice?,* pp. 124–26; Norton, "Moral Minimalism," p. 183; Pincoffs, ibid., pp. 21–27.

53. Nussbaum, *Fragility of Goodness,* p. 306–8. See also MacIntyre, *After Virtue,* pp. 60, 154, 161–62, and *Whose Justice?,* pp. 116, 124–26, 136; Sherman, *Fabric of Character,* pp. 44–50. Cf. Pincoffs, ibid., pp. 58–63, 69.

54. Cf. Solomon, "Internal Objections," pp. 429–30; and Spohn, "The Return of Virtue Ethics," p. 65. I am unaware of any account of consequentialism that makes the acquisition of virtue a central aim. Rather, consequentialism usually reduces the virtues to an instrumental role: the virtues are those dispositions or traits that assist our obtaining other "nonmoral" consequences or goals.

55. MacIntyre, *After Virtue,* pp. 150–51, and "Plain Persons and Moral Philosophy: Rules, Virtues and Goods," *American Catholic Philosophical Quarterly* 66 (Winter 1992): 10; Nelson, *Priority of Prudence,* pp. 131–35; Sherman, *Fabric of Character,* p. 51.

56. See also n. 31.

57. Pincoffs, *Quandaries and Virtues,* p. 171; Sherman, *Fabric of Character,* pp. 71, 87, 92, 114–15; cf. Keenan, "Die erworbenen Tugenden als richtige," pp. 19–20. As far as I can tell, a concern with consequences is always assumed but seldom stated in neo-Aristotelian virtue accounts. According to virtue ethics, one issue surrounding many actions is whether they will direct one to or away from the virtues. This issue certainly concerns consequences, but authors seldom explicitly note the need for calculating these consequences. Similarly, the focus of virtue ethics on friendship is unintelligible without attention to consequences, but this fact is seldom noted.

58. For example, Solomon, "Internal Objections," pp. 429–30; Trianosky, "What Is Virtue Ethics All About," p. 335.
59. See, for example, MacIntyre, *After Virtue*, 60, 118–20.
60. Nussbaum, *Fragility of Goodness*, p. 302.
61. Nussbaum, ibid., pp. 302–5; Trianosky, *What Is Virtue Ethics All About*," p. 342. See also nn. 50–52.
62. MacIntyre, *After Virtue*, pp. 150–52, 258; Sherman, "Common Sense," p. 98. Cf. Pincoffs, *Quandaries and Virtues*, pp. 29, 31.
63. *Fragility of Goodness*, p. 299; cf. id., "Non-Relative Virtues," p. 44.
64. Nelson, *Priority of Prudence*, pp. 80, 102, 132, 138.
65. *Fragility of Goodness*, p. 304.
66. Nussbaum, ibid. See also MacIntyre, *After Virtue*, pp. 52–55, and "Plain Persons and Moral Philosophy," p. 10; Pincoffs, *Quandaries and Virtues*, p. 173; Sherman, *Fabric of Character*, p. 181.
67. *Fragility of Goodness*, p. 304.
68. *Quandaries and Virtues*, p. 25.
69. For example, MacIntyre, *After Virtue*, pp. 52–55.
70. Most deontological theories start with a set of rules and introduce the virtues as dispositions to follow the rules. Thus, deontologists almost always relegate the virtues to an instrumental and subservient role (e.g., William K. Frankena, *Ethics*, 2nd ed. [Englewood Cliffs: Prentice-Hall, 1973], pp. 65, 67; John Rawls, *A Theory of Justice* [Cambridge: Harvard University Press, 1971], p. 192). In virtue theory, however, it is the rules or principles that are derivative and thus subservient. In addition to the citations already listed, see Michael Davis, "Civic Virtue, Corruption, and the Structure of Moral Theories," in *Midwest Studies XIII*, p. 353; MacIntyre, *After Virtue*, pp. 232–33; Trianosky, "What Is Virtue Ethics All About," p. 340; cf. Walter Schaller, "Are Virtues No More than Dispositions to Obey Moral Rules?" *Philosophia* (July 1990): 195–207.
71. See nn. 16 and 17.
72. For example, Sherman, *Fabric of Character*, pp. 30, 54, 133; Nelson, *Priority of Prudence*, pp. 52–53. The emphasis on examples and role models (also called "experts" and "masters") differs according to author but is usually a prominent feature in virtue ethics. See Alderman, "By Virtue of a Virtue," p. 61; MacIntyre, *Three Rival Versions*, pp. 60–66; Nussbaum, *Fragility of Goodness*, pp. 248–50, 290, 300; Pincoffs, *Quandaries and Virtues*, pp. 165–66; Roberts, "Virtues and Rules," p. 328. See also Lawrence A. Blum, "Moral Exemplars: Reflections on Schindler, Trocmes, and Others," in *Midwest Studies XIII*, pp. 196–221.
73. I take this perfectionism as implicit in the logic of a teleological virtue ethic. The most helpful explication is David Norton, "Moral Minimalism," pp. 180–95. But see also Keenan, "Virtue Ethics: Making a Case," p. 123–24; Sherman, "Common Sense," pp. 101–102; Pincoffs, *Quandaries and Virtues*, pp. 103–14, cf. pp. 13–52. Sherman and Pincoffs are dealing with somewhat different issues, but their discussions are relevant.
74. Norton, ibid., p. 185.
75. Ibid., p. 186.
76. Ibid., p. 187.

77. Ibid., p. 185; and see Putman, "Virtue and the Practice of Modern Medicine," p. 438.

78. Pincoffs, *Quandaries and Virtues*, pp. 107–9. See also Norton, *Moral Minimalism*, p. 185. Although dealing with somewhat different issues, other relevant sources are Adams, "Saints," pp. 153–60; Ray, "A Fact About the Virtues," pp. 436–37, 449–50; Sherman, *Fabric of Character*, 102–5.

3

Needed: a Christian Case for Virtue Ethics

Despite growing numbers of adherents to virtue theory, surprisingly little is said about why Christians in particular should develop a virtue ethic. Proponents of virtue theory have failed to explain why Christians might find virtue theory attractive. They have done little to suggest why Christians qua Christians might favor virtue ethics over nonvirtue theories.

Are there reasons for supposing that Christians have a stake in virtue theory? Or are nonvirtue theories equally good at giving expression to Christian moral insight? Indeed, is virtue theory even compatible with a thoroughly Christian morality? Theologians advocating virtue ethics have generally failed to answer such questions. They have failed to provide an explicitly Christian case for virtue ethics.

One need not look far to find those who question whether virtue is the best framework for expressing Christian concerns. For example, William K. Frankena notes:

> I do not see . . . why a religious framework requires us to think in aretaic or virtue, rather than in denotic or obligation, terms. My impression is that, in the Judeo-Christian tradition, the divine law conception of ethics has been at least as prevalent as the EV [ethics of virtue] one.[1]

Philip Quinn similarly suggests that the Christian tradition is about duty, not virtue, and is more at home with Kant than Aristotle. Quinn also raises doubts about whether virtue ethics is agreeable to a fully Christian emphasis on God's grace. He concludes that we cannot turn to an Aristotelian virtue ethic because such a turn would involve abandoning central Christian claims.[2]

Even some proponents of virtue theory are uneasy about whether and which Christian convictions fit with a virtue framework. Gilbert Meilaender, for example, repeatedly worries about the compatibility of virtue theory and Christian belief:

> Indeed, before a Christian ethicists latch too quickly onto an ethic of virtue, it is important to remember that an emphasis on character may sit uneasily with some strands of Christian belief.... Such an approach cannot without difficulty be incorporated into a vision of the world which has at its center a crucified God—which takes, that is, not self-realization but self-sacrifice as its central them.
>
> These words suggest a difficulty for anyone wishing to write about the virtues within a framework of Christian belief.... The entire effort may seem too self-centered, a failure to focus one's attention upon God and the neighbor. And the very fact that virtues are habits of behavior ingrained in one's character may suggest that they become our possession and that the moral life is not continually in need of grace.[3]

These concerns—that virtue theory may be self-centered or narcissistic and incompatible with a Christian understanding of God's grace—appear frequently in Meilaender's work.[4]

Richard Taylor, unlike Meilaender, does not hesitate on this question. According to Taylor, Christianity and virtue theory are antithetical. Taylor understands Christianity to be about obedience to God's demands and therefore blames Christianity for virtue ethics having been supplanted by an ethics of duty. Taylor also views Christianity's concern for the poor and oppressed and its extolling of traits like humility and meekness as diametrically opposed to virtue theory's aspiration to excellence. For Taylor, Christianity and true virtue are irreconcilable.[5]

The point of these illustrations is straight-foward: a defense of a Christian virtue ethic must show that virtue theory is compatible with and capable of expressing Christian convictions about the moral life. Authors trying to articulate a Christian moral vision are not going to adopt a virtue framework if it is unable to give voice to that vision. It is therefore important to show that virtue theory is compatible with and helpful in expressing Christian convictions.

ON NOT RECOGNIZING THE NEED

Lack of attention to the issue of the compatibility and continuity between Christian concerns and virtue theory is widespread among Christian ethicists favoring a virtue approach. Stanley Hauerwas provides a striking example. Hauerwas is widely known for his appropriation of virtue ethics, and his *Character and the Christian Life* explicitly links Christian convictions and virtue theory.[6] There Hauerwas shows that a virtue or character ethic helps articulate and make intelligible "some of the primary insights associated with the doctrine of sanctification."[7] He does this chiefly by explicating Calvin's, Wesley's and (to a lesser extent) Jonathan Edwards's views of sanctification and then showing how those views suggest and lend themselves to a virtue or character ethic. Hauerwas describes, for instance, how their understandings of "person" and "moral growth" lead toward virtue ethics.[8]

The link Hauerwas establishes between virtue ethics and sanctification is helpful. The problem is that his treatment of sanctification is very limited and is practically the only point at which Hauerwas has worked to establish such a connection. Indeed, as L. Gregory Jones has observed, "his discussion still tends to be too 'bilingual'; talk of character and the virtues here, then talk of sin and grace and discipleship and Jesus there, without carefully working out whether and how those vocabularies are related to each other."[9]

Hauerwas seems to assume that his theological discussions of the moral life easily and self-evidently connect with his attention to virtue and character. Yet these connections are not evident in his work. When attending to theological issues of discipleship, the centrality of Jesus, or the role of the church, particular virtues are sometimes mentioned, but virtue theory is not prominent.[10] Even more striking, when he is developing an account of character and virtue, theological concerns drop almost completely from the picture.[11] Thus, Hauerwas generally does not show how virtue ethics connects with and expresses Christian convictions.[12]

I believe that Hauerwas was headed in the right direction when he started to link sanctification with virtue ethics. But sanctification is not the only category Christians use to understand their faith or how they are to live morally. His case would have been more persuasive had he provided a fuller account of sanctification and similarly linked other Christian convictions with virtue ethics. Hauerwas's *Character and the Christian Life* embarked on an important task, but it leaves that task largely unfinished.

Hauerwas is not alone in this. Most discussions of virtue theory simply bypass the question of whether virtue ethics is adequate to Christianity's theological and biblical commitments. A good example of this oversight is the debate between proponents of an ethic of virtue and proponents of an ethic of duty held in the *Journal of Religious Ethics* from 1973 to 1976. Here, in a journal devoted to "religious ethics," we search almost in vain for accounts of the biblical and theological adequacy of virtue ethics. In numerous essays on virtue and duty, we find little explicit reference to Christian convictions.[13] Of the few theological or biblical claims made, the majority argue for the importance of obligation, not virtue.[14] The only major exception is an essay by Frederick Carney critiquing the work of William Frankena. Although Carney does not argue for virtue theory, he shows that Frankena's notion of morality and obligation is inconsistent with how morality is understood from a Christian perspective. Carney also suggests that general moral theories be tested against Christianity's background beliefs, commitments, and judgments.[15]

This testing against a broad background of Christian convictions is precisely what's missing among advocates of virtue theory. We are offered little in the way of theological or biblical arguments for a renewed interest in virtue. We are presented with few avowedly Christian reasons for thinking that a return to virtue theory is appropriate.[16]

JUSTIFICATIONS FOR NEGLECT

Why have authors concerned with virtue theory neglected to show its compatibility and connections with Christian convictions?[17] Among many possible answers, including the personal interests or temperaments of those writing in virtue theory, two will be discussed here: (1) the assumption that the connections between virtue theory and Christian convictions are obvious, and (2) the notion that everyone, Christians and non-Christians alike, should adopt virtue ethics. Either type of response could explain why questions of connections and compatibility are seldom addressed. One who thinks the connections are obvious will not recognize that there are questions of compatibility or will consider those questions trivial. One who thinks that everyone should adopt a virtue framework will not appeal to specific Christian concerns in advocating that framework. Instead, he or she will attempt to argue for virtue theory in more general or neutral terms.

Connections Are Obvious

Hauerwas often appears to operate from this first assumption. The disjunction of his use of virtue language from his use of theological language suggests that Hauerwas either assumes that the connections between these language forms are obvious or is himself unclear about their precise relationship. In either case, the divided nature of his work leads one to question whether the connections between virtue theory and Christian convictions are really obvious.

Another example of believing the connections to be obvious is found in James McClendon's *Biography as Theology*.[18] After outlining the notion of character or virtue ethics—which he prefers to call a "character-in-community" ethics—McClendon suggests that Christian ethics must shift from a focus on decisions to a focus on character and virtue.[19] McClendon offers little in the way of theological or biblical justification for this shift, however. One of his remarks helps to explain the lack of specifically Christian justification:

> There can be little doubt that if "character ethics" is understood in the terms now roughly indicated, it has many features which are compatible with Christian morality as widely understood by Christians of any age. Christians from New Testament times have been deeply interested in character, though more correctly in character as redeemed by Christ, rather than in character as a natural or personal achievement.... [Jesus'] character is a touchstone of Christian life (Phil 2:5ff).[20]

McClendon does not think it necessary to argue that a virtue framework is compatible with and can express Christian convictions. He views it as obvious. A virtue framework is, for McClendon, a natural way of expressing Christian concerns, whether biblical or more systematic. But the connections between virtue theory and Christian convictions are not obvious to everyone. Indeed, many writers would be surprised at the suggestion that there is "little doubt" about their compatibility.[21]

A further example of assuming compatibility is Romanus Cessario's *The Moral Virtues and Theological Ethics*.[22] Cessario's work attends more to Scripture than most contemporary studies in virtue theory.[23] One gets the impression, nevertheless, that Cessario assumes the connection between virtue theory and Scripture more than he shows it. Cessario claims in his opening paragraph that "even a casual perusal of the Gospels and the writings of the apostles reveals the specificity of Christian teaching on the virtues."[24] This statement sets the tone for the work, and one finds an almost proof-text approach. Rather than show the compatibility of virtue theory with the plausible exegesis of some biblical texts, Cessario periodically seeds the discussion of virtue with biblical citations. Occasionally the biblical texts fit his point well; most often they do not.

For example, Cessario uses Gal 4:19 to show our continued need for moral growth after conversion and Rom 8:22-23 to show the tension between our new self in Christ and the continuing need for moral growth.[25] While these themes are typical Pauline concerns, they are not the foremost issues in the cited texts. Gal 4:19 is primarily about the Galatians leaving, or having left, true faith in Christ. It is not primarily concerned with the process of moral growth after conversion. Similarly, Rom 8:22-23 deals with waiting, based on the promise of the Spirit, for the redemption of the whole of creation. The central issue in this passage is not our moral growth, but our hope in God's promise given in Christ and the Spirit.

Cessario offers biblical texts throughout to show the connection between virtue theory and Christian convictions. The problem is that the chosen biblical texts often do not relate directly to the point he is making. His opening assumption concerning the obvious connection between Scripture and virtue theory may explain this cavalier, haphazard selection. In any event, the case for connecting virtue theory and Scripture remains unresolved. Although an improvement over McClendon's "little doubt," Cessario also assumes too much.[26]

This tendency to assume rather than show the compatibility and connections between Christian convictions and virtue theory creates a difficulty precisely because the connections are not obvious to everyone. Many question how much harmony exists between virtue theory and Christian theology and Scripture. Given that the connections are not obvious to all, it would be better to point out some similarities and points of contact between virtue theory and Christian convictions.[27]

Besides, it is likely that nearly every author in Christian ethics makes similar assumptions about his or her adopted ethical theory. Most Christian authors advocating proportionalism, deontology, divine command ethics, or situational ethics believe that their emphases are adequate to Christian convictions. Some have tried to show this adequacy; most have simply assumed it. Their certainty notwithstanding, it is not evident to everyone that each of these theories is sufficient for expressing Christian moral convictions.[28] So why assume that virtue theory's sufficiency is self-evident? The case for Christians adopting virtue theory would be strengthened by showing its compatibility and connections.

Everyone Should Adopt Virtue Ethics

The notion that everyone should adopt virtue ethics is another reason authors neglect questions of virtue theory's compatibility with Christian convictions. If there are reasons for thinking that everyone (irrespective of one's religious, cultural, or philosophical tradition) should hold to a virtue framework, then there is no need for an explicit appeal to specifically Christian ideas.

McClendon again serves as an example. He sets an agenda early in his chapter on character ethics: "I will argue that the hope of ethics, both secular and religious, lies in the recovery of what may be called an ethics of character."[29] The claim is not limited to Christians, or even to religious people of whatever persuasion, but extends to everyone interested in ethics. Given this agenda, it is little wonder that McClendon affords slight attention to Christian convictions. Why should he? If the "hope of ethics" is in virtue theory, then Christians, like everyone else, must adopt some form of virtue ethics.[30]

But why would authors assume that everyone should adopt virtue ethics? A variety of reasons or assumptions could lead in this direction, but all of them are problematic. For instance, one may believe that virtue theory is the only alternative to the particular nonvirtue theories that one is critiquing. Something like this idea seems to be at work in Alasdair MacIntyre's *After Virtue*. MacIntyre paints the contemporary picture as if the only live option is "Nietzsche or Aristotle."[31] Since most readers will find the consequences of a Nietzschean view unacceptable, they are thrust into a neo-Aristotelian virtue framework.

MacIntyre seems to believe, or would have us believe, that virtue theory is the only available option. Therefore, it is not necessary to ask whether virtue theory is compatible with Christian moral convictions (or, for that matter, with the convictions of Buddhists, Hindus, Muslims, or Marxists). The problem is that no one, MacIntyre included, has shown that virtue theory is the singular alternative.[32] To show this would require a dialog with adherents of a wide variety of communities and traditions. Such dialog has not been initiated.

It is unlikely that we have exhausted the variety of ethical schemes within the West. It is certain that we have barely touched the possibilities outside the West. As Nripinder Singh notes:

> Western ethicists have betrayed a relative neglect of non-Western ethical systems. The work of a handful of social anthropologists apart, the moral claims advanced in the religious traditions of humankind have elicited, especially of outsiders from those traditions, not more than a passing interest.[33]

Many doubt that we have spent the ethical resources of modern Western moral philosophy. But even if we have, other traditions may have ways of envisioning the moral life that we have not even begun to explore. Thus, we cannot adopt virtue theory solely because we assume it to be the only alternative to the ethical theory or theories we reject.

Another factor lending support to the idea that everyone should adopt a virtue framework is the presumption that virtue theory is tradition neutral. That is, one might suppose that virtue theory provides an impartial account of human morality and is thus applicable to all traditions despite their differences.[34] After all, if virtue theory is true, it must be true for everyone.

The difficulty here is with the notion of a tradition-neutral ethical theory. How would one develop an ethical theory that does not reflect the language, practices, and beliefs of some particular group and its history? Moreover, how would one determine that the theory was truly neutral? Authors like Wittgenstein, Sellars, Quine, Kuhn, and Berger have helped us to see that we lack access to an Archimedean point from which to judge between competing practices or moral theories.[35] It is therefore unclear how we would develop an ethical theory that could be judged a priori to apply to all significant human communities and their commitments. This limitation is as applicable to virtue theory as to any other.

There is no obvious way to develop a substantive ethical theory that we can safely assume is free from bias and applicable to every important human community. Indeed, theories claiming neutrality actually begin with a historically particular understanding of the moral life, which is then elevated to the claimed status of neutrality. Virtue theory is no different. Its view of the human moral condition is not, and could not be, an impartial one.

But if ethical theories are not neutral, if there is no Archimedean point, then such theories need to be tested against the actual convictions and practices of various human traditions. Theories must be tested community by community, tradition by tradition. They must show that they can account for the convictions and practices of the specific tradition or traditions to which they are meant to apply. This book argues that virtue theory is compatible with and helpful in expressing the moral convictions of the Christian tradition. Whether or not that theory is helpful for other traditions can be explored in conversation with members of those groups.[36]

A third reason one might think that virtue theory is applicable to everyone is the idea that different traditions have the same basic understanding of ethics. This idea is a variation of the tradition-neutral idea, except the emphasis is on the equivalence of traditions rather than the neutrality of a theory. One might assume, for instance, that Christians, Muslims, Sikhs, and Buddhists are all saying basically the same thing (at least about how we should live our lives). The same ethical theory would then be applicable to everyone because everyone is engaged in the same task.[37]

John Hick often appears to view various religious traditions as using different languages and practices to talk about the same experiences and goals.[38] Similarly, Harold Alderman's argument for a virtue or character ethic is largely based on the assertion that good character is transculturally recognizable. Alderman claims "that there are no irresolvable conflicts" between paradigmatic individuals like Christ, Lao Tsu, and Socrates and that they endorsed "a common core" of traits and behaviors.[39]

The problem with this view is the overwhelming evidence against it. As William Placher observes, "the great world religions seem to have quite different views on whether there is a personal God (or more than one), how and where that God has been revealed, what awaits us after death, how we ought to live our lives, and so on."[40] The aims and practices of Theravada Buddhists, for example, are not the aims and practices of Christians. Buddhists are not seeking salvation in Christ but are trying to reach nirvana. Christians are not trying to achieve nirvana but are looking to Christ for their salvation.[41]

Different religious traditions, like Christianity and Buddhism, provide different pictures of the nature of reality as well as different understandings of how we should live. Given this, it is likely that different traditions will authorize different, even somewhat incompatible, ethical systems or theories. The goals, practices and convictions of various traditions are different. Traditions will therefore likely endorse differing accounts of the moral life. To assume otherwise disregards what are often basic convictions about the world.[42]

It is uncertain, for example, whether most Muslims would find a virtue framework helpful in expressing their moral vision. The ethical self-understanding of Islam is tied extensively to notions of submission, obedience, rights, duties, and law. These concepts are not dominant in virtue theory. Thus, whether virtue theory and its concerns can be reconciled with Islam and its moral concerns remains an open question. It is possible that Islam endorses an ethical theory different from, and at points incompatible with, virtue ethics.[43] Similarly, because Islam's ethical self-understanding is based on Allah's revelation in the Quran, traditions that lack the idea of a personal and revealing God may accept an ethical theory different from an Islamic one.

Since basic religious convictions may make a moral theory more or less attractive, and since there are reasons to doubt whether virtue theory in particular is compatible with some other traditions (e.g., Islam), why assume the connection between virtue theory and Christianity? Instead, we should test whether virtue theory is congruent with Christian convictions. We should no more assume a harmony between virtue theory and Christianity than we should assume harmony between virtue theory and Islam.[44] Instead of presuming a fit between virtue theory and Christian convictions, we need to show the former's suitability to the latter.

EPISTEMOLOGICAL ISSUES AND TRUTH CLAIMS

Some will view my focus on Christian convictions as implying a radical epistemological relativism or a kind of sectarian withdrawal. The insistence that religious traditions not only differ from each other but may also endorse substantially different ethical theories will appear especially troublesome, suggesting to some the moral equivalent of Babel.

But my argument is not meant to imply radical relativism or the need for Christians to isolate themselves from others. It is, rather, an attempt to acknowledge the difference between "truth" claims and claims concerning "justification."[45]

Put succinctly, I see no way to argue for a belief, practice, or theory except from the context of a historically particular setting and tradition. The justification of claims is thus always dependent on context. Truth claims are different, however. I believe many things to be true, not only for people at a certain time or place, but always and everywhere. Two examples of truth claims concern slavery and God. I believe that slavery is wrong, not just for twentieth-century Western society, but always and everywhere wrong. I also believe that the cosmos is the creation of a loving God who reaches out to the creation. I do not think this is true only for adherents of monotheistic religions; it is true for all people, whether they are aware of it or not. Still, I know of no way to argue for or to justify these claims concerning slavery and God so that everyone, irrespective of his or her tradition, will find the claims compelling. Rather, these claims must be justified and argued in conversations among and between members of different communities and traditions.

This appeal to "conversation" reflects ideas suggested by the work of Hans-Georg Gadamer and Alasdair MacIntyre.[46] The basic notion is that the search for truth (in this case, truth concerning such things as right and wrong behavior and ethical theory), does not start with the suspension of our previous beliefs and commitments or with the search for an Archimedean point from which to judge all positions objectively. Instead, the search for truth involves dialog, discussion, and argument among conversation partners. The conversation begins with whatever ground is shared among those particular partners. As shared ground is discovered, it provides a position from which to discuss and argue agenda that is not shared. What is shared can be assumed among participants without requiring the added judgment that the shared ground has a privileged epistemological status. Common ground in one discussion can be the disputed ground in another. All that is required for conversation to begin is some common ground.

These few comments obviously do not do justice to the complex epistemological and hermeneutical issues dealt with by Gadamer, MacIntyre, and others. But pointing briefly to notions like "justification" and "conversation" helps locate my argument: I am suggesting to those who share the Christian tradition that virtue theory provides a helpful framework for expressing Christian moral convictions. Thus, this work is part of a conversation within the Christian tradition. It is part of the conversation between traditions only in the sense that articulating our Christian understanding of the truth is a necessary component of that larger discussion.

The consequence of so locating my argument is that I can assume as common ground the basic catholic beliefs and appeal to Scripture widely shared among Christian people. I present here no general argument in defense of those beliefs. Instead, I presume that the basic theological and biblical convictions of the Christian tradition are true. This common ground is a necessary assumption if the appeal for a Christian virtue ethic is to proceed. Debates concerning the truth of any specific Christian conviction can be carried out in other conversations within or between traditions based on whatever ground is shared among the participants.

Similar kinds of assumptions must be made concerning virtue theory. Any aspect of virtue ethics can be challenged by someone from some specific context. For example, the kind of virtue theory outlined in chapter 2 relies on the notion of a human *telos*—that is, that humans have an essential nature, purpose, and function. But the idea of a human *telos* is certainly controvertible. Some philosophical, scientific, and religious traditions will not agree that humans have a *telos*. Those that accept the basic notion of a human end or good may well dispute its nature or constitution. I will not, however, directly address these issues. Instead, I will argue that virtue theory, including the notion of a human *telos*, makes good sense from a Christian perspective.

TOWARD AN ECUMENICAL CHRISTIAN VIRTUE ETHIC

Up to this point I have made frequent reference to "Christian convictions" without any acknowledgement of the plurality of Christian traditions. This oversight may appear egregious, especially given the above insistence on the differences between religious traditions. Indeed, some may want to argue that there is no single Christian faith, only several, significantly dissimilar, Christian faiths. My argument would then fail, not because it is relativistic, but because it does not take denominational distinctions seriously.[47]

While admitting substantial differences between Christian traditions, this work does not focus on denominational or sectarian distinctions. Rather, it argues that a virtue framework is helpful in expressing the basic Christian journey founded in Scripture and classical catholic doctrine.

There are many differences within Christianity. Lutherans are not Mennonites, and neither group is Roman Catholic. Still, it is likely that Orthodox Christians, Roman Catholics, and Reformation Christians (including groups from the "radical" end of the reformation) share substantial ground. This shared ground makes it intelligible to speak about the Christian tradition, however difficult it may be to define its boundaries. We can talk about the Christian tradition without additional qualifiers like "Roman Catholic" or "Lutheran." After all, it makes sense to have a "Dictionary of Church History" or a "Dictionary of Christian Theology." While we may disagree on what to exclude from such dictionaries, we will agree on much that must be included.

Rather than focus on denominational distinctions, this work focuses on convictions widely shared among Christian traditions. In dealing with theological categories, appeal is made to representatives from several Christian traditions who hold similar positions. Such argument shows that my proposed interpretations of theological categories are possible readings in more than one Christian tradition. Similarly, substantial appeal is made to New Testament exegesis. Since the whole church claims the New Testament as Scripture and Canon, plausible readings of those texts should carry considerable weight across denominational lines.

Of course, any interpretation can generate objections. Even a rudimentary Christology or appeal to sanctification can cause disputes—so can almost any biblical text. There is no way around this plurality. I will endeavor, however, to provide readings of Scripture and theological categories that are plausible within the larger Christian tradition. Moreover, my appeal for a Christian virtue ethic does not rest on one or two areas of theology and Scripture. Instead, I appeal to several different areas in both systematic theology and biblical studies. If a reader objects to the interpretation offered in one area, the other areas may prove persuasive.

A caveat is needed here. I do not wish to argue that we need a single, comprehensive and fully detailed Christian virtue ethic. Details and specifics of the theory may differ among Christian communities. A fully specified Lutheran virtue ethic will not look exactly like a fully developed Orthodox account, and neither will look precisely like a Mennonite virtue ethic. The argument is not that every Christian community must subscribe to the *same* virtue ethic. As important differences persist within Christianity, so we cannot expect our ethical understandings to match precisely. Besides, even if we disregard theological differences, Christianity is embodied in diverse settings and cultures. It is unreasonable to think this diversity will have no impact on one's account of ethical theory.

I argue that virtue theory is helpful in expressing the basic Christian journey founded in Scripture and classical catholic doctrine. The implication is that differing Christian communities will find a general Christian virtue ethic, in its basic framework and outline, helpful in expressing their moral convictions. This does not require that every community embrace the same ethic in every detail. Many specifics will undoubtedly differ from community to community.[48]

I argue for the Christian appropriation of virtue theory, not that every Christian community should have exactly the same ethic, or that Christians should adopt virtue theory (as developed in chapter 2) without modification. In many instances virtue theory needs to be developed, filled out, and reformulated to be properly Christian.

As this work proceeds (especially in chapters 4 and 5), I will suggest areas in which virtue theory requires modification. The themes of forgiveness and reconciliation, for example, are important in Scripture but are absent from most virtue accounts. If a virtue ethic is to be truly Christian, it must include the elements of forgiveness and reconciliation. It must also include Christian belief in a human end or good that is in some important sense beyond this world—usually referred to as "union with God," "kingdom of God," "resurrection of the dead," or "heaven." If it is to be genuinely Christian, virtue theory must be adapted to express this end that reaches beyond our world. To be thoroughly Christian, virtue theory must be filled with Christian content and altered to fit a Christian conception of the world.

NOTES

1. "Conversations with Carney and Hauerwas," *Journal of Religious Ethics* 3 (Spring 1975): 53. See also David Schenck, Jr., "Recasting the 'Ethics of Virtue/Ethics of Duty' Debate," *Journal of Religious Ethics* 4 (Fall 1976): 284. Likewise, when G. E. M. Anscombe ("Modern Moral Philosophy," *Philosophy* 33 [1958]: 1–19) equated Christian ethics with divine law ethics, she expressed a common understanding of what Christian ethics entails.

2. Philip L. Quinn, "Is Athens Revived Jerusalem Denied?" *Asbury Theological Journal* 45(1): 49–57. Oliver O'Donovan, *Resurrection and Moral Order:*

An Outline for Evangelical Ethics (Grand Rapids: Wm. B. Eerdmans, 1986) also rejects much of virtue theory as incompatible with the Christian moral life (e.g., pp. 204–25).

3. Gilbert C. Meilaender, *The Theory and Practice of Virtue* (Notre Dame: University of Notre Dame Press, 1984), pp. x, 36.

4. Ibid., pp. 13–17, 100–126, and cf. Gilbert C. Meilaender, *Faith and Faithfulness: Basic Themes in Christian Ethics* (Notre Dame: University of Notre Dame Press, 1991), pp. 73–88; Don H. Zinger, "Are Grace and Virtue Compatible," *Lutheran Forum* 23 (February 1989): 12–13.

5. Richard Taylor, *Ethics, Faith, and Reason* (Englewood Cliffs: Prentice-Hall, 1985), pp. 22–25, 77–87. This book was later reprinted as *Virtue Ethics: An Introduction* (Interlaken: Linden Books, 1991).

6. Stanley Hauerwas, *Character and the Christian Life: A Study in Theological Ethics* with new introduction (San Antonio: Trinity University Press, 1985).

7. Ibid., p. 179; also see, p. 10.

8. Ibid., pp. 179–228, especially pp. 195–226. Earlier parts of this book are concerned with developing a character ethic (pp. 35–128) and responding to Barth's and Bultmann's objections to character ethics (pp. 129–78).

9. L. Gregory Jones, *Transformed Judgment: Toward a Trinitarian Account of the Moral Life* (Notre Dame: University of Notre Dame Press, 1990), p. 17. Jones offers a brief sketch of this disjunction on pp. 15–18.

10. For example, Stanley Hauerwas, *A Community of Character: Toward a Constructive Christian Social Ethic* (Notre Dame: University of Notre Dame Press, 1981), pp. 36–52, 53–71.

11. See, for example, Stanley Hauerwas, "Virtue," in *Powers That Make Us Human: The Foundations of Medical Ethics,* ed. K. Vaux (Urbana: University of Illinois Press, 1985), pp. 117–40, and *Vision and Virtue* (Notre Dame: Fides Publishers, 1974), pp. 48–67, *Dispatches from the Front: Theological Engagements with the Secular* (Durham: Duke University Press, 1994), pp. 31–57; and Stanley Hauerwas with Richard Bondi and David B. Burrell, *Truthfulness and Tragedy: Further Investigations into Christian Ethics* (Notre Dame: University of Notre Dame Press, 1977), pp. 40–56. A similar problem is evident in Richard Bondi, "The Elements of Character," *Journal of Religious Ethics* 12 (Fall 1984): 201–18.

12. Hauerwas's articles in *The Asbury Theological Journal* 45(1): 5–48 are a slight improvement on this point. In them, Hauerwas treats the Aristotelian themes of happiness, virtue, and friendship. He then adds to each article a theological postscript indicating how Christians might appropriate those themes. Although interesting, these articles are at most suggestive; they still exhibit the "bilingual" and disjunctive approach noted by Jones.

13. See n. 1 and the following articles in the *Journal of Religious Ethics*: Frederick S. Carney, "The Virtue-Obligation Controversy," 1 (Spring 1973): 5–19, and "On Frankena and Religious Ethics," 3 (Spring 1975): 7–25; Arthur J. Dyck, "A Unified Theory of Virtue and Obligation," 1 (Spring 1973): 37–52; William K. Frankena, "The Ethics of Love Conceived as an Ethic of Virtue," 1 (Spring 1973): 21–36; Stanley Hauerwas, "Obligation and Virtue Once More," 3 (Spring 1975) and reprinted in *Truthfulness and Tragedy,* pp. 40–56; Thomas W. Ogletree, "Values, Obligations, and Virtues: Approaches to Bio-Medical

Ethics," 4 (Spring 1976): 105–30; J. Wesley Robbins, "Professor Frankena on distinguishing an Ethic of Virtue from an Ethic of Duty," 4 (Spring 1976): 57–62.

14. See, for example, Dyck, "Unified Theory," pp. 43–46; and Ogletree, "Values, Obligations, and Virtues," p. 115. Dyck's essay is interesting and somewhat troubling. He appeals to biblical and theological notions to show an obligation to develop certain virtues. Virtues thus serve and develop from a sense of obligation rather than the opposite. Nor does Dyck view biblical and theological appeals as essential to his argument. He is convinced that the relation between obligation and virtue holds true irrespective of religious convictions or heritage.

15. Carney, "On Frankena," pp. 13–14, 16–17, 23.

16. An example of this failure is seen in Eilert Herms, "Virtue: A Neglected Concept in Protestant Ethics," *Scottish Journal of Theology* 35(6): 481–95. Herms's call for Protestant theologians to renew attention to virtue is unsupported by any theological or biblical rational. The closest he comes is a suggestion that an adequate notion of agency requires attention to virtue, perhaps implying that virtue is necessary to an adequate theological anthropology. He does not say or show this to be the case, however.

A more recent example is James A. Donahue, "The Use of Virtue and Character in Applied Ethics," *Horizons* 17(2): 228–43. Donahue provides an overview of virtue or character ethics and suggests several norms that arise from this ethic. But Donahue, like our other authors, provides no direct appeal to common Christian convictions or Scripture to justify this form of ethical theory. In addition, Donahue spends so much time developing norms that it is unclear in the end whether he is advocating a virtue-based or principle-based ethic.

A lack of engagement with theological and biblical issues is also evident in Jean Porter, *The Recovery of Virtue: The Relevance of Aquinas for Christian Ethics* (Louisville: Westminster/John Knox Press, 1990). Porter's book contains little explicit theological reflection and no interaction with the biblical text. There are indications that Porter views direct appeal to theology—specifically to theological anthropology and the doctrine of God—as crucial to the full justification of virtue theory. Porter has yet to develop those theological ties, however. See Porter, ibid., pp. 56, 175–79, and "Basic Goods and the Human Good in Recent Catholic Moral Theology," *Thomist* 57 (January 1993): 48–49.

17. One exception to this general neglect is Paul Wadell's *Friendship and the Moral Life* (Notre Dame: University of Notre Dame Press, 1989). Wadell asks whether friendship understood in a virtue context is compatible with Christian convictions and shows how to formulate a virtue understanding of friendship that is candidly Christian. In view of Wadell's strong contribution, I need not rehearse the potential link between friendship and Christian convictions.

18. James Wm. McClendon, Jr., *Biography as Theology: How Life Stories Can Remake Today's Theology* (Nashville: Abingdon Press, 1974).

19. Ibid., pp. 29, 32.

20. Ibid., p. 33. To back these assertions, McClendon cites the transition in Rom 12:1-2 and the catalogs of virtues and vices in Gal 5:19-24; Rom 1:28-31; Eph 5:3-5, 6:14-20; Phil 4:8; and Col 3:5-15. Ibid., p. 33nn.26–27.

The only other significant theological or biblical citation in McClendon's work is on p. 19. Here he offers the story of the sheep and goats in Matt 25:31-46 to illustrate that deliberate choice is not central. The biblical text instead focuses on those situations "in which they acted unknowingly, and yet showed themselves for what they truly were."

21. The relationship between my claims and McClendon's more recent *Systematic Theology: Ethics* (Nashville: Abingdon Press, 1986) is more complicated. In *Ethics*, McClendon attends to Scripture throughout and is always aware of the dual question "what must Christian ethics be to be *ethics*, and what must it be to be *Christian*" (p. 63). However, *Ethics* does not develop a virtue ethic but considers broader questions. Elsewhere I have suggested that a virtue ethic can fulfill the criteria McClendon sets forth in *Ethics* (Joseph J. Kotva, Jr., "An Appeal for a Christian Virtue Ethic," *Thought* 67 [June 1992]: 176–78). Thus, I see my claims as a supplement or corollary to *Ethics*, not as a challenge to or rejection of it.

22. Romanus Cessario, *The Moral Virtues and Theological Ethics* (Notre Dame: University of Notre Dame Press, 1991).

23. Another important work in this regard is Stephen E. Fowl and L. Gregory Jones, *Reading in Communion: Scripture and Ethics in Christian Life* (Grand Rapids: Wm. B. Eerdmans, 1991). However, see my comments in n. 44.

24. Cessario, *The Moral Virtues*, p. 1.

25. Respectively, ibid., pp. 24 and 30.

26. Cessario's use of Scripture is not the only reason to find his argument for virtue theory unpersuasive. Cessario's real priority is the infused moral virtues, so the acquired moral virtues get too little attention. He also gives very little attention to communal aspects of existence. Thus, two key aspects of an adequate virtue theory—acquired virtue and communal existence—are inadequately developed by Cessario. Cessario also makes numerous, unargued assertions about things like the Magisterium's moral authority (pp. 90, 133, 153) and the imprudence of homosexual practice (p. 143). These kinds of unsupported statements do not help his case. Simply put, Cessario's work has too many difficulties to stand alone as an appeal for a Christian virtue ethic.

27. Cf. Alasdair MacIntyre's hasty assertion that a virtue scheme is compatible with Christian, Jewish, and Islamic theological frameworks. MacIntyre begins his brief discussion of theistic morality by claiming that a virtue scheme "is complicated and added to, but not essentially altered, when it is placed within a framework of theistic beliefs, whether Christian ... or Jewish ... or Islamic" (Alasdair MacIntyre, *After Virtue*, 2nd ed. [Notre Dame: University of Notre Dame Press, 1984], p. 53).

To his credit, however, MacIntyre admits on the last page of the second edition that *After Virtue* lacks "anything like an adequate treatment of the relationship of the Aristotelian tradition of the virtues to the religion of the Bible and to its theology" (p. 278).

28. I will argue in chapter 6 that these nonvirtue theories are insufficient for expressing the full wealth of Christian moral convictions.

29. McClendon, *Biography as Theology*, p. 14; cf. pp. 35–36.

30. That everyone should adopt a virtue ethic is McClendon's assumption, not his argument. He provides no conceptual or historical justification for suggesting that the "hope of ethics" rests in a virtue or character ethic. In fact, McClendon later admits that he is not refuting other ethical systems but suggesting that the dominant ways of thinking about morality are giving way to concern with character or virtue (ibid., p. 27).

31. MacIntyre, *After Virtue*, pp. 109ff, 256ff.

32. MacIntyre does provide a type of historical argument to support the idea that we are caught in a dilemma. By tracing several failed attempts at finding an alternative to Nietzsche and Aristotle, MacIntyre reinforces the notion that we must choose between them. However, the specifics of MacIntyre's history have not met with especially wide acceptance. Moreover, MacIntyre only covers a portion of Western intellectual history. He does not discuss whether forms of life and convictional systems outside his select history might provide real alternatives to Nietzsche and Aristotle.

33. Nripinder Singh, *The Sikh Moral Tradition* (Columbia, MO: South Asia Publications, 1990), p. 9.

34. Cf. Paul Nelson, *Narrative and Morality: A Theological Inquiry* (University Park: The Pennsylvania State University Press, 1987), pp. 54–61. Nelson views MacIntyre as attempting to develop a concept of virtue common to various moral traditions. But this attempt, as Nelson points out, conflicts with MacIntyre's general historicism. Nelson thus views MacIntyre as succumbing to one of the problems I discuss below: viewing virtue theory as tradition-neutral or viewing various traditions as having the same ethic.

35. Among the more obvious texts, see Ludwig Wittgenstein, *Philosophical Investigations*, 3rd ed. trans. G. E. M. Anscombe (New York: Macmillan Publishing, 1953); Wilfred Sellars, *Science, Perception and Reality* (New York: Humanities Press, 1963); Willard Van Orman Quine, *From a Logical Point of View*, 2nd ed. (New York: Harper and Row, 1963); Thomas S. Kuhn, *The Structure of Scientific Revolutions*, 2nd ed. (Chicago: University of Chicago Press, 1970); Peter L. Berger, *The Sacred Canopy: Elements of a Sociological Theory of Religion* (Garden City: Anchor Books Edition, 1969).

For a lucid, compact, and helpful treatment of these issues and their theological ramifications, see William C. Placher, *Unapologetic Theology: A Christian Voice in a Pluralistic Conversation* (Louisville: Westminster/John Knox Press, 1989).

36. I do not deny that some formal features of morality are universal in scope. For instance, it should be possible to articulate certain requisites of human social existence. One such requisite would be truth-telling. It is difficult to conceive of any human social group extending over a significant period of time without some concept or activity that we can recognize as truth-telling.

This admission does not, however, reduce the strength of my argument. Admitting a formal similarity between various communities' truth-telling practices does not provide a substantive description of those practices. Some elements that may differ from one community to another include deciding to whom the truth is due, what constitutes the truth, and under what circumstances truth should be spoken. The only way to arrive at a substantive description of a community's morality, including the formal aspects that every community must share, is through observation and dialog.

Moreover, it is unlikely that formal resemblances among communities will amount to a meaningful ethical theory. Deontology, consequentialism, and proportionalism provide a place for truth-telling, but the practice of truth-telling does not tell us which theory is correct. In addition, it is questionable whether formal resemblances are central to the self-description of particular moralities. That is, just because communities share the formal feature of truth-telling does not mean that they see truth-telling as a lynch pin of their moral self-understanding.

In short, acknowledging certain universal features of morality does not amount to developing a substantive ethical theory that is safely assumed applicable to every human community. Cf. Nelson, *Narrative and Morality*, pp. 122–30, especially pp. 128–29; and Stanley Hauerwas, "The Difference of Virtue and the Difference It Makes: Courage Exemplified," *Modern Theology* 9 (July 1993): 249–64.

37. This section focuses on the convictions of religious traditions and communities. It is clear, however, that most of these arguments could apply to any set of basic or fundamental convictions about the world, for example, to political and economic systems as well as to religious communities.

38. E.g., John Hick, *Problems of Religious Pluralism* (New York: St. Martin's Press, 1985), p. 102, and "The Outcome: Dialogue Into Truth," in *Truth and Dialogue in World Religions: Conflicting Truth-Claims*, ed. John Hick (Philadelphia: Westminster Press, 1974), p. 151.

39. Harold Alderman, "By Virtue of a Virtue," in *The Virtues: Contemporary Essays on Moral Character*, ed. Robert B. Kruschwitz and Robert C. Roberts (Belmont: Wadsworth, 1987), pp. 52–54. Cf. also n. 14.

40. Placher, *Unapologetic Theology*, p. 17.

41. Cf. ibid., p. 145. Placher also quotes the Buddhist scholar Edward Conze: "I once read through a collection of the lives of Roman Catholic saints, and there was not one of whom a Buddhist could fully approve. . . . They were bad Buddhists though good Christians" (p. 143).

42. The connection between religious convictions and ethical theory admittedly runs both ways. While basic religious convictions or beliefs can make some theories more attractive than others, one who is committed to an ethical theory will likely shape some religious convictions to fit the theory.

The priority I give Christian convictions over ethical theory rests on the notion that many religious convictions are more basic and fundamental to a tradition's system of convictions than are ethical theories. That is, ethical theories tend to be secondary notions; religious convictions tend to be nearer the center. Said differently, if convinced of an irreconcilable conflict between certain basic religious beliefs and an ethical theory, most committed Christians (or Buddhists, Hindus, or Muslims) would reject the ethical theory. Thus, for example, if confronted with the choice of rejecting Jesus as the Christ or rejecting virtue ethics, I would reject virtue ethics.

Granted, these kinds of direct conflicts seldom surface, but that is not the point. The point is which convictions are central or most basic. If, as I suggest, religious convictions are more basic than ethical theories, then the theories need to justify themselves in relation to religious convictions. There is an important sense in which religious convictions authorize ethical theories, but that ethical theories do not authorize religious convictions.

43. This judgment relies on conversations with Muslim friends and the following works: John L. Esposito, *Islam: The Straight Path,* expanded ed. (New York: Oxford University Press, 1991), pp. 25–33, 74–76, 88, 94–101; Shaikh Shaukat Hussain, *Human Rights in Islam* (New Delhi: Kitab Bhavan, 1990); Mahmud Shaltout, "Islamic Beliefs and Code of Laws," in *Islam: The Straight Path,* ed. Kenneth W. Morgan (Delhi: Motilal Banarsidass, 1987), pp. 87–143.

Apparently, the great Muslim theologians and philosophers who appropriated Greek philosophy were and are viewed by the majority in Islam as rationalists, nonbelievers, and unorthodox. These theologians and philosophers are not accepted as sufficiently expressing Islamic theological and ethical convictions. Indeed, Esposito suggests that Islamic philosophers have had a greater impact on the West than on Islam (Esposito, ibid., p. 75).

44. This assumption is a problem (or at least a limitation) even in some very fine works like L. Gregory Jones's *Transformed Judgment* and Stephen E. Fowl and L. Gregory Jones's *Reading in Communion.* These works strive to be thoroughly Christian—filling virtue theory with Christian content and attending to specifically Christian beliefs and practices. Yet both books still assume too much. Because Jones is trying to develop a specifically Trinitarian virtue ethic, he generally fails to ask the antecedent question of whether virtue theory is actually suited to a Christian morality. Similarly, Fowl and Jones seldom present biblical texts that suggest or lead toward a virtue ethic. Instead they assume that virtue theory is essentially correct and offer an understanding of Scripture and ethics that is congruent with their approach. Both books contribute to our understanding of what a fully developed Christian virtue ethic would look like. But the force of their arguments largely depends on one's having already accepted virtue theory's basic premises and its suitability to Christian convictions.

45. On this distinction and the following discussion, see Placher, *Unapologetic Theology,* pp. 123–24 and Stout, *Ethics After Babel,* pp. 23–28. Cf. Porter, *Recovery of Virtue,* pp. 57, 175.

46. See especially Hans-Georg Gadamer, *Truth and Method,* 2nd revised ed., trans. revised by Joel Weinsheimer and Donald G. Marshall. (New York: Crossroad, 1989); and Alasdair MacIntyre, *Whose Justice? Which Rationality?* (Notre Dame: University of Notre Dame Press, 1988). Placer, *Unapologetic Theology,* pp. 55–73, 105–53 is concise and very helpful. See also Joseph Dunne, *Back to the Rough Ground: "Phronesis" and "Techne" in Modern Philosophy and in Aristotle* (Notre Dame: University of Notre Dame Press, 1993), pp. 106–23, 132–44, 150. Although different in approach, Fowl and Jones, *Reading in Communion,* pp. 110–34, is instructive. Fowl and Jones suggest that Christians' own convictions drive them to conversation with others.

47. Cf. the new (1995) journal *Christian Bioethics: Non-Ecumenical Studies in Medical Morality,* which takes the differences among Christian communions as its starting point:

Because Christians are separated, united neither in one communion nor in one baptism, *Christian Bioethics* will address differences, not just agreements. *Christian Bioethics* will attend to the differences among the Christian faiths and underscore the content-full moral commitments that separate and give moral content. It will seek to take seriously the commitments that divide Christians and which are appropriately bridged by conversion rather than by discounting differences (H. Tristram Engelhardt, Jr., "Towards a Christian Bioethics," *Christian Bioethics* 1(1): 1–2).

48. The father we move from Western society, the less certain I am about these claims. Virtue ethics may not be so helpful for Christians in Africa, Asia, or South America. Indeed, Christians in other parts of the world may have ethical theories that will even be more helpful for us in expressing Christian convictions than virtue ethics. We have not had enough intercultural discussion about ethics to rule out this possibility. Thus, my argument is best viewed as part of the dialog within Western Christianity. Only secondarily is it part of the dialog within the larger Christian tradition.

4

Theological Links

This chapter's central aim is to establish points of similarity, contact, and correlation between virtue theory and contemporary Christian systematic theology. It explores numerous potential links and parallels between virtue theory and Christian convictions, and it also indicates some areas where a virtue framework needs to be altered, filled out, and reformulated to be properly Christian.

The argument unfolds in three primary sections. The first section concerns sanctification and personal or individual eschatology. The primary focus here is on sanctification as a teleological process that involves the transformation of the self and is radically dependent on God's grace. The second section deals with Christology. This section's dominant claim is that an adequate Christology includes the notion that Jesus of Nazareth embodies the true human *telos* or end. The third section offers some brief observations on Christian anthropology. The emphasis here is on similarities between Christian anthropology and virtue theory's notions of human agency and our communal nature.

The theological treatment in these sections is not comprehensive. I do not attempt to develop a full or even minimally sufficient Christology, for example. Instead, this chapter focuses on some aspects of Christology (and sanctification and anthropology) that readily connect with or correct a virtue framework.

Nor have I attempted in this chapter to survey a truly representative cross section of theologians or schools of theology to see what each says about sanctification, Christology, and anthropology. A handful of theologians has of necessity been chosen with full knowledge that there is no satisfactory way to justify choosing any particular theologian. Indeed, it seems to me that the selection of authors can be validated only in the course of the work. That is, if the ensuing discussions of sanctification, Christology, and theological anthropology prove to be insightful, or at least occasionally plausible, then the choice of authors will have proved a good, or at least minimally sufficient, choice.

Nevertheless, I offer three comments as a partial explanation of my choice and use of authors. First, the discussion of each theological category draws on authors from more than one Christian tradition. This is done to show that the proposed correlations between the theological categories and virtue theory are possible readings across denominational lines. I am not interested in merely showing that virtue theory is compatible with Mennonite theology, for example. Rather, I want to suggest that virtue theory is compatible with and helpful in expressing convictions widely shared among Christian traditions.

Second, I use different theologians for each of the three major sections.[1] Different readers will find different authors helpful, but my hope is that readers will find in each section at least one author who is helpful. However, even if a reader objects to all the authors in one section, it is possible that he or she will find the authors in other sections more useful.

Third, although I endeavor to provide readings of theological categories that are plausible within the larger Christian tradition, it cannot be denied that these readings are informed by my perspective or "bias." My theological perspective is probably most noticeable in the selection of authors for the Christology discussion (C. Norman Kraus, Hendrikus Berkhof, and Edward Schillebeeckx). Roughly speaking, I chose theologians who in various ways root and focus their Christologies in critical appropriations of the New Testament and its testimony about Jesus Christ. This general approach to Christology differs, for example, from one that concentrates on interpreting ecumenical creeds and ecclesiastical pronouncements.[2]

This is not to imply that the theologians appearing in the Christology section all say the same thing or work from identical methodologies. Their Christologies are substantially different from each other in both approach and content. My comments merely allude to my theological perspective and acknowledge that my biases might be detectable in the section on Christology, given the "family resemblance" in the various authors' approaches to Christology.[3]

My theological predisposition is less obvious in the selection of authors for the sections on sanctification and theological anthropology. The account of sanctification draws on authors (Hendrikus Berkhof, Millard J. Erickson, and John Macquarrie) who are very different from each other in terms of theological influences and methods. This choice of authors is meant to help distinguish my treatment of sanctification from Stanley Hauerwas's treatment in *Character and the Christian Life*.

The latter concentrates somewhat narrowly on Calvin and Wesley.[4] Similarly, because I attempt to discuss some trends or directions in contemporary Christian anthropology, I chose authors (primarily Thomas N. Finger and John R. Sachs) whose anthropologies are in dialog with numerous theologians. My agenda in the sections on sanctification and anthropology thus encouraged the selection of diverse authors. That selection, in turn, makes my theological bias less conspicuous.

It is, of course, true that this entire book is informed by a perspective or bias. The interest in virtue theory, for example, informs the whole project and undoubtedly influences the questions I raise and the themes I emphasize. Acknowledgment of "biases" or "prejudices" does not, however, make this work an illegitimate exercise. The deployment of prejudices is unavoidable in the reading of any text or discussion. But, as Joseph Dunne points out, "it becomes disreputable only when one is unaware, or does not make a clean breast, of the prejudices that one brings, or when one allows them to be so blaring that the text has no chance to speak back."[5] I hope it is evident throughout this work that others (in the form of modern and ancient texts) are continually "speaking back" to me and forcing me to refine and refocus this project.[6]

SANCTIFICATION AND PERSONAL ESCHATOLOGY

Stanley Hauerwas in *Character and the Christian Life* began the task of linking virtue ethics to the systematic category of sanctification. This section will not duplicate his work or discuss his contribution in any detail. For our current purposes, the issue is not what Hauerwas said but what he left unsaid. The notion of sanctification provides both links and corrections to virtue theory that Hauerwas left largely unexplored. The concern here is to discuss those underemphasized or omitted aspects of sanctification that connect with or alter virtue theory.

This section is not strictly limited to "sanctification" but also touches on the individual or personal component of eschatology—that is, what happens to the individual after death. Sanctification and personal eschatology are treated together because the latter concerns the fruition of the former. This will become clear as we proceed.

This discussion of sanctification and personal eschatology draws on three very different theologians: Hendrikus Berkhof (Dutch Reformed), Millard J. Erickson (Baptist General Conference), and John Macquarrie (Anglican).[7] While these authors are from varied traditions and use different theological methods, they agree on key points concerning sanctification and eschatology.[8]

A Teleological Concept

A key point at which our authors agree is that sanctification is a teleological concept.[9] More specifically, sanctification involves the growth and transformation of oneself and one's character toward a partially determinate picture of the human good or end.[10]

According to Berkhof, the process that starts in repentance, justification, and faith has as its goal our "conformity with Christ." Noting that the goal of sanctification is described in various ways—Calvin's "servant of God," Luther's "child of God," Wesley's "perfect man in the full stature of Christ"—Berkhof thinks that "the concept of conformity with Christ can embrace the others and do justice to them."[11]

As Berkhof depicts it, God's purpose for humanity involves encounter and covenant relationship between us and God. But for this encounter to happen, we must be transformed into the image of the true covenant partner—Christ. Thus Christ-likeness is the goal or end of the process of sanctification.[12]

According to Berkhof, the process of sanctification should be viewed not as an inevitable organic progress but as a "training school." It involves struggle, both within oneself and with forces and social structures outside the self. There also is a continual need to fall back on God's gracious forgiveness. Nevertheless, "the Christian life is indeed a matter of goal and an advancing towards it." It involves "a growing, a going forward, a pressing on, a straining toward what lies ahead." It involves a life ever more in conformity with Christ.[13]

Berkhof's understanding of the goal or *telos* involves becoming a certain kind of person. On analogy with Christ, it involves a posture of love, surrender, trust, and obedience before God. It also involves freedom from destructive customs and practices, and freedom for a transforming love of the world and neighbor. It involves becoming the sort of person who often performs acts of faith and love spontaneously, out of who one is, without taking notice of oneself. But there is also concern with self-examination. If we are to progress in faith toward the goal, we must sometimes ask if we are acting and growing in freedom and love.[14]

Erickson also uses Christ to indicate the goal of sanctification. According to Erickson, the process that starts in conversion, repentance, faith, and the new birth "continues throughout one's lifetime."[15] The goal or end of the process gets various designations from Erickson. When talking about the process as beginning in "regeneration," the goal is the transformation and restoration of humans to their original goodness—that is, to their state before the fall.[16] When discussing the process as "sanctification," Erickson mentions "likeness to God" as its goal, but the dominant image is "likeness to Christ."[17]

This is not, Erickson says, a superficial or external resemblance. Likeness to Christ involves a "whole set of characteristics or qualities which makes something what it is."[18] Thus the life-long process of sanctification involves the transformation of character and the development of certain kinds of virtues. As examples of these virtues, Erickson lists the fruits of the Spirit of love, joy, peace, patience, kindness, goodness, gentleness, faithfulness, and self-control.[19]

Macquarrie's account of sanctification is similar to Berkhof's and Erickson's at key points. Indeed, Macquarrie's concluding statement on growth in the Christian life could be offered by either Berkhof or Erickson:

> So the life that begins with conviction of sin, repentance, election, justification, passes into the progressive work of sanctification, in which the Holy Spirit more and more conforms this life to Christ, deepening and extending it in faith, hope, and love.[20]

"Conformity to Christ" is again the dominant image of sanctification's goal,[21] and sanctification is again a process that spans one's entire life.[22] It is a process that requires transformation at the depths of one's character and the development of specific virtues.[23]

Macquarrie talks about those virtues by using the traditional tripartite division of faith, hope, and love. Faith concerns obedience to God, in conformity with Christ's own obedience, and the freedom ("from the tyranny of things... [and] from the frustration and meaninglessness of a life impotent in the face of guilt") that comes with that obedience.[24] Hope looks forward to God's continuing activity of creation and reconciliation. Love leads to community in which we help others reach their potential.[25]

It should be readily apparent that our authors' descriptions of sanctification resemble virtue ethics at key points. Sanctification is a teleological process that involves the transformation of the self and the development of character traits or virtues. The end or goal of sanctification can be variously designated but is frequently discussed in terms of likeness or conformity to Christ. "Conformity to Christ" thus provides a sense of sanctification's goal. It provides each author with a broad vision of the end to which sanctification moves, an end that includes certain traits or virtues. Sanctification is also a process through time, one's lifetime. It is a process (begun in conversion, justification, and faith) where one moves from the kind-of-person-one-is to the kind-of-person-one-is-called-by-God-to-be.[26]

A Concept Tied to Grace

While the idea of sanctification resembles virtue theory in important ways, the Christian belief in sanctification involves a major affirmation that the earlier account of virtue theory does not mention: dependence on God's grace. The initiation and continuing journey or process of sanctification depends on God's prior initiative and loving forgiveness. This dependence does not negate our participation and struggle in moral transformation, but the process is empowered by and dependent on God's previous and ongoing activity.

Berkhof clearly views sanctification as based and rooted in justification.[27] According to Berkhof, in the act of repentance that occurs when we encounter God and God's love, we accept or own up to our sinful past and who we have become.[28] But it is God's receiving us in justification that sets us free for a new future and a new direction. We are not strictly determined by our past because God reaches out to us as lost children. When we hear that God accepts us, "it enters our experience as a sense of liberation, joy, release, and security." In God's loving forgiveness "we derive strength to fight against sin, to endure, and to serve."[29] In short, justification empowers change.

The process of sanctification finds its beginning in justification and goes forward because we can continually "fall back on God's grace as the decisive foundation of our life."[30] We persevere in the struggle only through God's faithfulness and help. Without a sense of God's initial and continuing grace, we succumb either to despair or a grim determination and works righteousness.[31]

Dependence on God's grace does not mean we are passive. Berkhof talks about "faith"—our response, affirmation, and trust in what God is doing—as the point at which justification becomes operative in our lives.[32] He also rejects an organic notion of moral growth because it views us as passive. He insists instead that one's will is helping or obstructing renewal at every step. Life is a training ground that involves continual struggle and striving. We are active (though not equal) partners in the process of sanctification. Trusting in God's grace, we go forward.[33]

Erickson makes similar statements but places even greater emphasis on God's activity. For Erickson, the very possibility of repentance, conversion, and faith is dependent on a "special action by God."[34] We are so entangled in sin that we are unable to respond to God's general call to salvation. Thus, only those who receive a special or effectual call from God are able to respond to the offer of salvation.[35]

Erickson obviously works with a strong notion of predestination. There is no need here to debate the merits of this notion.[36] The significant thing for us is Erickson's strong emphasis on God's activity. Conversion, which lies at the very beginning of sanctification, is a human response enabled by God's gift.[37]

The process of sanctification finds both its introduction and sustenance in God's activity. As the divine side to the human response of conversion and faith, the "new birth" involves God changing our basic "inclinations and impulses." Sanctification continues the change. "Sanctification is the continuing work of God in the life of the believer, making him or her actually holy."[38]

While sanctification is a "supernatural work" and "something done by God," we are not passive.[39] We are "exhorted to work and to grow," urged to the "practice of virtues and avoidance of evils," and commanded to "strive by grace" to attain the goal.[40] Thus, for Erickson as for Berkhof, we are active partners in the transformative process of sanctification.

Macquarrie also talks about sanctification as a joint work. He enjoins us to think "in terms of a work that is initiated and carried through by God working in human lives, and yet a work which needs man's response, cooperation, and highest effort if it is to go forward."[41]

This dual emphasis on God's grace and human effort is evident throughout Macquarrie's discussion. The Christian life begins in the combined process of the Holy Spirit's convicting us of sin and our response of repentance and turning toward God. It is a life that involves our growth in righteousness, but it is also a life founded on God's initiative of choosing, accepting, and forgiving us. Growth continues throughout one's life, but growth is possible only because of divine grace working in us. Thus, Macquarrie, like Erickson and Berkhof, teaches that we both depend on God and participate with God in the transformative processes of sanctification.[42]

Each author finds a way to emphasize the priority of God's grace without negating either moral growth or our responsibility for that growth. This is significant, for some suspect that virtue ethics cannot accommodate the central Christian conviction of the priority of God's grace.[43]

An ethic concerned with moral growth and desiring the designation "Christian" must emphasize God's gracious activity. Christians believe that our starting and continuing on the Christian journey depends on God's prior and sustaining initiative. Note, however, that these authors discuss our need for and dependence on grace without denying human participation in moral growth. They honor the priority of God's grace without rejecting growth or the agent's efforts.

On this important point, virtue theory must be amended to be genuinely Christian. For an ethic to be Christian, it must emphasize our dependence on God's grace, but our discussion suggests that an ethic concerned with grace can also be concerned with the moral transformation of the agent and the agent's role in the transformation. Thus, we can develop a teleological virtue ethic that does not abandon central Christian convictions about God's grace.[44]

A Telos beyond This World

We noted in chapter two that the *telos* is an ideal of human excellence and perfection that can never be fully actualized. We can move toward a fuller realization of the human good, but we never completely realize the goal. The Christian idea of sanctification is similar: we can become more like Christ but we are never (in this life) fully conformed to Christ's image.

The phrase in parentheses points to an important dissimilarity between virtue theory and the Christian belief in sanctification. Sanctification reaches or approaches its goal after or beyond this life. Standard neo-Aristotelian accounts of virtue theory do not entertain the idea of continuing growth after death or of a *telos* beyond this world.

This dissimilarity between Christian belief and virtue theory should not be exaggerated. Christians believe in an end beyond this life, but it only completes the renewal begun in this world. The goal after death is the consummation of a journey or process begun in repentance and continued in sanctification.

According to Berkhof, Christians believe in continuing beyond death precisely because we do not reach the ultimate goal of renewal in this life. Our realization of the goal in this life is partial and fragmentary. The goal is so great it cannot be realized within the confines of our provisional and sinful existence. Death, moreover, seems to rob us of all hope of reaching the goal.[45] Death, Berkhof says, cannot be the last word:

> God will have to finish beyond death what he started here—or death would be more powerful than God and thus the real god and ultimate, chill mystery of human life. On the ground of this alternative or, rather, in virtue of the encounter with this faithful God, the Christian believes in what is called, using traditional language for it, a "life after death." We believe in the completion of the renewal.[46]

Berkhof notes that we cannot say much about what awaits us on the other side of death. But we believe that "God's faithfulness holds on to us even in death and guarantees our identity even in discontinuity."[47] The gift of the Spirit guarantees that God will not let go of us and that the process of renewal will be completed.

Berkhof stresses the continuity and "close tie between life on both sides of the death crisis." He notes that the "New Testament speaks about the completion as 'fruit,' 'harvest,' and 'wages' of the sowing and struggling in this life."[48] He also expresses preference for "conformity with Christ" as the description of the ultimate goal. Unlike other descriptions—for example, "vision of God" and "eternal rest"—conformity with Christ "clearly maintains the connection with Christ's earthly work and that of the Spirit." It also avoids the impression of "individualism and passivism" that can follow from the images of vision and rest.[49]

Erickson similarly stresses the continuity of life on the two sides of death. The life beyond, termed "glorification," involves the perfecting of our current life. It is the final stage and culmination of the process of salvation. We do not reach in this lifetime the ideal toward which we press, but we aim to come as close to that ideal as possible, knowing that perfect sanctification will be reached in eternity.[50]

Erickson is somewhat more willing than Berkhof to speculate on the nature of "glorification." He talks about a "fullness of knowledge" of God and about the resurrection and perfection of the body.[51] Still, our knowledge of what awaits us is limited and can be variously characterized—"adoption by God, redemption of the body, an undefiled inheritance guaranteed by the Spirit."[52] What is certain is a "future completion of the process begun in regeneration and continued in sanctification."[53]

Macquarrie also stresses the continuity between life on the two sides of death. For instance, when interpreting the term "heaven," Macquarrie says we should not view heaven as a "reward that gets added on to the life of faith, hope, and love." Instead, "heaven" is the "working out of the life that is oriented by these principles." Heaven is a symbol that stands for "fullness of being" and the perfection toward which we advance. It is not a goal attained within the confines of historical existence, but one toward which we continue after death.[54]

Macquarrie, like Berkhof, warns against overly detailed speculation about what follows death. However, he affirms the New Testament belief that our ultimate destiny will conform to what we learn of God in Christ.[55] Macquarrie uses various terms or symbols for this destiny— for example, beatific vision, likeness to God, and deification—but the terms are always tied to what we encounter in Christ and Christ's going before us as "first fruits." Thus, for Macquarrie, like Berkhof and Erickson, what follows death continues the process that preceded death.[56]

In this overview of personal eschatology or "life after death," we can see both correlation with and correction to virtue theory. In Christian theology, like virtue theory, the process of growth is not completed in this life. But Christianity offers a hope that our earlier account of virtue theory did not offer: hope that the process will not be incomplete. In this life we make gains, great or small, toward our *telos*. Christianity holds out the hope that the gains do not end in death. Because of God's faithfulness and Christ's going before us, we trust that the journey continues beyond the grave.

CHRISTOLOGY

In our discussion of sanctification, the *telos* was often designated as "conformity with Christ" or "being in the image of Christ." This section expands on the idea of Christ as our *telos*. Its central claim is that an adequate Christology includes the notion that Jesus of Nazareth embodies the true human good or end. Jesus Christ is not just another human being, but the paradigmatic human being.[57]

The effort to develop this point draws on three authors: C. Norman Kraus (Mennonite), Hendrikus Berkhof (Dutch Reformed), and Edward Schillebeeckx (Roman Catholic).[58] Despite their varied traditions, each author sees in Jesus our true end and nature.

C. Norman Kraus

Kraus opens his one volume overview of Christian theology, *God Our Savior*, with a discussion of Christology.[59] According to Kraus, "Christian theology begins with the fundamental conviction that Jesus Christ is the normative relevation of God to us." This norm does not exclude other sources of knowledge about God or imply that God is done teaching us. It is a final norm "in the sense that we do not expect a revision that would change our understanding of God's character and purpose for the world."[60]

Why do Christians make such strong claims about Jesus? What gave rise to the conviction that Jesus is the "normative self-disclosure of God"?[61] Kraus argues that it was Jesus' total identity or *"gestalt"*: the impact of Jesus' way of living and relating to others and God, combined with his teaching and power over the demonic, combined with his righteous death, combined with the resurrection of the same Jesus and the experience of the Holy Spirit. As Jesus' followers reflected in the light of the resurrection and Pentecost on the sum of his life, teaching, and death, "they began to see with increasing clarity that he was God's self-revelation."[62]

According to Kraus, this historical encounter with Jesus gave rise to new and exalted terminology for Jesus—for example, Savior, Messiah, Lord, Word, Son of God. These expressions were not originally metaphysical explanations, but confessions of "God experienced in Christ." In terms that strain the limits of language, Christians in various new contexts strove (and continue to strive) to voice the conviction "that Jesus was 'Immanuel, God with us.' "[63]

This is, for Kraus, one side of what we mean by "incarnation." Incarnation means that God was present and disclosing God's way and work within the boundaries of our historical existence in the person of Jesus Christ. In Jesus, God was present and expressing God's self.[64]

The other side of the incarnation is Jesus' full humanity. Kraus tries to give equal weight to Jesus' humanity because "Jesus not only reveals God to us, he shows us what it means to be fully human." In Jesus, "God *shared our humanity*, thus revealing its true meaning and dignity."[65]

Kraus notes that Jesus' humanity is taken for granted throughout the New Testament and affirmed by the Apostles' Creed and the ecumenical creeds. Kraus stresses that it was totally from within human boundaries that Jesus became everything we were created to be.

> What is extraordinary and even miraculous in all of this is that Jesus realized the full potential of the image of God within the existential boundaries of sinful humanity.... Thus Jesus fulfilled the sinless image of God in and for humanity and became the paradigm for all humanity as "children of God" (John 1:12–13).[66]

Christ became the human paradigm because he realized our full human potential. He resisted selfish temptations, identified with the weak and oppressed, made love his motivation and guide, responded in love to both friends and enemies, was obedient to God (even to death), and found self-fulfillment in relationship with God rather than in autonomy. In short, the same way of being and acting that moves Christians to see God in Christ is what makes Christ our model and paradigm. In his complete identification with humanity, humanity reaches its goal in him.

Kraus believes Christians know something about their true *telos* because we have seen that end in Christ. We have an idea of what it means to be a truly excellent human being, to fulfill our potential, because Christ has reached the goal ahead of us. Christ was more than a prophet or sage or seer. He was God's personal self-revelation to us.[67] But he was also one of us. In his full humanity and solidarity with us, he became what we were created to be: the image of God. Our ultimate goal is known in the person of Christ.[68] Thus, by looking to a specific, concrete life within history we find clues to our true nature and end.

This knowledge is one possible link between virtue ethics and Kraus's Christology; there is another. The quest to know Christ and his import for our lives is not, according to Kraus, limited to the intellect. It is in discipleship, following Christ, that we both learn who he is and are ourselves transformed toward that goal. This discipleship is, says Kraus, best understood in terms of master and apprentice:

> A *disciple* is an apprentice, that is, one who places himself or herself under the discipline of a *master* (a person who has mastered the art or craft one wants to learn).

> When such an apprenticeship involves a conscious quest for the source and meaning of life, the relationship between disciple and master is unique. The master (*rabbi, guru*) becomes an authority to whom the disciple freely submits in order to learn. Such learning involves one in absorbing the influence and style of the master by intimate relationship ... observation, and imitation. In such a relationship, one learns to know not only the discipline but also the person of the master. In this way the follower of Jesus learns to know who he is.[69]

The similarity between this vision of discipleship and our second chapter is striking. There we discussed the need for mentors and exemplary figures in both moral education and decision making. Indeed, virtue theory often uses the master/apprentice model to describe the process of moral education and the acquisition of the virtues. It is in being guided by, following after, and imitating masters or worthy examples that we learn to recognize and embody the emotional and intellectual dispositions, habits, and skills designated by the virtues.[70]

This element of virtue theory is obviously close to Kraus's understanding of discipleship. Kraus even talks about growth in "life's integration and wholeness" through our "*submission* to Jesus as *Master*." Note, however, that for Kraus this is a christological issue, not just a matter of ethics or sanctification. In being "transformed" by this relationship, we learn to understand better our goal in Christ and his significance for the world.[71] Thus, according to Kraus, an adequate Christology must be accompanied by the transformation of the self under Christ's tutorage.[72]

There may be other elements in Kraus's Christology that fit with virtue ethics. However, enough has been said to suggest that major themes in his Christology can be linked to a virtue framework. According to Kraus, Christians know something of our true end because we have seen that end in Christ. Moreover, our journey toward understanding that end involves the transformation of the self through a master/apprentice relationship with Christ.

Hendrikus Berkhof

The theme of Jesus as our true *telos*, as the one who embodies the full human potential, runs throughout Berkhof's Christology. His

Christology cannot be reduced to this theme, but it plays a prominent and sometimes dominant role.

It is seen, for example, in Berkhof's discussion of "the person" of Jesus. By "the person" Berkhof means to get at Jesus' question to the disciples: "Who do you say that I am?"

Historical investigation cannot, according to Berkhof, answer this question for us. Rather, such investigation forces on us the same type of personal choice concerning Jesus that confronted the people of Jesus' day. Historical investigation leaves us with the same question about Jesus: Who is he?[73]

Faith's answer to this question, an answer that concurs with Peter's, requires "a leap, a decision" that is not simply given by the data.[74] But faith's decision about Jesus is not a blind leap. It is a decision justified by the total picture of Jesus' person and life. Some are first moved to faith by Jesus' authority or his radical love of people or his discourse and parables or by his death or his resurrection. Whatever initially moves one to faith, "when one is gripped by one aspect it leads to the recognition of the other aspects."[75] It is this total picture of Jesus that grounds faith's response to him.

Berkhof's own attempts to call this picture to the reader's mind vary according to context. When discussing the relationship between the historical Jesus and the kerygmatic Christ, Berkhof offers a brief narrative history of Jesus, focusing on elements widely accepted among biblical scholars. When talking about Jesus as the "Son of God," Berkhof highlights several elements of Jesus' life: love and obedience before God, reaching out to the neighbor, freedom in relation to established powers and traditions, and control over destructive forces of sickness and demonic possession. When discussing Jesus' human life, Berkhof underlines Jesus' intimate relationship with God and the way he represented God to humanity in forgiveness, compassion, healing, and freedom. In these and similar instances, Berkhof tries to recall several elements and events in Jesus' life.[76] The effort is to get the reader to imagine the "total picture" of Jesus and not isolate one aspect or event. Berkhof views the Christian faith as grounded in Jesus' entire life and way, and the faith becomes distorted when we lose sight of that large picture.

So what does faith see in Jesus? Berkhof notes that the title "Son of God" has been prominent with the Christian community from shortly after the resurrection until today. He therefore starts with the title "Son of God."

The first thing Berkhof notes about the title is its roots; it is a redemptive, historical, and covenantal term. In the Old Testament, Israel, and sometimes the king, is addressed by God as son. This address does not refer to physical origin, but to the "convenantal relationship of mutual love and (with man) of obedience."[77]

According to Berkhof, Jesus' sonship also

> stands in this covenant tradition. He is preeminently the obedient and therefore beloved covenant partner. His relationship with God meets the requirements of the representative purpose with the king and other types of mediators in Israel. . . . Through this representation, he becomes as son "the first-born among many brethren."[78]

While emphasizing that Jesus stands within this convenantal context, Berkhof also wants to highlight Jesus' uniqueness. Berkhof says that the covenant "had come to a dead end" and was in need of a new beginning. The prophets knew such a beginning could not come from this world. Instead,

> God himself must provide the true man, the faithful covenant partner. That new beginning from above is called "Jesus." He finally fulfills the sonship. He is the Son *par excellence*. And he is that not as the fruit and climax of human religious and moral purity, but in virtue of a unique and new creative act of God.[79]

Thus Jesus, "the true man," is unique because of his origin in God.

One notes here a dual emphasis concerning Jesus that is best expressed in Berkhof's own words:

> As regards its origin . . . Jesus' sonship is unique. But as regards its content it is that to which all of mankind is called through the covenant way of Israel. Here we see what we, what Israel, what Israel's representatives should have done and are, but in which all have obviously failed. Jesus' sonship . . . is that in which he . . . wants to involve us. . . . We must become like him, but in virtue of his going-before and in abiding dependence on it.[80]

Berkhof stresses Jesus' humanity, his normative and paradigmatic humanity, but he always joins that emphasis with an assertion of Jesus' uniqueness. Jesus went the way before us and faith sees in him God's new creative act.

Indeed, for Berkhof it is Jesus' humanity that leads faith to make claims about his unique origins. The historical encounter with Jesus and the way he realized his human existence (seen in light of both God's previous dealings with Israel and the resurrection) drives faith to view him as the true human come from God. In other words, faith sees a new creative act of God in Jesus because Jesus fully realized human existence as it was divinely intended.[81]

The emphasis on Jesus' paradigmatic humanity continues throughout the remainder of Berkhof's Christology. After asking about Jesus' person, Berkhof asks about the kind of life Jesus led. Berkhof notes Jesus' life is often "summed up as his *sinlessness*." Berkhof views this term as unfortunate. It is "too negative, too static, too limited." Berkhof prefers the word "*humanity* to express the core of Jesus' life." Berkhof applies this term to Jesus' unique life to highlight the connection between Jesus and us. In Jesus we see

> the depth and the breadth of God's purpose for man.... Here is the complete structure of what it is to be man, in his threefold relationship to God, the neighbor, and nature. Here is also the highest quality of what it is to be man, as love and freedom. Here human existence has reached its full maturity and therefore has fully become God's partner and instrument.[82]

This emphasis on Jesus' normative humanity continues in Berkhof's discussions of Jesus' death and resurrection. Berkhof's first point in discussing the resurrection is its relationship to Jesus' life. The resurrection "did not ... happen to a random individual, but to someone whose life called for it."[83] The resurrection is

> the divine validation of the way of Jesus in his life and death. Without this exceptional sign from God we would have no certainty about the exceptional nature of his life and his surrender of it.... It is only through the resurrection that we know that God was in Jesus.... [God] declares only this life as valid, as a life in agreement with his design.[84]

Although the theme of Jesus' normative humanity continues throughout the remainder of Berkhof's Christology, enough has been said to show the prominence of this theme. Berkhof, like Kraus, believes that as Christians, we know something of the *telos,* of our true end, because we have seen that end in Christ.

Edward Schillebeeckx

Although Kraus and Berkhof are interested in the historical Jesus, Schillebeeckx pays greater attention to historical investigation. Indeed, he devotes most of two large volumes on Christology to biblical exegesis.[85]

Schillebeeckx's emphasis on historical investigation has at least three interrelated functions. First, it helps us see and understand what occasioned the claims made by early Christians concerning the historical Jesus. Those claims were generated by an encounter with Jesus of Nazareth, who in light of his death and resurrection was experienced and understood as offering salvation. Jesus' earthly life and ministry, viewed from the perspective of his death and resurrection, provided the foundation for the extraordinary claims the early Christians made concerning Jesus and his relation to God and salvation.[86]

Second, the same historical investigation confronts us with the question of Jesus. Historical research can raise the same question among us that confronted the Jews of Jesus' day: how are we to interpret Jesus of Nazareth? Is he, for example, the bearer of salvation or illusion and ill?[87]

Third, since Christians answer the last question with the affirmation that Jesus is the "bringer" of salvation, we need historical investigation to guide our faith. In light of the resurrection and God's judgment on Jesus, our faith and life must be subject to the historical Jesus of Nazareth.[88]

As this three-pronged use of historical investigation suggests, Schillebeeckx, like Kraus and Berkhof, stresses the "total picture" of Jesus. Schillebeeckx does not use the language of "total picture." Instead, he notes our need of a narrative Christology. If we are going to encounter and communicate Jesus of Nazareth, we need to tell and retell his story—a story that starts with Israel, continues in Jesus' life, teaching, death and resurrection, and persists in the life of the church and the promise of a future not yet realized.[89]

Schillebeeckx's use of historical investigation is in the service of this narrative Christology. He uses it to provide a loose historical narrative or rough biographical sketch of Jesus of Nazareth. The sketch helps us understand what occasioned early Christian claims about Jesus. It also provides the foundation for both our encounter with Jesus and our search for fresh ways to express his identity.[90]

As the third use of historical investigation suggests, Jesus is for Schillebeeckx the norm and criterion of faith and practice. According to Schillebeeckx, the language, concerns, and concepts used to express Christian faith change with the differing social and cultural contexts within which Christians live. However, Schillebeeckx does not accept unaltered the language, concerns, and concepts of one's society. Rather, they are reshaped to be consistent with the memory of Jesus.[91] Concepts like "justice," "freedom," and "liberation," and titles like "Messiah," "Son of God," and "Lord" are not used to measure Jesus, nor do we come to him knowing what they mean when applied to him. Instead, says Schillebeeckx, the Christian strives to learn from Jesus' career what such words as "justice" and "liberation" really mean.[92]

This reshaping of concepts also applies to the notion "human." While seldom using traditional incarnation language, Schillebeeckx asserts that "Christians learn to express stammeringly the content of what 'God' is and the content of what 'humanity' can be from the career of Jesus."[93] We learn from Jesus' life, message, death, and resurrection what it really means to be human. And while we inevitably come to faith with some notion of what it means to be "human," Jesus is the test of that concept; it is not the measure for assessing him. Moreover, in Jesus we do not simply see what humanity is, but "what 'humanity' can be." In Jesus we see our true potential, purpose, and end. Thus Jesus provides us with a glimpse of the human *telos* or end.[94]

Thus, Schillebeeckx believes—as do Kraus and Berkhof—that Christians know something of our *telos,* of our true end, because we have seen that end in Christ. By looking to a specific, concrete life within history, we find clues to our true nature and end. This is not to deny that we know something of "humanity" apart from Christ. Rather, Jesus is the test and criterion of our understandings of the meaning and goal of humanity.[95]

Better Expressed in Virtue Terms

Jesus is our true nature and end. This assertion goes beyond what was earlier said about sanctification. In discussing sanctification, "conformity to Christ" was a designation for our true end that had not yet been given content. We also have various other ways of referring to that end—for example, "child of God" and "perfection."

By looking at Christology, we see that the life and way of Jesus of Nazareth help provide the end's content. Although we do not grasp the human *telos* in every detail, we discover substantial clues to its nature and content in Jesus' life, teaching, death, and resurrection.

This claim that the human *telos* is seen in Christ is not trivial. It asserts that we can find clues to our true nature and end by looking at a specific point in history. It claims, moreover, that such clues are normative. Whatever else we may say or discover about our true end, it must conform to the shape and pattern of Jesus' entire way.

This important theological insight seldom receives voice among Christian ethicists for at least two reasons. First, Christian ethicists tend to declare Jesus irrelevant in the constructing of ethics. Various arguments account for this supposed irrelevance. One argument views Jesus as offering a spiritual message that is distinct from the material and ethical. Another argument says that Jesus was a simple rural figure whose way of life cannot be transferred to our complicated and cosmopolitan situation. Another argument is that Jesus' world view was apocalyptic and interim. He lived and taught under the assumption that the world was soon passing away, but Jesus was mistaken about this ending and we must have an ethic that deals with duration. What these and similar arguments share is the assertion that Jesus' life and way are immaterial for understanding ethics.[96]

This tendency to declare Jesus irrelevant for ethics cannot be reconciled with the above christological discussion. Our authors make claims about Jesus' normative humanity that do not vanish simply because one is now talking about "ethics." What, for instance, is the possible content of Kraus's understanding of incarnation if Jesus is not decisive for our life and action?

Second, even when Christian ethicists see Jesus as somehow normative, they often reduce that norm to an abstract rule or principle. The most common example of this reduction is seeing Jesus as bearer of the law of love. Following Jesus' example, we are to love God and neighbor.[97]

This view is, however, an inadequate expression of Jesus' paradigmatic humanity. It seldom grounds the use of "love" in a discussion of Jesus' life, teaching, and death or discusses how his way enlightens and alters our previous understanding of love. It is as if we totally understand what love is without his specific example.

Besides, it is difficult to sum up an entire life with one word. Jesus loved people. He also prayed, told stories, went to and hosted dinner parties, healed the sick, debated intellectuals, and died on a cross. It is unlikely that we can encapsulate and communicate such a life in a single principle like "love."

To understand the inadequacy of viewing Jesus' normative humanity in terms of a rule or principle, consider our three authors. Kraus claims that faith finds its start in Jesus' total identity or *"gestalt"* and that a fuller understanding of Jesus requires a master/apprentice type of relationship. Berkhof talks about and continually calls to mind the total picture of Jesus' person and life as the grounds of faith. Schillebeeckx develops a loose historical narrative or biographical sketch that both encourages our encounter with Christ and allows Christ to serve as norm for theology and practice.

In each author we see an emphasis on Jesus' entire life against which appeals to "love" seem meager and deficient. Their discussions of Jesus' humanity resist reduction to a single term. Indeed, each author pushes hard in the direction of a large, complex picture of Jesus' humanity.

Adopting several rules or principles does not solve the problem. With multiple rules or principles, we still have the problem of the rules being separated from their norm. As Schillebeeckx reminds us, Christians do not, for example, come to Christ fully knowing the meaning of "justice." Instead, Christians strive to learn the meaning of justice from Christ's life and way. Thus, an appeal to multiple rules or principles needs to show how one understands those rules and principles in light of Christ. But when one makes this move, rules and principles are no longer the real guide for life and action. Jesus' total life story is the guide.

In other words, a view consistent with the above christological discussion sees rules and principles as subordinate to Jesus' life. Rules can serve to remind us of his life (each rule or principle possibly highlighting certain features of that life), but they are not the most basic or foundational guide. How could they be, if they must be tested against our example in Christ?

Moreover, Christ is not simply the giver of rules and principles, but humanity's goal. In Jesus, we see not only the acts we are to perform or the rules we are to follow. In Jesus, we see the kind of people we are to become, the kind of humanity we are to embody.

Let us again consider our three authors. According to Kraus, we see our full humanity in Jesus. We see in him what it means to realize the full human potential as intended by God. In addition, discipleship is a quest for the "source and meaning of life" in which the self is transformed by absorbing the "influence and style of the master" through relationship, observation, and imitation. For Berkhof, Jesus is the goal to which all humanity is called. Humanity sees in Jesus its full maturity and full partnership with God. Jesus is the "new man, the eschatological man." According to Schillebeeckx, we see in Jesus our true potential, purpose, and end. Jesus is "what 'humanity' can be."

When we combine these comments with each author's insistence on a full-bodied, rich picture of Jesus' life, it is clear that each views Jesus as the goal, not only of our behavior, but of our humanity. Christian faith is a matter of becoming a certain sort of person. It is a matter of becoming like Jesus. Rules and principles can help us toward that goal, but the goal involves more than following rules. It is a goal that involves a way of being in the world. It is a goal seen in the totality of Jesus' life and way. It is a goal that requires the transformation of the self into his likeness.[98]

The point here is that standard ways of dealing with Jesus in Christian ethics are inadequate to the claims Christians make about him, and attempts to declare Jesus irrelevant to ethics cannot be reconciled with Christian claims. The Christian confession of Jesus Christ is impoverished if Jesus is not our exemplar, if his path does not provide the form and shape to which our lives are directed.[99]

Attempts to view Jesus' paradigmatic humanity in a rule or principle (or a series of rules and principles) are similarly ill suited. How does one compact an entire life and way into a rule or principle? Moreover, since Jesus is the criterion and norm for those rules and principles, their meaning is dependent on his life story. Our real guide for life and action are not the rules, but the life those rules help us recall. Finally, the goal is not simply to follow certain rules or principles; rather, it involves our transformation into Christ's likeness.[100]

Virtue ethics, unlike other approaches, can fully embrace the claims Christians make about Jesus' normative humanity. Theology sees in Jesus the new Human (cf. Rom 5:14; 1 Cor 15:22, 45) and views him as exhibiting our true purpose, potential, and end.[101] A virtue framework can affirm this language because it points to Jesus as manifesting our true *telos*.

A virtue framework can also affirm Jesus' normative humanity without trying to reduce that norm to rules or principles. Chapter 2 noted that rules can play an important part in virtue ethics but that more important are the pictures we have of our true nature or end.

A Christian adoption of virtue theory could affirm Jesus as providing essential clues to our true nature. Because of Christ we have a vision of where our journey should take us. Because of Christ, we can contrast who-we-are with who-we-could-be and focus on habits, capacities, interests, precepts, injunctions, prohibitions, and skills consistent with the move from the former to the latter.

CHRISTIAN ANTHROPOLOGY

My strategy for reviewing Christian anthropology is somewhat different from the way that sanctification and Christology were discussed. Instead of reviewing what various authors say about the subject, I will summarize certain basic trends in Christian theological anthropology. This shift in style results primarily from the rudimentary character of the claims I make here. The treatment is so basic that it is unlikely to occasion dissent among most Protestants or Catholics.

Human Freedom

Virtue ethics presupposes an understanding of human agency that falls midway between behaviorism and voluntarism (see chapter 2). Christian accounts of human freedom concur with this judgment: we are neither totally determined nor totally free.

Christianity can never accept an anthropology where human action is solely the product of forces external to personal choice. After all, we believe ourselves to be made for encounter and response to God—a response that does not merely mirror God's action but is voluntary on our part. Christians believe we are called to a relationship with God in which we have a voice.[102]

Christian anthropology does not, however, believe human freedom is unlimited. It is limited in two ways. First, because we are finite, embodied creatures, we are shaped in profound ways by biological, social, and historical forces. Our exercise of freedom must take place within the constraints of these forces. Second, human freedom is limited by "sin." The sin that limits freedom includes both the personal turning away from God and the corporate power of corrupted social structures, institutions, and relationships.[103]

The reality of sin means that freedom itself needs liberating. In turning from God, we can become imprisoned by self-centeredness and addiction to security or material things. Moreover, the very social and historical structures that shape us are disordered and incapacitating. Thus, Christian theology speaks about freedom as a gift from God. True freedom comes only in response to God's self-giving grace.[104]

Without God's grace, our freedom is negligible. But even in the setting of God's freeing grace, we are still finite creatures limited by the biological, social, and historical contexts we inhabit. Thus theological anthropology sees the human person as neither completely determined nor completely free.

Consider for example the traditional Christian image of the human person as a unity of body and spirit. If we envision ourselves as only "body," then we naturally develop a mechanistic vision of the person. If we envision ourselves as solely "spirit," then our vision of the person is of one totally free of constraints. But when we conceive of ourselves as a unity of body and spirit, it is natural to see the person as embodying both limits and freedom. "Body" symbolizes our solidarity with the rest of creation and the way it shapes us. "Spirit" symbolizes that we are transcendent beings who act and share in relationships.[105]

Here is an obvious link between virtue theory and Christian theology—each views our choices and actions as neither completely determined nor completely free. However, the link is both weaker and stronger than this statement implies. The link is weaker because theology does not believe that we inhabit this midway point between determinism and freedom on our own or as we are. Human freedom unfolds only in response to God's Spirit. The link is stronger because there is a growing tendency in theology to view freedom as a capacity for choosing and intending who one is going to become. In other words, theology increasingly sees the exercise of freedom as involving self-formation. In the midst of our many choices and actions, we help shape ourselves and others. Freedom allows us to choose between competing options, but it also means that through our choices we play a key role in the development of our character, goals, and desires.

God's grace does not merely free us from sin. God's grace also frees us for a certain kind of life—one that exhibits service, love, peace, patience, kindness, faithfulness, and self-control. The freedom discovered in grace involves more than freedom among choices; it involves freedom to become a certain kind of person through our choices and actions. Indeed, if the freedom we gain in grace is to be lasting and substantive, we need to choose the kinds of activities, practices, and disciplines that will shape us in a way consistent with the gospel.[106]

Our Communal Nature

We noted in chapters 1 and 2 that relationships and corporate activity are central to virtue ethics. We acquire the virtues in the company of others. And while the goal of our journey involves individual growth, it also involves common projects, shared activities, and intimate relationships.

Theological anthropology agrees that relationships are crucial. Consider, for instance, the stories of creation. Genesis 1:27 implies that our relational character ("male and female") is an essential component of our being in God's image. Similarly, according to Genesis 2:18–25, "man" is incomplete without a partner.[107]

Whether it is God's creating a people by liberating them from Egypt or Paul's image of the church as a body, the Bible continually views us as communal in nature. This dimension is seen preeminently in Jesus' preaching of the kingdom of God. Jesus neither embodies nor preaches an individualistic gospel. Instead, he serves others, celebrates with others, and proclaims a community of mutual service and love.[108]

Christians believe that in Jesus we see the potential and goal of human existence. Accordingly, life's goal is not complete solitude or absorption into God but fellowship with and service to God and others. Life's journey is meant to culminate in shared activity and intimate relationships, not in isolation or detachment.

What is true of the journey's goal is also true of the journey. From the moment of birth, we are dependent on others for everything from food and clothing to the acquisition of language. We do not outgrow this basic need for others. We continue throughout our lives to be influenced, informed, and shaped by others. Thus, if we are to reach our goal in Christ, we need appropriate relationships of mutual submission, affirmation, confession, and guidance.[109]

According to theological anthropology, both the journey and the goal involve shared activity and intimate relationships. If space permitted, an examination of ecclesiology and eschatology would further show that relationships are indispensable to the journey and goal.[110] It is enough, however, to observe that Christian anthropology always views the individual in community. The self does not exist in a vacuum, and self-realization requires the presence of others.

Here then is another potential link or correlation between theology and virtue theory. Both Christian theology and virtue theory view community as nonnegotiable: the individual cannot realize his or her potential in isolation.

CONCLUSION

This chapter establishes points of similarity, contact, and correlation between virtue theory and contemporary Christian theology. The first section described sanctification as a teleological concept that concerns moral growth and transformation. This section also argued that the *telos* of sanctification is one toward which we continually strive but never fully reach in this life. The second section viewed Christology as providing essential clues to the content of sanctification's *telos*. This section also suggested that viewing Jesus as embodying the human *telos* gives voice to Jesus' paradigmatic humanity in a way that is difficult to express in other ethical schemes. The third section claimed that Christian anthropology sees us as neither completely determined nor completely free. This section also suggested that theology increasingly views us as self-forming agents and that community is essential to the Christian life. Together these sections point to several potential links between Christian theology and virtue theory. Many of the themes from chapter 2 find parallels and counterparts in this chapter.

This chapter also highlighted some areas wherein a virtue framework needs to be altered, filled out, and reformulated in order to be properly Christian. A major emphasis here concerned our dependence on God's grace. Sanctification and human freedom were described as dependent on God's self-giving love. An equally significant addendum comes from Christology: normative clues to our true nature and end are provided by a specific life within history.

NOTES

1. The one notable overlap is the use of Hendrikus Berkhof, *Christian Faith: An Introduction to the Study of the Faith*, Revised ed. trans. Sierd Woudstra (Grand Rapids: Wm. B. Eerdmans, 1986) in both the sanctification and Christology sections. This overlap reflects my theological inclinations. That is, Berkhof's work more closely reflects my theological perspective than any other theologian cited in this chapter.

2. This assertion does not mean that virtue theory is incompatible with a christological approach centered on the creeds. Many of the christological claims I advance are basic and might be affirmed by most contemporary approaches to Christology. I do not explore that possibility in this work, however.

3. For more on this see n. 58.

4. Stanley Hauerwas, *Character and the Christian Life: A Study in Theological Ethics* with new introduction (San Antonio: Trinity University Press, 1985).

5. Joseph Dunne, *Back to the Rough Ground: 'Phronesis' and 'Techne' in Modern Philosophy and in Aristotle* (Notre Dame: University of Notre Dame Press, 1993), p. 231.

6. I did not, for example, begin this chapter intending to include a discussion of "life after death." I felt pushed into it by the authors I had chosen to discuss sanctification. Each of them so links the discussions of sanctification and personal eschatology that I did not feel justified in using their treatments of one without the other.

7. Berkhof, *Christian Faith;* Millard J. Erickson, *Christian Theology*, 3 vols. (Grand Rapids: Baker Book House, 1985); John Macquarrie, *Principles of Christian Theology*, 2nd ed. (New York: Charles Scribner's Sons, 1977).

8. Allowing for the limits of labels: Berkhof is "neo-Barthian"; Erickson is a well-known, conservative evangelical; and Macquarrie's work is influenced by existentialism and transcendental Thomism.

9. Although each author used here refers to "sanctification," the language for moral regeneration often differs between Christian traditions. Eastern Orthodoxy prefers *theosis* or *theopoiesis*. The West refers variously to the process as "growth in sanctification," "created grace," "increase in justification," "regeneration," and "perfection." This differing terminology can embody subtle but real distinctions. Nevertheless, each term reflects similar or related ideas of a God-given process or journey toward becoming holy or being made saints. See, for example, *The Westminister Dictionary of Christian Theology,* 1983, s.v. "Sanctification," by Geoffrey Wainwright, and Berkhof, *Christian Faith,* pp. 431–32, 454–56, 474.

I highlight this similarity or commonality because I do not want my linking of sanctification and virtue theory to suggest that this link is limited to only those traditions in which the term "sanctification" is frequently used. I believe similar links with virtue theory could be argued in traditions where other terms are more common. For a Lutheran example suggestive of this link, see Gilbert C. Meilaender, *Faith and Faithfulness: Basic Themes in Christian Ethics* (Notre Dame: University of Notre Dame Press, 1991), pp. 74–84, and *The Limits of Love: Some Theological Explorations* (University Park: The Pennsylvania State University Press, 1987), pp. 35–36. For an Orthodox example, see Joseph Woodill, "Virtue Ethics: An Orthodox Appreciation," *Thought* 67 (June 1992): 181–82.

10. In the new introduction to *Character and the Christian Life,* Hauerwas notes that he paid insufficient attention to the teleological character of the Christian life (p. xxv).

11. Berkhof, *Christian Faith*, p. 432; also pp. 429–31; cf. pp. 491–92.
12. Cf. ibid., p. 467.
13. Ibid., pp. 457, 476, 475. See also pp. 468–69, 472.
14. Ibid., pp. 443–44, 450, 459–65, 477–78.
15. Erickson, *Christian Theology*, p. 945.
16. Ibid., pp. 944–46.
17. Ibid., pp. 967–75.
18. Ibid., p. 970.
19. Ibid., pp. 970–71. Also of interest to us is Erickson's depiction of the Christian's relationship to the "law"—that is to biblical commandments.

Although his comments are somewhat vague, he seems to view these commandments as related to our moral growth. They help us understand what living in Christ's image means and are guideposts of God's wisdom along the way (ibid., pp. 977–78). They do not dictate or cover all of our behavior, but they help depict the goal and the behavior consistent with growing toward that goal. This treatment resembles our discussion in chapter 2 of rules as guidelines in moral development and as depicting the *telos*.

20. Macquarrie, *Principles of Christian Theology*, p. 350.
21. Ibid., pp. 345–46, 358, 367–68.
22. Ibid., p. 344. Indeed, for Macquarrie the goal is never reached, even after death, but we grow toward greater and greater perfection (ibid., p. 361).
23. Macquarrie's language is striking. He talks about growth in the "right ordering" of our existence, growth as a "unified self," and growth and perfection of "the very potentialities" of our being (ibid., pp. 343, 344, 345).
24. Ibid., p. 347.
25. Ibid., pp. 347–49.
26. Chapter two discussed the *telos* in terms of our "true nature," which is not completely foreign or unrelated to the notion of growing in the "image of Christ" or "conformity to Christ."

Berkhof talks about our "potential and future" as seen in Christ (*Christian Faith*, p. 430). Christ embodies the kind of humanity God had in mind since the beginning of creation. This does not mean a return to an imaginary Adam. It means God's goal for us was always that which became embodied in Christ. See also pp. 288, 291, 297, 444, 462, 473.

Erickson says of regeneration:

> It does not result in anything foreign to human nature. Rather, the new birth is the restoration of human nature to what it originally was intended to be and what it in fact was before sin entered the human race at the time of the fall. It is simultaneously the beginning of a new life and a return of the old life and activity (*Christian Theology*, p. 944.)

Macquarrie talks about grace perfecting nature and the fulfillment of human "potentialities" (e.g., *Principles of Christian Theology*, pp. 259, 339, 359, 361).

Here each author would add caveats concerning human sinfulness. Our true human nature as seen in Christ is not unproblematically related to our current state or nature, and we do not enjoy simple organic progress from the latter to the former. Still, in each author the goal seen in Christ concerns our "true human nature."

27. For example, Berkhof, *Christian Faith*, pp. 436–37, 442, 456. Berkhof does not use the term "perfection" in relation to sanctification because current usage of this term gives insufficient voice to God's forgiving and empowering grace (p. 431).
28. Ibid., pp. 432–33.
29. Ibid., p. 437.
30. Ibid., p. 475.

96 Theological Links

31. Ibid., pp. 476-77, 480-81.
32. Ibid., pp. 443-48.
33. Ibid., pp. 456-57, 472-77, 483; cf. pp. 427-29.
34. Erickson, *Christian Theology*, p. 925.
35. Ibid., pp. 925-41.
36. I do not extensively discuss Erickson's notion of predestination because it does not necessarily conflict with a virtue ethic. I will suggest below that Erickson believes that those who are called by God actively participate with God in sanctification. Since Erickson's notion of predestination allows for our active participation in moral growth, the potential correlation between sanctification and virtue theory remains.

The problem with Erickson's notion of predestination is that it potentially views all non-Christians as incapable of true moral growth. But even this arguably objectionable view is not conceptually incompatible with a virtue framework. Instead, it would make virtue theory applicable only to those called by God. I will argue in chapter 5 that a virtue framework is capable of such restrictions but that we can easily conceive of a virtue ethic that resists them.

37. Ibid., p. 941.
38. Ibid., pp. 945, 967.
39. Ibid., p. 969; cf. p. 983.
40. Ibid., pp. 971, 973.
41. Macquarrie, *Principles of Christian Theology*, pp. 343-44.
42. Ibid., pp. 338-45, 364.
43. Cf. Hauerwas, *Character and the Christian Life*, p. xxxi; Gilbert C. Meilaender, *The Theory and Practice of Virtue* (Notre Dame: University of Notre Dame Press, 1984), p. 36; Philip L. Quinn, "Is Athens Revived Jerusalem Denied?" *Asbury Theological Journal* 45(1): 51-53; Don H. Zinger, "Are Grace and Virtue Compatible?" *Lutheran Forum* 23 (February 1989): 12-13.
44. Another helpful account of sanctification is found in Thomas N. Finger, *Christian Theology: An Eschatological Approach*, vol. 2. (Scottsdale: Herald Press, 1989), pp. 197-23. Finger's account includes all the elements discussed above—that is, our efforts as part of the grace-dependent transformation of the self toward the goal of "fullness in Christ" and thus full "humanization" (p. 211). The potential link to virtue theory is especially evident in Finger's work. He explains the importance of disciplines (e.g., prayer, study, mutual submission, guidance and celebration) in the process of personal sanctification by deferring to "Thomas Aquinas's notion that character forms through the development of 'habits' " (pp. 214-15).
45. Berkhof, *Christian Faith*, pp. 486.
46. Ibid., p. 487.
47. Ibid., p. 490. Berkhof offers somewhat more speculation on what follows death in later sections (pp. 529-45).
48. Ibid., p. 491.
49. Ibid., p. 492.
50. Erickson, *Christian Theology*, p. 973-74, 985, 997, 999.

An interesting disagreement between the three authors concerns how quickly this culmination is achieved after death. Erickson views it as an instantaneous act of God (p. 1001). Berkhof suggests that a continuing process of growth is more likely. He bases this guess on observation of God's renewing activity in the rest of creation and the close connection between life on the two sides of death (*Christian Faith*, p. 491–92). Macquarrie also views it as a process, but a process that in an important respect never ends: "the goal of a human existence cannot be static, but, even if we call it a 'perfection,' must be an expanding perfection within the continually expanding perfections of Being" (*Principles of Christian Theology*, p. 361).

51. Erickson, *Christian Theology*, pp. 1000–1001. Cf. n. 47 above.
52. Ibid., p. 999.
53. Ibid., p. 1000; also see, p. 1002.
54. Macquarrie, *Principles of Christian Theology*, p. 365; see also p. 344. Macquarrie's interpretation of "purgatory" expresses a similar continuity (pp. 367–69).

For Macquarrie, consummation on the other side of death is only a part of a single dynamic work by God. Our growth through and beyond this life is part of "one great action of holy Being." Creating, reconciling, and consummating are "three distinguishable but inseparable aspects" of God's single activity (p. 355). In other words, consummation is coextensive with God's work of creation and reconciliation (p. 357). Thus, our hope for continuity in life on the other side of death is rooted in God's single ongoing activity. The continuity is not limited to our experience of continuing growth but is based in God's own movement (cf. pp. 358–60).

55. Ibid., pp. 358, 361; cf. p. 363.
56. Ibid., pp. 363–66. Macquarrie uses terms for our ultimate destiny that Berkhof is hesitant to use (e.g., beatific version). However, Macquarrie rejects images of that destiny that are passive or dissolve the individual into God. Thus, despite differing reactions to the terms, Berkhof and Macquarrie have similar concerns about what those terms convey (ibid., pp. 356, 360–61, 369; cf. pp. 348–49).
57. Concentration on Christ as the excellent and paradigmatic human does not necessitate Arianism or reduce soteriology to Jesus as moral example. The claim is not that Christology is summarized in a focus on Jesus' normative humanity, but that this focus is an essential part of a complete Christology.
58. The introduction to this chapter suggested a "family resemblance" among these authors. I believe the resemblance is apparent in the christological discussion that follows. However, further delineation of this resemblance is difficult. A helpful place to start is Elizabeth A. Johnson's chapter on "The History of Jesus" in *Consider Jesus: Waves of Renewal in Christology* (New York: Crossroad, 1992), pp. 49–65. Johnson there outlines a "second wave of renewal in Catholic christology," in which "theologians now began christology by reflecting not on the Chalcedonian dogma but on the scriptural stories and testimony about Jesus Christ, leading to ideas which have a concrete and historical flavor to them" (p. 49).

Also helpful in this regard is Robert A. Krieg, *Story-Shaped Christology: The Role of Narrative in Identifying Jesus Christ* (New York: Paulist Press, 1988). Krieg's proposal includes a complimentary relationship between a historical reconstruction of Jesus' ministry, suffering, and death (e.g., Schillebeeckx) and a more Kerygmatic/Gospel Realism approach (e.g., Karl Barth, Hans Frei). Kraus and Berkhof both fall somewhere within this spectrum.

59. C. Norman Kraus, *God Our Savior: Theology in a Christological Mode* (Scottdale: Herald Press, 1991).

60. Ibid., p. 20; cf. p. 56.

61. Ibid., p. 21.

62. Ibid., p. 27; see also pp. 22–26.

63. Ibid., pp. 27, 28; see also pp. 29–31.

64. Ibid., pp. 24, 28.

65. Ibid., p. 31.

66. Ibid., p. 32.

67. See Kraus's chapter on revelation: ibid., pp. 41–67, and also his *Jesus Christ Our Lord: Christology from a Disciple's Perspective*, revised ed. (Scottdale: Herald Press, 1990), pp. 102–21.

68. Indeed, Kraus's chapter on theological anthropology is entitled, "Humanity in the Image of Christ" (*God Our Savior*, pp. 102–30). Cf. Kraus, *Jesus Christ Our Lord*, pp. 63–74.

69. *God Our Savior*, p. 40.

70. For example, Stanley M. Hauerwas, *Christian Existence Today: Essays on Church, World and Living In Between* (Durham: Labyrinth Press, 1988), pp. 103, 141; Alasdair MacIntyre, *After Virtue*, 2nd ed. (Notre Dame: University of Notre Dame Press, 1984), p. 258; Meilaender, *Theory and Practice of Virtue*, pp. 70–72; Nancy Sherman, *The Fabric of Character: Aristotle's Theory of Virtue* (Oxford: Clarendon Press, 1989), pp. 152, 179–80. Cf. G. Simon Harak, *Virtuous Passions: The Formation of Christian Character* (New York: Paulist Press, 1993), p. 103.

71. This idea is similar to MacIntyre's notion that the depiction of the *telos* is not adequately characterized from the start but is altered and refined as the moral journey progresses (MacIntyre, *After Virtue*, p. 219; cf. Sherman, *Fabric of Character*, pp. 43–44, 89, 94). For both Kraus and MacIntyre, a better understanding of the goal is accompanied by a transformation of the self.

72. Kraus, *God Our Savior*, p. 40. Discipleship as a christological issue is a recurring theme in Mennonite theology. For example, Thomas N. Finger, "The Way to Nicea: Some Reflections from a Mennonite Perspective," *Journal of Ecumenical Studies* 24 (Spring 1987): 212–31; Harry Huebner, "Christology: Discipleship and Ethics," in *Jesus Christ and the Mission of the Church: Contemporary Anabaptist Perspectives* (General Conference Mennonite Church and the Mennonite Church, 1989), pp. 31–48.

73. Berkhof, *Christian Faith*, p. 284. For Berkhof's full discussion of the merits and limits of critical biblical study and historical research, see pp. 273–84.

74. Ibid.

75. Ibid., p. 285.

76. Ibid., pp. 279–80, 287–88, 300–301. See also pp. 271–72.

77. Ibid., p. 286.

78. Ibid., p. 286–87.

79. Ibid., p. 287.

80. Ibid., p. 288.
81. For example, ibid., pp. 256–72, 291–96, 314–15.
82. Ibid., pp. 302–3.
83. Ibid., p. 313.
84. Ibid., p. 314.
85. Edward Schillebeeckx, *Christ: The Experience of Jesus as Lord*, trans. John Bowden (New York: Crossroad, 1980), and *Jesus: An Experiment in Christology*, trans. Hubert Hoskins (New York: Crossroad, 1979). These works are cited hereafter as *Christ* and *Jesus*.
86. *Jesus*, pp. 17, 21, 34, 318–19, 385–87, 392–97; also see, pp. 154, 170–71, 177, 182–83, 191, 203, 206, 212–13, 229, 384–91, 639–49. Historical investigation cannot prove the validity of their response to Jesus. History is always ambiguous and open to various interpretations. It is the believer who sees God's activity in Jesus. The very fact that Jesus was an earthly, historical, and therefore contingent being makes different interpretations of him possible (ibid., pp. 73–75, and see Edward Schillebeeckx, *On Christian Faith*, trans. John Bowden (New York: Crossroad, 1987), pp. 36–39.
87. *Jesus*, pp. 171, 182–83, 269–71, 295.
88. *Jesus*, pp. 36, 76; cf. pp. 39, 639–49; Schillebeeckx, *On Christian Faith*, p. 26–27. I emphasize these three uses because they are the most obvious and most important for our purposes. However, historical research also serves the apologetic concern of showing that Christian belief in Jesus is rationally justifiable belief. Christian claims are intelligible and justifiable because Jesus' earthy life provides grounds for seeing in him God's definitive saving action (e.g., *Jesus*, pp. 627–37). In addition, research into the early church's response and interpretation of Jesus is meant both to stimulate further insight into Jesus' identity and guide our search for new ways of expressing that identity. Thus, for example, *Christ*, pp. 65–71, 112, 463, 631–34, 638–43. See also Krieg, *Story-Shaped Christology*, pp. 66–80.
89. *Jesus*, pp. 77–80; cf. pp., 104, 673. In my estimation, Schillebeeckx's discussion of "formal structural elements" also directs us to a narrative Christology (*Christ*, pp. 638–43).
90. See: Krieg, *Story-Shaped Christology*, pp. 79–80.
91. Examples of this reshaping are found in *Jesus*, pp. 60, 403–37, 559–70.
92. For example, *Christ*, pp. 837–38; Schillebeeckx, *On Christian Faith*, pp. 40.
93. Schillebeeckx, *On Christian Faith*, p. 28.
94. *Jesus*, pp. 598–607; *Christ*, pp. 639–40; Schillebeeckx, *On Christian Faith*, pp. 18–19, 23–24, 40–41. For Schillebeeckx, Jesus' "universality" or "universal significance," is located in Jesus' "manner of being-man" (*Jesus*, p. 598ff). The meaning, end, and purpose of life, including God's relationship to us, is disclosed in Jesus' way of being human.
95. Cf. *Christ*, pp. 731–42. It is instructive that section 3 of *Jesus* is entitled, "Jesus, parable of God and paradigm of humanity" (p. 626ff; see especially, pp. 669–73).
96. John H. Yoder summarizes various arguments used by Christian ethicists to declare Jesus irrelevant in the constructing of ethics. See John H.

100 Theological Links

Yoder, *The Politics of Jesus* (Grand Rapids: Wm. B. Eerdmans, 1972), pp. 16–19. See also Jürgen Moltmann, *The Way of Jesus Christ: Christology in Messianic Dimensions*, trans. Margaret Kohl (New York: Harper & Row, 1990; reprint ed., Minneapolis: Fortress Press, 1993), pp. 116–18.

97. For example, Reinhold Niebuhr, *An Interpretation of Christian Ethics* (New York: Harper and Brothers, 1935); Paul Ramsey, *Basic Christian Ethics* (New York: Charles Scribner's Sons, 1950). Niebuhr and Ramsey exhibit the common tendency to combine points one and two. Both ascribe to Jesus the eschatological mistake mentioned above and then suggest that the ethically normative thing about Jesus is absolute love.

98. We saw this, for example, in Kraus's concern for the transformation of the self in the context of a master/apprentice relationship. We also saw the need for transformation into Christ's likenesses in the section on sanctification.

Interestingly, Berkhof not only talks about our need to become like Christ but also about Christ's need to become who he was. As a human within history, Jesus starts his way as a carpenter's son and goes through turmoil and struggle to end up participating fully in the life and work of God. Thus, even the one who exhibits humanity as God intends it, "had to become what he was" (Berkhof, *Christian Faith*, p. 302; see also pp. 290–93).

99. Cf. these claims with Moltmann, *The Way of Jesus Christ*, pp. 116–19. Moltmann rejects attempts to declare Jesus irrelevant for ethics and argues that "the confession of Jesus as the Christ also involves a practical discipleship that follows the messianic path his own life took" (p. 118). Moltmann goes on to say that

> the *solus Christus* of the Reformers cannot be normative merely for the doctrine of faith. It must be the rule for ethics too, for *solus Christus* also means *totus Christus*—the whole Christ for the whole of life, as the second thesis of the Barmen Theological Declaration of 1934 says. But this means that christology and christopraxis become one, so that a total holistic knowledge of Christ puts its stamp not only on the mind and the heart, but on the whole of life in the community of Christ; and it also means that Christ is *perceived and known* not only with mind and heart, but through the experience and practice of the whole of life (pp. 118–19).

100. Cf. Hans Küng, *On Being a Christian*, trans. Edward Quinn (New York: Wallaby Books, 1976), pp. 544–53. Küng argues that a "person cannot be reduced to a formula" (p. 547) and suggests that the norm for Christian ethics is not abstract principles but the "concrete Jesus as the Christ . . . in the totality of Jesus' person and fate" (p. 549). As norm, Jesus does not call for a "literal imitation" or mimicking, but for the kind of "personal discipleship" (p. 545) that alters one's basic view and practice of life, including the transformation of one's attitudes, tendencies, and dispositions (551–52).

101. I hope neither this particular allusion to the Pauline image of a "new Adam" nor my general focus on Jesus and use of male theologians suggests that the human good or *telos* is more appropriately embodied or better

exemplified in men than in women. Such a suggestion is as improper as arguing that the human good can only be realized in a first-century Jewish prophet.

I argue that Christianity sees in Jesus Christ the paradigm, the vital example, of what it means to embody the human good. But as an example of the *human* good, Jesus of Nazareth was a historically particular agent whose person and identity involved his race, sex, "occupation," language, and so on. None of these specific aspects of Jesus' own person are privileged or necessary elements of the human end. In other words, claiming that Jesus is our example and model does not mean that we must be like Jesus in the historical particularities of his person—which is as true of Jesus' gender as it is of his race and language. Cf. also the section on *multiple forms of life* in chapter 2, and see Elizabeth A. Johnson, *She Who Is: The Mystery of God in Feminist Theological Discourse* (New York: Crossroad, 1992), pp. 154–56, 166–67; and *The Westminister Dictionary of Christian Ethics*, 1986, s.v. "Imitation of Christ," by E. J. Tinsley.

102. For example, John R. Sachs, *The Christian Vision of Humanity: Basic Christian Anthropology* (Collegeville: Liturgical Press, 1991), pp. 27–28; Berkhof, *Christian Faith*, pp. 186–90; cf. Finger, *Christian Theology*, vol. 2, pp. 94–96. In the following discussion, Sachs (Roman Catholic) and Finger (Mennonite) are helpful representatives of contemporary Christian anthropology. Both Sachs and Finger offer basic, accessible treatments in dialog with several theologians.

103. For the first limit on freedom, see, for example, Berkhof, ibid., p. 189; Edward Farley, *Good and Evil: Interpreting a Human Condition* (Minneapolis: Fortress Press, 1990), pp. 47, 68–74, 79–82, 85, 135–36, 159; Finger, ibid., p. 96, 121, 126–28; Wolfhart Pannenberg, *Anthropology in Theological Perspective*, trans. Matthew J. O'Connell (Philadelphia: The Westminster Press, 1985), pp. 225, 240 (and cf. pp. 315–84); Sachs, ibid., p. 29; cf. Stephen J. Duffy, *The Dynamics of Grace: Perspectives in Theological Anthropology* (Collegeville: The Liturgical Press, 1993), pp. 319–22, 359, 387, 390. For the second limit see n. 104.

104. For example, Duffy, ibid., pp. 323–30, 359–68, 387; Farley, ibid., pp. 127, 130, 135–37, 158–64, 255 (also cf. pp. 144, 146, 152, 178); Finger, *Christian Theology*, vol. 2, pp. 128, 134–36, 159–62, 208–9; Wolfhart Pannenberg, *Systematic Theology*, vol. 2, trans. Geoffrey W. Bromiley (Grand Rapids: Wm. B. Eerdmans, 1994), pp. 255–57; Sachs, *Christian Vision of Humanity*, pp. 33–34, 61–64, 68–69, 73.

105. Cf. Duffy, *Dynamics of Grace*, pp. 279, 320–26; Farley, *Good and Evil*, p. 71; Finger, *Christian Theology*, vol. 2, pp. 120–21; Pannenberg, ibid., pp. 181–202; Sachs, *Christian Vision of Humanity*, pp. 55, 57, 90.

106. Farley, *Good and Evil*, pp. 68–74, 159, 168–69, 181, 226–30; Sachs, *Christian Vision of Humanity*, pp. 29–31, 33; Finger, *Christian Theology*, vol. 2, pp. 134–36, 214–20; cf. Duffy, *Dynamics of Grace*, p. 278, 353–56, 359, 379, 388; Gal 5. Pannenberg, *Anthropology*, pp. 225–242, 502–515 is somewhat relevant. Note also the previous discussion of our active role in sanctification: this role clearly presupposes the idea that freedom involves self-formation.

107. Finger, *Christian Theology*, vol. 2, pp. 102–6; Sachs, *Christian Vision of Humanity*, pp. 18–19, 49.

108. Finger, ibid., pp. 97–100; Sachs, ibid., p. 40; cf. Pannenberg, *Systematic Theology*, vol. 2, p. 224.

109. Duffy, *Dynamics of Grace*, pp. 281–83, 347, 354, 363, 377, 387, 392; Finger, *Christian Theology*, vol. 2, pp. 101–2 (cf. pp. 110–12, 218–20); Sachs, *Christian Vision of Humanity*, pp. 36, 41. Cf. also Farley's discussions of the interhuman and social spheres of life: Farley, *Good and Evil*, pp. 28–62, 119–20, 190–93, 242–50, 266–92.

110. For example, the authors we used to discuss personal eschatology view our ultimate end in terms that are active and social. Each envisions the ultimate end in communal terms. See Berkhof, *Christian Faith*, pp. 492, 538–44; Erickson, *Christian Theology*, pp. 997, 1001–2, 1230–31; Macquarrie, *Principles of Christian Theology*, pp. 348–349, 360–61, 365, 369.

5

Biblical Connections

This chapter's central aim is to establish points of similarity, contact, and correlation between virtue theory and the New Testament. I also want to indicate some areas in which a virtue framework needs to be altered, filled out, and reformulated if it is to reflect New Testament priorities. Since a survey of the entire New Testament is not practical in a work of this size, we will use the Gospel according to Matthew and Paul's letters as representative.[1]

One benefit of choosing Matthew and Paul is that they represent the predominant New Testament genres (gospel and epistle). Another benefit is that a cursory view of either Matthew or Paul suggests incompatibility with virtue ethics. Matthew can be read as supporting either a law-based ethic (5:17–18) or an ethic based on the principle of love (22:36–40). Similarly, the popular image of Paul as preoccupied with grace and faith leaves little room for ethics, let alone an ethic focusing on the formation of virtuous people. However, if, as I will argue, the first Gospel and Paul's letters readily connect with virtue theory, then the case for a Christian virtue ethic is that much stronger.[2]

This is not to imply that Matthew and Paul developed a virtue ethic or intentionally work from a virtue framework. They do not. Indeed, one searches the New Testament in vain for a systematic account of ethics or an explicit ethical theory. Thus, instead of attempting to show that Matthew and Paul work from a developed virtue theory, I will argue that their concerns, themes, patterns of moral reasoning, and uses of language fit well with the basic virtue framework discussed in chapter 2.

With this objective in mind, my discussion of Matthew concentrates on the following: the role of "internal" qualities like feelings and dispositions, Matthew's perfectionist thrust, the relationship between master (Jesus) and disciples, the understanding of morality as both individual and corporate, the use of devices such as the depiction of character traits, and Matthew's view and use of the Mosaic law. My discussion of Paul examines his appeal to specific persons as moral examples, his interest in internal qualities, his view of morality as individual and corporate, his understanding of moral discernment, his use of images suggesting moral growth, and his movement between the "indicative" and "imperative."

Not everything in Matthew and Paul has an obvious correlative in virtue theory. This chapter therefore also highlights some cases where Matthew and Paul push us to fill out, alter, and reformulate a virtue framework. I focus in particular on Matthew's emphases on forgiveness and the centrality of Jesus and on Paul's emphasis on grace.

THE GOSPEL OF MATTHEW

Internal Qualities

Possibly the most obvious similarity between Matthew and virtue theory is Matthew's concern with the "internal" qualities of human action, not just the overt acts themselves. The importance of feelings, dispositions, and inclinations is a repeating theme in the first Gospel.

Consider, for example, the Sermon on the Mount. The Beatitudes depict the kinds of people and actions that will receive a full share in God's coming kingdom. In pronouncing blessings on the "poor in spirit" (5:3), on those who "hunger and thirst for righteousness" (5:6), and on those who are "pure of heart" (5:8), Matthew's Jesus promises God's reign to those who are humble before God, who yearn for and desire God's justice, and who live from a position of genuineness and integrity.[3] While these and other blessings presuppose action, they also commend a posture reflecting certain attitudes and feelings.[4]

Similarly, in at least two of the six "antitheses" (5:21–48), we see a change in focus from external action to internal dispositions.[5] Jesus never denies that killing is wrong, but he explicitly warns about anger (5:21–22). Jesus assumes that adultery is illicit, but he makes a point of condemning lust (5:27–28). While the teachings about retaliation and love of enemies probably also involve dispositions and feelings, Jesus' words about anger and lust emphatically move the spotlight from overt actions to dispositions and feelings.[6]

The remainder of the Sermon expresses similar concern with intentions, feelings, and attitudes.[7] The Sermon is not, however, the only time the internal is emphasized in Matthew. Matthew's Jesus calls repeatedly for a posture and attitude of humility, especially the socially powerless humility symbolized by children (18:2–4; 19:14; 23:12).[8] Similarly, Jesus condemns some Pharisees as hypocrites because they do not practice what they preach and because, instead of expressing an interior reality, their actions are done for show (23:2–7, 25–28).[9]

Concern with the "internal" does not mean that Matthew is unconcerned with overt action. Matthew does not advocate a morality of pure intention and never rejects action as unimportant. Indeed, the parable of the two sons (21:28–31), the parable of the talents (25:14–30), and the judgment of the sheep and the goats (25:31–46) make clear the considerable weight Matthew attaches to action (cf. 16:27). Matthew stresses both the internal and the external.[10]

Matthew also presumes a connection between the internal and the external: one's conduct (the external) flows from and reflects one's inner character (the internal). Thus, good or evil fruit is the manifestation of a good or evil tree (3:8, 10; 7:15–20: 12:33); and people will render account at the judgment for every careless word because such words manifest the true character of one's disposition and heart (12:34–37). Similarly, defilement comes not from what enters the mouth but from what comes out of the mouth, for it is one's speech, and not what one eats, that expresses the true state of one's innermost being (15:10–11, 17–20).[11] Even Jesus' activities of healing and feeding the crowds are portrayed as flowing from the disposition or emotion of "compassion" (14:14; 15:32; 20:34; cf. 9:36).[12]

Matthew's concern with the internal and Matthew's understanding of the relationship between the internal and the external have obvious similarities to our earlier discussion of virtue theory. Like Matthew's concern with the internal, virtue theory focuses on tendencies, feelings, and dispositions. Like Matthew's understanding of the connection between internal and external, virtue theory sees an intimate link between states of character and action, between "being" and "doing."

Virtue theory sees a reciprocal or circular relationship existing between states of character (that is, virtues and vices, including feelings, tendencies, and dispositions) and action. States of character inform, direct, and execute perception, choices, and actions. Conversely, actions express and help to develop states of character.

Actions and character states are not equally emphasized, however. Virtue theory is more concerned with the kind of person one becomes than in judging particular actions, because the former largely determines the latter. Without excluding the importance of actions, virtue theory stresses the need to become the right sort.

There are important parallels here between Matthew and virtue theory. Both see an important link between internal and external, being and doing, character states and action. And both Matthew and virtue theory stress the role of interior states in shaping action. In addition, Matthew, like virtue theory, seems to view the internal as having a kind of priority—after all, it is the tree's state that decides the quality of its fruit.[13]

There is, in short, a definite similarity, even parallel, between virtue theory and Matthew's concern with the internal.[14] Both Matthew and virtue theory emphasize feelings, attitudes, and dispositions, and both see a correlation between character and conduct.

A Perfectionist Ethic

Virtue theory is, as we have noted, a perfectionist ethic. One is encouraged to continually improve one's character, to move toward the *telos*. We are, for example, to work continually at becoming more just, more courageous, and more generous. Not that we can always be at work on every aspect of our character, and not that the ideal must be realized before we can receive a positive evaluation. The point is simply that the *telos*, as an ideal of human excellence, is always in front of us, always calling us forward toward a fuller realization of the human good.

There can be little doubt that Matthew also espouses a kind of perfectionist ethic.[15] The rigorous teaching of the Sermon on the Mount is held up "as an ethic disciples are to live."[16] Within the Sermon, Jesus demands a "righteousness" exceeding that of the scribes and Pharisees (5:20) and calls us to be "perfect" as God is perfect (5:48; cf. 19:21).[17] Outside the Sermon, we are told that disciples must be willing to give up everything, including their families and their lives (10:35–39; 16:24–26). Similarly, the parables on watchfulness invoke the parousia to reject a sense of attainment or self-satisfaction: one must remain "awake" and seek to increase his or her "talents" (24:37–25:30).[18] Even the Gospel's closing words require followers to observe "everything" Christ has taught (28:20). Matthew's ethic is, then, a perfectionist ethic. The ideal is held up as the guiding and determining factor.[19]

Note, however, that Matthew's perfectionism is not the "brittle perfectionism" rejected in chapter 2's discussion of virtue theory. The first Gospel is not under the illusion that the kingdom of heaven is fully here (cf. 24:37–25:30). Matthew is aware of the difficulty and struggle involved in entering the perfection that summons us as disciples. He does not, for instance, idealize the twelve or obscure their proneness to "little faith" and failure (e.g., 8:26; 14:31; 16:8; 17:20). And while Matthew does not condone "little faith," he never equates it with "unbelief." Indeed, Jesus is depicted as standing ready to save those who succumb to bouts of doubt or little faith.[20] Likewise, Matthew's emphases on seeking reconciliation and granting forgiveness show intense concern for human frailty and finitude (5:21–26; 6:12, 14–15; 18:15–35).

In short, though Matthew's ethic, like virtue theory, is a perfectionist ethic, it is not destructive or unrealistically idealistic. Matthew does not expect the ideal to be fully realized.[21] Yet Matthew holds to the ideal as the norm and guide.[22] Matthew does not, for instance, make a distinction between obligations and works of supererogation.[23] All Christians are called to wholehearted discipleship; all are summoned by the norm of the "kingdom of heaven."[24]

Master and Disciple

In chapter 4, we observed the importance of the master/disciple relationship to both virtue theory and C. Norman Kraus's Christology. I noted in particular that virtue theory often uses a master/apprentice model to describe the process of moral education and the acquisition of the virtues. According to virtue theory, it is in being guided by, following, and imitating masters or worthy examples that we learn to recognize and embody the emotional and intellectual dispositions, habits, and skills designated by the virtues.

One finds a comparable relationship in Matthew's depiction of Jesus and the disciples. The relationship is one of teacher and learner, master and slave (10:24–25; cf. 23:10). The disciples come after or follow Jesus, address him as Lord, and share in his mission (4:19–20; 8:19–23; 9:9; 9:37ff; 14:28; 16:22; 20:34).[25] And while Jesus is not only a teacher, Matthew views Jesus' teaching as a central component of his ministry (4:23; 5:1–2; 9:35; 11:1; 13:36; 13:54; 26:55).[26]

Without denying that Matthew's vision of Jesus and the disciples is unique, the similarity between this vision and virtue theory is striking.[27] At the heart of each is an intimate master/learner relationship that shapes every aspect of the learner's life.[28] At the heart of each is a relationship that shapes not only through explicit teaching but also through the associations and activities of daily life.[29]

If there is an important difference, it is that the relationship between Jesus and the disciples goes deeper and is more demanding. Following Jesus can mean a total break with piety, convention, and natural ties (8:21–23; 10:21–22, 35–37; 12:46–50; 19:29). And sharing in Jesus's life and mission includes sharing in his fate and suffering (10:24–25; 38; 16:24).[30]

The point here is that central to Matthew's vision of being Christian is a relationship remarkably similar, although probably more intense, to virtue theory's master/apprentice model.[31] Indeed, my description of the virtue model could almost function as a description of Jesus' relationship to the disciples: in being guided by, following, and imitating the master, they learn to recognize and embody the emotional and intellectual dispositions, habits, and skills appropriate to the Christian life.[32]

Individual and Corporate

Virtue ethics is both individual and corporate. Its task and hope is that the individual will move toward his or her *telos*, toward the true human good. But the good is not conceived solely in individual terms. Virtue theory views relationships and corporate activity as essential to both the true human end and the journey toward that end. Thus, for example, the individual's moral improvement requires the presence of others. Similarly, the significance of many virtues (e.g., justice and generosity) depends on social connections.

Matthew's ethic is also individual and corporate.[33] The concern for individuals is obvious. Jesus calls specific individuals to be his disciples (e.g., 4:18–22; 9:9). He interacts with crowds, but also specific, concrete individuals (e.g., 8:2–15). He talks about socially observable actions but also about the individual's attitudes and feelings (e.g., 5:21–24). And, most strikingly, Jesus tells us that God rejoices more over finding one lost "sheep" than over ninety-nine that were never lost (18:12–14; cf. 12:11–12).

Matthew's ethic also involves relationships and corporate activity. This is already apparent in the discussion of discipleship: discipleship involves a close association of "slave" and "master" (10:24–25). It surfaces again in Matthew's concern with the regulation and life of the

Christian community, especially in 16:13–18:35.[34] Here, for example, are the only references (16:18; 18:17) to the "church" (*ekklesia*) in the Gospels. Chapter 18 is particularly helpful for our purposes. Its basic concern is life within the Christian community and it deals with issues like status-seeking, scandal, and a process for church discipline.[35]

One significant element of chapter 18 is Matthew's procedure for dealing with sins (18:15–20). Two aspects of this procedure are worth noting.[36] First, moral discernment and moral wrongs ("sins") are not simply personal matters. The text assumes that such matters affect and are of concern to the larger group. Thus, if problems cannot be worked out between individuals, then other members of the local church are gradually included (vv. 15–17). Similarly, heavenly ratification of decisions and Jesus' presence are promised when two or more are gathered in his name (vv. 18–20).[37] And, most tellingly, the text realistically views the possibility that the process will fail and the offending member will need to be expelled (v. 17). Such action would be unnecessary if moral concerns were solely individual matters.[38]

The second aspect worth noting about the procedure for dealing with sins is that this procedure is directed at restoration and reconciliation. This aspect is reflected, for instance, in verse 15's "you have regained that one," and in verse 18's "whatever you loose on earth shall be loosed in heaven."[39] This focus on restoration suggests that the first Gospel presumes our moral interdependence. It is precisely because we are not morally self-sufficient that Matthew's Jesus outlines a process for helping one who is straying from the path.[40]

This is comparable to virtue theory's claim that from infancy onward we depend on each other for our moral development. We depend, for example, on instruction and guidance from parents, models, and friends. Although Matthew does not fully develop or spell out this view, he appears to agree: our moral development depends on the presence and help of others.[41]

Another significant element of Matthew 18's focus on the Christian community is its underlining of humility and forgiveness (18:4; 18:21–35).[42] As Ogletree points out, these qualities are essential to community maintenance:

> The early church was a community gathered from the nations. Many natural supports for human association—family, kinship ties, a common language and culture, ethnic and racial identity— could no longer contribute directly to stable social order. The

diversity of the community with regard to these factors actually increased the likelihood of unintended misunderstandings and injuries.... Communities transcending family, language, culture, and national identity could only sustain themselves through continual acts of forgiveness.[43]

In other words, humility and forgiveness are important because they are social attributes. Since the church's cohesion is not predicated on ordinary human ties (cf. 10:35–37; 12:46–50), Matthew views characteristics like forgiveness and humility as essential to the church's unity.[44] Matthew thus envisions a community whose cohesion is based in part on certain personal qualities or characteristics, on certain "virtues," not on violence or kinship or common culture.[45]

This emphasis on the qualities or "virtues" of humility and forgiveness is comparable to virtue theory. Both Matthew and virtue theory assume a link between virtues and relationships. At least part of Matthew's incentive for underlining certain qualities relates to their communal role and resembles virtue theory's claim that many virtues are not simply individual qualities but have social import—indeed, some virtues are important only because of relationships and shared activity. Virtue theory's emphasis on the social significance of some virtues thus anticipates the type of link between virtues and social setting exhibited in Matthew.

In sum, Matthew, like virtue theory, envisions the individual's journey within a social/communal context. Examples of this are seen in the disciples' relationship to the master and in the procedure for dealing with sin. The procedure for dealing with sin also suggests that Matthew, like virtue theory, presumes that our social context is more than merely scenery or backdrop: we are morally interdependent. Finally, Matthew, like virtue theory, assumes a link between certain personal qualities and certain relationships. One example of this is the stress on forgiveness and humility within chapter 18's focus on the Christian community.

Matthew as Narrative

That Matthew is a narrative is obvious, but this fact also might provide a meaningful link with virtue ethics. There has recently been much talk in virtue theory concerning the importance of narrative and narrative ethics. The problem, however, is knowing what people are talking about and finding any actual point of agreement.[46] While many authors view the story genre as philosophically and morally significant, there is little agreement as to where that significance lies.[47] The only certainty is that many concerned with virtue theory are also exploring the moral and philosophical implications of narrative.

This assertion says very little; still, it must be pointed out. Given virtue theory's current intensive exploration of narrative, Matthew's genre may turn out to be the most significant link between this Gospel and virtue ethics. Moreover, we discover some significant connections with virtue theory when we put aside the broad category "narrative" and briefly explore some of Matthew's literary and rhetorical devices. That is, various elements of Matthew's narrative—for example, pointing to specific people as moral examples, the depiction of character traits, and the use of eschatological blessings and warnings—are consistent with the expectations arising from virtue theory.

For instance, we learn from Matthew 5:20 that "righteousness" is a key term. In this passage, Jesus tells us that one's righteousness must exceed that of the scribes and Pharisees. This teaches us to watch for instances of "righteousness." The term's periodic appearance thereafter functions, in part, to point out persons who are examples of righteousness. The prophets (5:10–12), Abel and the martyrs (23:35), John the Baptist (21:32), and Christian missionaries (10:41) are identified by Matthew as moral examples, as examples of righteousness.[48]

Of course, Jesus is the preeminent model or example in Matthew. Jesus, the "innocent" and "righteous" man (27:4, 19), is baptized to fulfill all "righteousness" (3:15) and is obedient even when tempted (4:1–11) or facing death (26:39, 42).[49] Jesus is also the teacher and master (10:24–25), and anyone who wishes to find life must take his or her cross and "follow" Jesus (10:38–39; 16:24).

Matthew's pointing to Jesus and others as examples or models is significant from the perspective of virtue theory. As noted in chapter two, virtue theory claims that we can learn from persons of practical wisdom even if they are not present. We gain insight by observing how such persons handled situations similar or analogous to our own. Thus, from virtue theory's perspective, Matthew's offering of specific people and groups as models or examples is noteworthy. Such models are an important part of discernment and the gaining of practical wisdom.[50]

Another connection with virtue theory is found in Matthew's depiction of various characters and character traits. Jack Kingsbury's literary-critical reading of Matthew discusses the Gospel's characterization of Jesus, the disciples, religious leaders, and many minor characters. According to Kingsbury, Matthew uses each of these to display character traits. For example, he sees Matthew depicting the disciples as loyal, loving, attentive, obedient, trusting, authoritative, servant-like, and vulnerable. But they are also doubting, fearful, prone to despair, self-deluded, and so on.[51]

It does not matter for our purposes whether Kingsbury is correct in describing each character trait. What is important is that Matthew uses the depiction of characters and traits to school the reader in the characteristics and traits appropriate to discipleship. The reader learns with which actions and attitudes to identify through the narrative portrayal of the various characters and their laudatory or reprehensible actions and attitudes.

For example, Kingsbury notes that

> Because the disciples possess conflicting traits, the reader is invited, depending on the attitude Matthew as narrator or Jesus takes toward them on any given occasion, to identify with them or to distance himself or herself from them. It is through such granting or withholding of approval on cue, therefore, that the reader becomes schooled in the values that govern the life of discipleship in Matthew's story.[52]

In short, the first Gospel encourages or discourages various character traits through such mechanisms as the narrator's comments, Jesus' explicit acceptance or rejection, or Jesus' actions and attitudes as examples and counterexamples.[53]

This narrative development of characters and their traits reminds us that Matthew is interested in the kind of people we become. Matthew is concerned with our "being," not just our "doing."

In making this point we return to where this chapter started: Matthew's concern with the internal qualities of human action. However, in emphasizing Matthew's depiction of character traits we go "deeper" than that earlier discussion. Matthew's presentation of various characters and traits is not neutral or dispassionate. The presentation is meant to invite and encourage certain responses and to discourage others. The first Gospel does not merely talk about actions, attitudes, beliefs, dispositions, and feelings. It also works at *shaping* and *informing* them. Matthew's concern with the internal goes beyond merely discussing a normative code or ethical theory. Matthew attempts to influence and form the Christian's total self—that is, to make it consistent with the invitation to become Jesus' follower.[54]

Matthew's portrayal of character traits is not the only way he tries to influence and shape the reader.[55] He also identifies certain people as moral examples or models. Such identification is an invitation to learn from and emulate the model.

Jesus' use of eschatological blessings and warnings of judgment also makes sense in this context of influencing and shaping the reader (e.g., 5:3–12; 7:15–27; 25:13–46). One function of these blessings and warnings is to encourage certain behavior and attitudes.[56] This tactic may seem antiquated (even barbaric) to philosophers who view ethics in terms of pure moral persuasion or one's self-legislating will, but it makes good sense both to parents and virtue theory. As every good parent knows, reward and punishment are essential equipment in the struggle to influence a child's attitudes and behavior. And with its understanding of human agency, virtue theory also sees praise and blame, encouragement and censure, as important components in the shaping of character.

Whether or not Matthew's genre eventually provides a significant connection with virtue theory, some of Matthew's literary and rhetorical devices already furnish links to virtue ethics. Matthew's use of role models, his depiction of character traits, and his various efforts to influence and shape the readers are congruent with expectations arising from virtue theory.

Matthew: Love and Law

A cursory reading of Matthew can suggest a law-based ethic or an ethic of love. It is a mistake to reduce Matthew's ethic to either of these. The language of both law and love plays an important role in Matthew's narrative, but Matthew's ethic is reducible to neither.

The principle or law of love plays an important role in Matthew. Matthew's Jesus teaches love of enemies (5:44), the "golden rule" (7:12), and that the law's greatest commands are love of God and love of neighbor (22:36–40; cf. 19:19; 23:23).

However, the import of the law of love is easily overstated. To say that it is the key or center or standard or hermeneutical principle of Matthew's ethic is an exaggeration.[57] Such language suggests that the meaning and implications of love are obvious and that the remainder of

Matthew's ethics can be deduced from this law. But this is clearly not so in Matthew.

The single biggest objection to seeing love as the key is the vast quantity of other types of ethical material in Matthew. It is difficult to reduce everything to love when one compares the relatively few texts that cite the law of love with, for instance, the wealth of parables and specific commands. Matthew's ethic includes specific commands, eschatological warnings, parables, Jesus' example, and the call to discipleship.[58] Matthew's ethic is also an ethic of justice (12:18, 20; 23:23), mercy (9:13; 12:7), and cross bearing (10:38; 16:24). Love is important, sometimes prominent. But love is not a comprehensive principle that allows dispensing with the remainder of Matthew's ethical concerns.[59]

Let me be clear: I have no wish to deny that love plays a vital role in Matthew's gospel. For example, love has a critical function in Matthew's appropriation of the law. Love is the epitome of the law's moral demands (7:12; 22:40), and it serves as a "critical principle by which the individual commandments of the law and tradition are to be read, interpreted and evaluated."[60]

Yet Matthew's ethic cannot be adequately summarized as an expression of love alone. Besides the other kinds of ethical material in Matthew, there is the problem of love's form and content. The word "love" can mean many different things. We learn what love means to Matthew by attending to Jesus' teaching and example. Love includes praying for one's enemies (5:44), "doing good" on the sabbath (12:12), and eating with sinners (9:13; cf. 21:31f).[61] But we do not know that these actions extol love's meaning until after we have read the story.

To the extent that we accept love as a key or hermeneutical principle in Matthew's ethics, we must be clear as well that this principle is neither self-interpreting nor individually sufficient.[62] We do not know what love means until after we have read Matthew's narrative. And Matthew's ethic includes much besides the formal imperatives to love God and neighbor.

A similar assertion must be made concerning the role of law in Matthew: Matthew's ethic cannot be reduced to an affirmation of the Mosaic law.[63] Not that Matthew is an enemy of the law; the first Gospel assumes that Christian behavior concurs with the law.[64] It is, after all, the Matthean Jesus who says,

> Do not think that I have come to abolish the law or the prophets;
> I have come not to abolish but to fulfill. For truly I tell you . . .

not one letter, not one stroke of a letter, will pass from the law until all is accomplished (5:17–18).

The first Gospel clearly holds the law in high esteem. It is a mistake, however, to reduce or limit Matthew's ethic to an ethic of law. Although the sense in which Jesus "fulfills" the law is notoriously difficult to interpret, Matthew's moral vision cannot be restricted to a discussion of the law.[65]

The norm in Matthew is Jesus, and the law's force remains only "as it has passed through the crucible of Jesus' teaching."[66] It is Jesus' words that the church is to hear and do (7:24; 28:18) and Jesus' words that will never pass away (24:35). Jesus claims authority over the sacred institution of Sabbath and claims to be superior to the Temple (12:1–8). And it is Jesus who rejects the Hebrew Bible's regulation of divorce in favor of God's original will (19:3–9).

The importance of reading the law through Jesus' teaching and example is particularly apparent in the "antitheses" (5:21–48). A contrast between Jesus and the scribal interpretation of the law is already established in the formulation of the antitheses: "You have heard that it was said to those of ancient times. . . . But I say to you" (5:21, 33; cf. 5:27, 31, 38, 43).[67] Moreover, the various antitheses extend, surpass, devalue, and even abrogate the law.[68]

This movement is especially evident in Jesus' rejection of oaths (5:33–37) and retaliation (5:38–42).[69] In the Hebrew Bible, oaths and vows constitute an esteemed institution whose use is sometimes not merely permitted but required.[70] Thus, it is difficult to view Jesus' rejection of oaths and vows as merely clarifying the law. Similarly, the Pentateuch repeatedly enunciates the law of retaliation.[71] Thus, when Jesus rejects retaliation and retribution of any kind, he does not simply intensify the law or make it more humane. There is, rather, an important note of contrast, probably abrogation.[72]

Some commentators may respond by arguing that Matthew's Jesus is merely extending or intensifying the law's intention.[73] In other words, Jesus should not be seen as breaking with the law, but as holding to its deepest purposes. Hence, both the law's prescription of oaths and Jesus' rejection of oaths are trying to ensure fidelity in one's speech. Similarly, both the *lex talionis* and Jesus' rejection of retribution aim at reducing the total level of violence.

For our purposes, this argument is beside the point. If one accepts Jesus' teaching on these matters, the Mosaic law cannot function as a direct action-guiding rule or law. The law requires vows and oaths but Jesus rejects them. The law requires retribution in kind; Jesus rejects retribution of any kind. Thus, whatever underlying connection exists between the intentions of Jesus and the law, the Mosaic law no longer functions as we normally anticipate rules or laws to function. The law prescribes a specific course of action; Jesus prescribes the opposite. Matthew may have seen Jesus as keeping with the law's deepest intent, but the actual effect of the antitheses is to undermine and annul the Torah's precepts in favor of Jesus' teaching and example. While Matthew views the law as revealing God's will, Matthew's ethic cannot be reduced to an affirmation of the law. Whatever authority the law has, that authority depends on Jesus.[74]

The objection might be raised that while Matthew's ethic is not a simple affirmation of the Torah, it is a deontological ethic—an ethic of rules, laws, and commands. There is some merit in this objection. The Mosaic law is important to Matthew and Jesus' commands are to be treated with the utmost seriousness. However, when considering whether Matthew's ethic can be understood solely in deontological terms, we must recall its various elements. Matthew's ethic is a perfectionist ethic that is concerned with both our actions and the attitudes behind them. It is also an ethic concerned with both individual and community, and it views the master/disciple relationship as essential. It is an ethic that uses rules and commands but also warnings and blessings, models or examples, parables, and even prayer.[75] In short, although rules and commands play a vital role in Matthew, the first Gospel's ethic cannot be discussed solely in deontological terms.

This is a negative judgment. But I want to argue also for the more positive judgment that the first Gospel is compatible with and has numerous potential links to virtue ethics. Several similarities and possible connections have been explored above. What remains to be done is an exploration of possible connections between virtue theory and Matthew's use of laws, rules, and commands (law language).

One potential link is found in Matthew's pedagogical use of law language. Many commentators do not see Matthew as developing a comprehensive set of rules. Instead, they view his use of law language as having an educative function. Wayne Meeks, for example, says that Matthew provides "no system of commandments." Rules and commands are important in Matthew, but they "are exemplary, not comprehensive, pointers to the kind of life expected in the community ... not a map of acceptable behavior."[76]

Meeks has company in this evaluation. Ulrich Luz views Matthew as holding the commands of the Mosaic law and Jesus as commands of God:

> But they are not laws which prescribe accurately how a Christian must act in every situation. They are not sentences of law but exemplary demands which portray in examples the manner and radicality in which God demands obedience. The Freedom to invent new examples is always a part of exemplarity.[77]

Others similarly view Matthew's use of law language, not as advancing a comprehensive law (new or old), but as paradigms, illustrations of wholeness, depictions of the greater righteousness required of disciples, and descriptions of behavior suitable to the coming kingdom.[78] Thomas Ogletree even argues that "laws and commandments function not simply as statements about what we are to do, but predominantly as specifications of who we are to become." In other words, Ogletree views Matthew as changing law language's "characteristic deontological thrust" into a "delineation of the wholeness of life to which God calls faithful disciples."[79]

These authors view Matthew's law language as having an educative function, often as sketching a picture of faithful discipleship and the kingdom of God.[80] This view finds parallels in the earlier discussion of virtue theory. Recall, for instance, Nussbaum's view of rules as summaries of previous wise decisions and as guidelines in moral development. As summaries, rules provide a reference point of previous good judgments but are valid only as long as they correctly describe the current particular case. As guidelines, rules function as guides in shaping character for those who do not yet possess practical wisdom.

The suggestions that commands in Matthew are exemplary and paradigmatic are similar to Nussbaum's ideas. Rules can function as reference points and guides without being comprehensive or always binding. Similarly, suggestions that commands in Matthew point at or portray the kingdom or faithful discipleship are analogous to an observation we saw, made by Pincoffs, namely, that rules can depict, or call one to become, a certain sort of person.[81]

Another way in which Matthew's use of law language is comparable to virtue theory is the need for "discernment, discretion, and judgment on the part of the disciple."[82] The application of rules and commands in Matthew is not straightforward and deductive. This is implicit in suggestions that law language in Matthew is paradigmatic or exemplary. It is also suggested by Jesus' observations that some commands are "greater" than others (22:37–40), some are "weightier" than others (23:23), and some are limited by love and mercy (e.g., 12:10–13). In short, the application of law language calls for interpreting discernment and wisdom.[83]

This need for discernment bears comparison with virtue theory, for law language in Matthew requires a quality of skillful judgment that resembles practical wisdom or "prudence." Law language in Matthew is insufficient without interpretation and judgment. Its use "calls for something akin to Aristotelian prudence."[84]

In sum, virtue theory and Matthew's use of law language are compatible. Indeed, they fit together nicely. Matthew views the law as revelation, but Matthew's ethic is not reducible to law (either specifically as Torah or in more general deontological terms). Instead, law language plays an educative role and calls for the exercise of discerning judgment.

Reformulating Virtue Ethics: Forgiveness and the Centrality of Jesus

I have left many aspects of Matthew's moral vision unexplored. I mentioned only in passing Matthew's eschatology or the significance of prayer, for instance. Still, I have suggested assorted points of similarity, contact, and correlation between virtue theory and the first Gospel. This chapter's central aim regarding Matthew is thus complete.

However, before discussing Paul, I must point out that attention to Matthew's ethic does not leave a virtue framework unaltered. One whose ethic is informed or influenced by the first Gospel will find it necessary to fill out and reformulate a virtue ethic. Examples of this point include Matthew's emphases on forgiveness and the centrality of Jesus.

I earlier observed the focus on forgiveness and reconciliation in Matthew 18. This focus is also evident in the "Lord's Prayer" (6:10–13), which links our seeking God's forgiveness with our willingness to forgive others (v. 12). Moreover, Jesus' only comment on the prayer is the assertion of correspondence between divine and human mercy: if we are willing to forgive, God will forgive us, but if we are unwilling to forgive, God will not forgive us (vv. 14–15; cf. 18:23–35).[85] A similar emphasis is seen in Jesus' contention that reconciliation takes precedence over liturgical rites (5:23–24) and in the resurrected Jesus' reference to the disciples as "brothers" (28:10) even after they deserted and denied him (26:56, 69–75).[86]

The centrality of Jesus appears at several points in this discussion. Jesus is the teacher and master. He is the preeminent model and his words have abiding validity. If you seek life, follow him. Even the law's authority depends on him. Jesus is, moreover, the Messiah/Son-of-Man/Son-of-God (16:13–17).[87] The church's moral discernment depends on the risen Christ's continuing presence (18:18–20).[88] Indeed, in the judgment that distinguishes the "sheep from the goats," Matthew appears to tie all morality to Christ. All nations are judged according to what they have done for the poor and the outcast, and what is done to them is done to the Son of Man (25:31–46).[89]

Virtue theory contains nothing concerning forgiveness or Jesus. Nor is there anything to suggest an inherent tension or opposition between virtue theory and these convictions. Rather, Matthew's focus on Jesus and forgiveness illustrates the kind of refinement and development that follows from the qualifier "Christian" being added to "virtue theory." From a standpoint influenced by the first Gospel, an adequate virtue ethic views the earthly/exalted Jesus as its center and norm (as its "*telos*") and forgiveness and reconciliation as essential to the community's life and practice. Although these are surely not the only points at which the first Gospel would modify a virtue perspective, the preeminence of Jesus and the importance of forgiveness remind us that a Christian appropriation of a virtue framework will not leave that framework unaltered.

THE LETTERS OF PAUL

Points Shared with Matthew

In looking for points of contact or correlation between Paul and virtue theory, there are several areas where Paul's outlook or concerns are similar to Matthew's. These areas include the appeal to models or examples, an interest in internal qualities, an outlook that is both individual and communal, and the need for the quality or skill of discernment. Since their correlation with virtue theory was discussed in covering Matthew, I want simply to call attention to these areas in Paul's letters.[90]

Models or Worthy Examples

Paul's ethic, like Matthew's, includes the appeal to specific people as models or examples.[91] Paul's use of models or examples is seen, for instance, in his frequent call to "imitate" him (1 Cor 4:16; Phil 3:17; cf. Gal 4:12; Phil 4:9) as he imitates Christ (1 Cor 11:1; cf. 1 Thess 1:6).[92] Similarly, there is at least an implied challenge to imitation in Paul's use of the Christ-Hymn in Phil 2:5–11, and Christ is our example in Paul's call to "please" and "welcome" our neighbors (Rom 15:1–7). In short, the Christian life is patterned after the work and lives of Christ and the apostle.[93]

Paul and Christ are not the only models or examples. In trying to generate enthusiasm for the collection for the Jerusalem church, Paul presents the Macedonians as examples to the Corinthians (2 Cor 8:1–15, 24; cf. 9:2). Likewise, in following Christ's example, the believers at Philippi "shine like stars in the world" (Phil 2:15; cf. 1 Thess 1:6–8). Thus, learning from and "imitating" models or worthy examples is a notable component of Paul's understanding of the Christian life.[94]

Internal Qualities

Paul, like Matthew, is concerned with both specific actions and internal qualities. This concern is evident, for instance, in Paul's appropriation of "virtue" and "vice" lists (Rom 1:29–31; 13:13; 1 Cor 5:10–11; 6:9–10; 2 Cor 12:20–21; Gal 5:19–23; Phil 4:8; cf. Col 3:5–17).[95] The "virtues" include love, joy, peace, patience, kindness, faithfulness, and purity, among others. The "vices" include idolatry, sorcery, meanness, arrogance, insolence, selfishness, envy, jealousy, greed, strife, sexual immorality, drunkenness, and carousing.

These lists do not show that Paul was explicitly working from a "virtue ethic." Such lists were common in Paul's milieu, both Jewish and Hellenistic, and he was simply adapting familiar material. Paul does not even refer to these lists as involving "virtues" and "vices" but as "fruits" of the Spirit and "works" of the flesh (Gal 5:19–23).

What these lists do show is that Paul considered dispositions and attitudes important and that he assumed that such interior aspects come to expression in action. By appropriating these long, unsystematic, and loosely connected lists, Paul depicts or portrays both the kind of people Christians are called to be and the kinds of actions appropriate to those people.

Virtue and vice lists are not the only places Paul shows an interest in these qualities. Paul's concern with both external actions and internal qualities is evident in his desire that we "cleanse ourselves from every defilement of body and of spirit" (2 Cor 7:1; cf. 1 Cor 7:34). The importance of attitudes and the inner life is similarly suggested by Paul's idea that the Spirit has transformed our "hearts" (Rom 5:5; 8:27; 2 Cor 1:22; 3:3; Gal 4:6).[96]

Several "inner" qualities are also evident in Paul's description of love in 1 Cor 13:4–8 and the exhortation of Rom 12:9–21. We are called to patience and kindness, but warned of jealousy, arrogance, rudeness, irritability, or resentment. We are called to self-control concerning boastfulness or insisting on one's own way. We are encouraged to rejoice in the right, and we are told to bear, believe, hope, and endure everything.[97]

In brief, Paul is concerned with concrete actions. But he is also concerned with the qualities, attitudes, and dispositions that give birth to actions.

Individual and Corporate

Paul, like Matthew, envisions the Christian life in terms that are both individual and corporate. For example, Paul chastises the Corinthians because their celebration of the Lord's supper does not reflect unity and mutual concern (1 Cor 11:17–34). Indeed, he insists that given their behavior, they are not in fact practicing the Lord's supper (v. 20; cf. 27–30). This emphasis on unity and mutual concern is also reflected in the collection for the Jerusalem poor (e.g., Rom 15:25–31; 2 Cor 8:1–15, 24; Gal 2:10) and in the practice of hospitality (e.g., Rom 12:13; 16:23; 1 Cor 16:5–7, 10–11; Phlm 22).[98]

Paul's individual and corporate moral vision is most obvious when he compares the church to a living human body (1 Cor 12:12–31; Rom 12:4–5; cf. 1 Cor 10:17).[99] Paul relates the individually gifted members of the church to the various parts of the physical body. Like the many parts of a body, the church includes many different people with many different abilities and gifts. Yet the individuals' abilities and gifts find their purpose in and are to be used for the benefit of one another (cf. 1 Cor 12:7; 14:12).[100]

Like the limbs of a body, each member is an integral part of a single whole. And like the limbs of a body, individuals depend in an important respect on their participation in a shared life. An individual member, like an arm or eye, cannot really be himself or herself, cannot do what an arm or eye does, apart from the whole (cf. 1 Cor 12:14; Rom 12:5).

As the body image suggests, Paul assumes our moral interdependence.[101] Thus, when calling for the excommunication of a man living with his stepmother (1 Cor 5:1–8), Paul's justification is based on the effect this one man's behavior could have on the entire community: "a little yeast leavens the whole batch of dough" (1 Cor 5:6). Similarly, Paul's discussions of meat sacrificed to idols (1 Cor 8, 10) and the conflict between "weak" and "strong" (Rom 14:1–15:13) presume our ability to influence each other.[102] Our moral interdependence also provides the underpinning for Paul's assertions that "bad company ruins good morals" (1 Cor 15:33) and that we should not associate with immoral persons within the church (1 Cor 5:9–11) or be mismated with unbelievers (2 Cor 6:14–7:1).

Lest we think that Paul views our interdependence only in negative terms, we must remember that the point of excommunication is to reform and reconcile the offender (2 Cor 2:5–11; cf. 1 Cor 5:5; Gal 6:1). We should similarly remember Paul's appeal to the Thessalonians: "admonish the idlers, encourage the fainthearted, help the weak, be patient with all of them" (1 Thess 5:14).

In emphasizing the corporate and interdependent side of Paul's ethic, it is important not to underestimate the individual's value and responsibility.[103] The corporate context of Paul's moral vision does not eliminate the importance of individual members and their moral improvement. Each believer has his or her own measure of faith (Rom 12:3; cf. 14:1; 15:1). Each will be judged by God according to what he has done (Rom 2:6, 16; 14:4, 10, 12; 1 Cor 4:5; 2 Cor 5:10), and thus each must test his or her own work (Gal 6:4). Even Paul must evaluate his work so as to be sure that he is not running in vain (Gal 2:2; cf. 1 Cor 9:24–27; Phil 2:16; 3:10–16; 1 Thess 3:5).

Although gifts are to be used for the benefit of the whole (1 Cor 12:7; 14:12), the Spirit gives different gifts to different individuals (Rom 12:6–8; 1 Cor 12:11), and speaking in tongues is largely a matter of individual edification (1 Cor 14:2–4). Moreover, as E.P. Sanders notes in a different context, Paul's message "is intended to elicit 'faith', and faith can only be individual."[104]

Paul's vision of the Christian life thus encompasses community and individuals. Individual gifts and abilities find their proper setting in the church. We are individually accountable before God, but we are also morally interdependent and can influence each other for good or for ill.[105]

Discernment

In discussing Matthew's view of the law, I noted the need for the quality or skill of discerning judgment, which was compared to wisdom or prudence. The need for this quality or skill is more pronounced (and less tied to the law) in Paul's letters.[106]

Paul challenges the Thessalonians to "test everything; hold fast to what is good" (1 Thess 5:21). Similar themes of "testing," "proving," and "discerning" are evident throughout Paul's letters (e.g., Rom 12:1–3; 1 Cor 2:14–16; 2 Cor 13:5–9; Phil 1:9–11; 1 Thess 5:19–22).[107] We even find Paul chastising the Corinthians for having lawsuits before unbelievers, for there ought to be someone in the church wise enough to judge the matters they are taking before pagan courts (1 Cor 6:1–8).

We also see discerning judgment at work in many texts. For example, Paul clearly knows Jesus' directive concerning divorce and that it permits no exceptions. Yet Paul submits this directive to critical evaluation and permits some type of separation for those married to pagans (1 Cor 7:10–16).[108] Discernment is also at work in Paul's treatment of meat sacrificed to idols (1 Cor 8, 10) and in the conflict between "weak" and "strong" in Rom 14:1–15:13. In both instances Paul concludes that though certain activities are not wrong of themselves, one may yet need to abstain from such activities for another's sake. We are thus privy to Paul's own discernment process: he first concludes that these things are acceptable but then modifies that conclusion in light of Christian relationships.[109]

Discerning judgment is not just a private or individual affair but involves a common, shared search for the right way.[110] Christians come together to test, investigate, and approve their actions. Thus, for instance, the concrete and situational utterances of prophets are to be tested by the congregation (1 Cor 14:29; 1 Thess 5:20–21). A prophet is not the sole judge of his or her own message. Indeed, since the Spirit gives different gifts or manifestations to each, we depend on each other for wisdom, knowledge, prophecy, and discernment (1 Cor 12:7–11).

In short, Paul continually exhibits and calls for a kind of discriminating wisdom or skillful judgment that seeks in the particular situation to "discern the will of God—what is good and acceptable and perfect" (Rom 12:2). This discerning judgment is not limited to individuals but involves the community's shared search.

This judgment provides a major connection with virtue theory. Few moral theories can abide Paul's relative lack of rules or principles or methods of moral calculation.[111] Yet Paul's ethic is concrete and specific without being a directionless "situational" ethic.[112] Virtue theory's notion of "practical wisdom" or "prudence" provides an important similarity or parallel (see chapter 2). Practical wisdom is sensitive to concrete particulars and relationships (without disregarding rules, principles, and consequences). It also depends on communal resources for discernment. Thus, a similarity or congruence between Paul's "testing" and virtue theory's "practical wisdom" is difficult to deny.

Other Connections with Virtue Theory

I now move to discuss some aspects of Paul's ethics that do not have obvious similarities to Matthew. I suggest in particular that potential connections with virtue theory are provided by (1) Paul's images of moral progress and (2) the relationship in Paul's thought between the "indicative" and the "imperative."

Images of Moral Progress

In chapter 4, I argued that the theological idea of sanctification provides important similarities and connections to virtue ethics. I cannot similarly appeal to this term in Paul's thought. "Sanctification" is not synonymous with moral growth in the Pauline letters. Instead, sanctification is one of many terms used by Paul to describe the effects of the Christ-event and its principal reference is the dedication of people or things to the service of God.[113]

Although we cannot directly appeal to sanctification, Paul uses several terms and images that suggest a moral journey of growth and progress. For instance, the verb "to walk" (e.g., Rom 6:4; 13:13; 1 Thess 2:12; 4:1, 12; cf. Col 1:10; 2:6; Eph 4:1) looks to the moral life and is often simply translated "to live."[114] In appropriating this term, Paul is using "a common Semitic idiom for a pattern of behavior."[115] Thus, for example, we should walk by the Spirit, not the flesh (Rom 8:4; Gal 5:16). Similarly, if there is jealousy and strife or if we injure others in the church, then we are walking by human standards and not by love (1 Cor 3:3; Rom 14:15).

By itself, "walking" does not imply moral growth or progress. But unlike many contemporary understandings of ethics, "walking" envisions continuity and patterns of behavior. Instead of seeing morality primarily as discrete acts, judgments, and dilemmas, "walking" or "living" pictures morality as patterns of behavior and a continuous journey.[116]

Paul also pictures the Christian life in terms of a race (1 Cor 9:24–27; Phil 3:11–17; cf. Gal 2:2; Phil 2:16; Heb 12:1–3).[117] The race's objective has not been obtained. Thus one should not run aimlessly, but strain forward and press toward the goal. One should run to win, exercise self-control, and train the body.

We see in this image that the Christian life for Paul is a goal-oriented endeavor. Perfection has not yet been reached, but like a race, we focus on and strain toward the end. Thus, we begin to see that morality for Paul is not just "walking," but a journey involving real effort and directed toward a goal.

Paul's references to "transformation" are also instructive. The term, deriving from Roman mythology, was current in Paul's day. He applies this term to the Christ-event and sees Christ gradually reshaping us. For instance, 2 Cor 3:18 pictures salvation as a process with the goal of conformity or likeness to Christ: "and all of us, with unveiled faces, seeing the glory of the Lord as though reflected in a mirror, are being transformed into the same image from one degree of glory to another; for this comes from the Lord, the Spirit."[118] Similarly, Rom 8:29 stresses God's antecedence in our growing conformity to Christ, and Rom 12:2 calls believers to a metamorphosis of the mind, not just external change.[119]

Paul's vision of the Christian life is not that of a static state of already achieved perfection. There is room for "progress" and an "increase" in faith (Phil 1:25; 2 Cor 10:15). Paul calls for an increase in love "with knowledge and full insight to help you determine what is best" (Phil 1:9–10; cf. 1 Thess 3:12; 4:9–10). The Corinthians, likewise, are chided for not having become more mature (1 Cor 3:1–2; 2 Cor 6:13; cf. Heb 5:13–6:1) and are challenged to "strive" both for "spiritual gifts" (14:1) and "to excel" (14:14). In short, there is need for growth in the Christian life.[120]

Although we cannot appeal to Paul's primary use of the term "sanctification," the theological category of sanctification has its roots in Pauline thought. Paul's vision of the Christian life includes the need for growth, increase, and progress toward the goal of conformity with Christ. It is then like virtue ethics at least to this extent: both involve goal-oriented moral growth and the transformation of the person and his or her character.

Paul, like virtue theory, focuses less on specific acts and more on continuities and patterns of behavior. Paul, again like virtue theory, also envisions the Christian life as a lifelong process or "walk" involving the transformation of oneself and one's character toward a partially understood goal (Christ-likeness).

Indicative and Imperative

Most treatments of Pauline ethics discuss the relationship between the "indicative" and the "imperative." Although catchwords, these terms remind us that Paul's letters contain theology and ethics, kerygma and injunction to action, proclamation and exhortation. In mentioning the indicative and imperative, authors are asking about the relationship between these two substantial aspects of Paul's letters. How is one to understand Paul's movement between kerygma and injunction, proclamation and exhortation?

There is a tendency to rigidly separate these two elements of Paul's thought or to treat them as if Paul's real interest was theological and the moral material simply an aside. Neither interpretation fits the evidence, however. Paul clearly presumes an intimate connection between the indicative and imperative.

This intimate relationship is seen in Paul's use of the consecutive conjunction "therefore" to introduce the specifically parenetic (that is, ethical) sections of Romans (6:12; 12:1), 1 Thessalonians (4:1), and Galatians (5:1). By so introducing these sections, Paul connects and correlates the two elements. He indicates not simply a transition of topic, but an inference. That is to say, the ethics follow from and are a consequence of the kerygma (cf. Eph 4:1; Col 3:1, 5).[121]

The intimate connection is also seen in that Paul often uses the same or similar language in both the indicative and imperative elements. For example, in Gal 5:25 we are told that we live by the Spirit but we are also encouraged to live by the Spirit (cf. Gal 5:16). Similarly, Rom 6:2 asserts that believers are dead to sin, but Rom 6:11 calls us to consider ourselves dead to sin.[122] This use of similar language in both the indicative and imperative shows their interconnection and forces us to give equal weight to both sides.[123]

Having argued that the indicative and imperative are closely related in Paul's letters, we must admit that their precise relationship is hotly debated and cannot be decided here. However, it seems likely that Paul's movement between them reflects his eschatology.[124]

According to Paul, we live at that point where one age is closing and another opening (1 Cor 10:11). Because of what God has done in Christ, salvation is now (2 Cor 6:2) and Christians possess the "firstfruits" and "pledge" of the Spirit (Rom 8:23; 2 Cor 1:22; 5:5). Similarly,

God through Christ has broken the power of sin and law and signaled the ultimate defeat of the last enemy, death (1 Cor 15:21–26; Rom 5:21; 6:7–10; 7:4–6; 8:1–5, 35–39). Yet, Paul never denies that the powers of sin, law, and death are still present and active. Because we await the final judgment and resurrection of the dead (Rom 2:6–11; 6:5; 14:10; 1 Cor 6:14; 15:13–20; 2 Cor 5:7, 10), we must continue the struggle against the powers. But because of what God has done in Christ, they now can be resisted successfully (Rom 6:1–14; 12:1–2; Gal 4:6–9; 5:24).[125]

This eschatological development is the context of Paul's movement between indicative and imperative. The indicative reflects what God has done, is doing, and will complete. The imperative reflects our wait for the final consummation. While living in this time, we strive to have our lives reflect both what God has done and will do (e.g., Rom 13:11–14; 14:7; Gal 6:9–10; Phil 2:16; 3:14; 1 Thess 2:12).[126]

Nothing said so far implies a connection between virtue theory and Paul's movement between the indicative and imperative. However, I suggest that this movement reflects potential connections with virtue theory. I suggest in particular that the indicative/imperative relationship (1) assumes a link between "being" and "doing" and (2) shows that the need for moral admonition derives from the discrepancy between who we are and who we are called to be.

First, note the relationship in virtue theory between "being" and "doing." There is an important sense in which "being" precedes "doing." That is, people with certain dispositions, attitudes, and beliefs will tend to act in certain kinds of ways.

We see something similar in Paul's movement from the indicative to imperative: our actions flow from our being. In the indicative mode, Paul recounts aspects of who Christians are and what God has done for us. He talks, for example, about salvation, the end of law, resurrection, the Spirit's transforming presence, and the church as Christ's body. When Paul moves to the imperative, he assumes that certain kinds of actions and attitudes follow naturally from what has been said in the indicative. That is why, for example, Paul begins the parenetic sections with "therefore." He presumes that a certain kind of people will act in a certain kind of way. It is almost like saying that since this is who Christians are and will be (the indicative), behave like this (the imperative). Paul takes for granted that the kind of people described in the indicative will behave in certain characteristic ways.

Understanding the relationship between indicative and imperative in this way does not negate Paul's emphasis on grace. In Paul's understanding, who we are, our "being," is the result of the Christ-event and the Spirit's continuing work.[127] But acknowledging that our "being" (the indicative) is indebted to God's gracious activity does not alter the basic logic in Paul's movement. When Paul freely moves from indicative to imperative, he is moving from who we are to how we should act. In so doing, he is working from a virtue-like presumption: being precedes doing; a certain kind of people will act in a certain kind of way.

Second, consider virtue theory's tripartite structure: (1) what-we-happen-to-be, (2) what-we-could-be, (3) those habits, inclinations, precepts, injunctions, and prohibitions that will move us from number one to number two. I suggest a resemblance between this structure and what we see in Paul. What-we-could-be (number two) is comparable to aspects of the indicative element in Paul's thought. The imperative element is comparable to those habits, inclination, precepts and injunctions (number three) that move us to what-we-could-be. The comparison with what-we-happen-to-be (number one) is found in those actions and attitudes that make the imperative sections necessary.

Paul's exhortations are more than a call for believers "to be who they are."[128] They are more than mere reminders of something already completed. The need for moral encouragement shows that believers do not yet fully embody their calling as Christians. It is, in a sense, a goal yet to be reached. Moreover, since the full consummation is ahead of us, we attempt to anticipate that future in our lives now. Because salvation is not complete, we strive toward, work out, and act in conformity with that which still lies ahead.

The need for Paul's moral encouragement, advice, and admonition thus derives from the discrepancy between who-we-are-called-to-be-as-Christians and who-we-actually-are (as shown by our actions and attitudes). Paul's advice, encouragement, and chastening help believers move from the latter to the former. This at least resembles virtue theory's tripartite structure: the imperative (e.g., precepts and injunctions) comes from the incongruity between our goal in Christ (what-we-could-be) and our actual state (what-we-happen-to-be).

Paul's eschatological framework is what makes this comparison to virtue theory possible. There would be no need for exhortation and human resistance to sin if the kingdom was fully here. But because we await the final consummation, there often is a discrepancy between what-Christians-are-called-to-be and who-we-actually-are. Without eschatological tension, there would be no need for the imperative. In light of that tension, there remains a need for moral encouragement and admonition—a need reflected in virtue theory's tripartite structure.

Reformulating Virtue Ethics: Grace

Before closing this chapter, I must point out, as I did with Matthew, that Paul's moral understanding does not leave virtue ethics unaltered. An ethic informed or influenced by the Pauline letters will necessarily fill out and reformulate a virtue ethic. Although I have mentioned it only in passing, Paul's emphasis on grace provides the most obvious example.

The emphasis on grace was implied in the discussions of moral growth and the relationship between the indicative and the imperative. For example, the language of "transformation" emphasizes God's prevenance in our moral growth. Similarly, the imperative rests on and assumes the indicative. It is because we have died with Christ to sin that we must now be instruments of God's righteousness (Rom 6:5–13).

A sense of grace permeates every facet of Paul's letters. God is the source of everything, including every right deed (Rom 8:28; 1 Cor 3:21–23; 8:6; Phil 1:6; 2:13). The contributions for the Jerusalem poor, for example, are attributed to God's grace (2 Cor 8:1; 9:8, 14). So is Paul's ministry (Rom 15:15; 1 Cor 3:5–7; 15:10; 2 Cor 3:5–6; 4:7; Gal 1:15–16).[129]

In Paul's understanding, humanity, when alienated from God, is incapable of consistently doing what is right, even when we want to do it (Rom 3:9–10, 22–23; 7:9–25; cf. 2:14–15). We are enslaved by the alliance of law, sin, and death. It is God's work through Christ that frees us from these powers (Rom 6:3–14; 7:4–6; 7:24–8:4; Gal 5:1). In Christ we are then set free for love and service (Gal 5:13). The Christ-event also creates community (Rom 12:3–8; 1 Cor 1:10–13; 3:3; 12:12–31) and tears down racial, social, and gender alienation (Gal 3:26–28; cf. Rom 1:16; 10:12; 1 Cor 7:22; Phlm 16).[130]

We depend on God's work through Christ; we also depend on the continuing work of the Spirit. Assorted qualities or virtues are "fruit" of the Spirit (Gal 5:22–24). The various "gifts" come from the Spirit and are for the common good (1 Cor 12:4–10). The Spirit also is the down payment on what is to come (Rom 8:23; 2 Cor 1:22; 5:5) and the active power behind the moral life (Gal 5:17–18; 25).[131]

In short, Christian living flows from God's act in Christ and is empowered by the Spirit's continuing presence. Within a Pauline framework, it makes no sense to talk about Christian morality without first, last, and always also talking about God's grace.[132]

Grace does not eliminate the need for human effort. Paul's stress on God's judgment indicates that responsibility for our actions accompanies our liberation in Christ (Rom 2:6, 16; 14:10–12; 1 Cor 3:8–15; 2 Cor 5:10).[133] Likewise, Paul's frequent moral exhortations are incomprehensible apart from the need for human striving. For example, the intelligibility of Paul's various challenges to the Philippians—to work out their salvation (2:12), help those who struggle with him in the gospel's work (4.3), and imitate him and other worthy examples (3:17; 4:8–9)—depends on human effort being necessary. God's merciful and empowering grace makes human effort possible but does not take its place.[134]

Nor does Paul's emphasis on grace establish a contrast between faith and ethics. Paul does reject the necessity of the Mosaic law, largely because he views the law as coming to an end in Christ (Rom 10:4; Gal 3:13). But this in no way establishes a gap between faith and praxis, grace and morality. Instead, Paul views the Christian life as requiring love's labor and the work of faith (1 Cor 3:13; Gal 5:6; Phil 1:22; 1 Thess 1:3). Indeed, Paul can even use "faith" as a synonym for "obedience" (Rom 1:5, 8; 10:16; 11:23, 30, 31; 15:18; 16:19). Grace is central in Paul's thought. But grace does not eliminate human effort or drive even a small wedge between faith and ethics.[135]

In summary, Paul's emphasis on grace provides a clear example of how the designator "Christian" can alter the meaning of "virtue ethics." Paul's vision of the Christian life does not exclude the need for human effort or separate the life of faith from the moral life, but Paul's focus on grace does add an element never mentioned in the earlier discussion of virtue theory. Thus, a virtue ethic claiming to be influenced by and compatible with Paul's moral vision would need to remain ever cognizant of our dependence on the Christ-event and the ongoing work of God and the Spirit. From a Pauline perspective, any growth and change in the self is a transformation made possible by God's grace.

CONCLUSION

This chapter undoubtedly leaves many aspects of Matthean and Pauline ethics unexplored. However, my objective was not to provide a comprehensive overview of Matthew or Paul but to note their possible correlation with and correction of virtue ethics. Several possible connections have been suggested. I noted both Matthew's and Paul's interest in "internal" qualities, their appeal to specific people as models or worthy examples, and their concern for an ethic that is both individual and corporate. I suggested, in addition, that Matthew's ethic is a perfectionist ethic and that his depiction of character traits and use of rules are congruent with virtue theory. I also pointed out Paul's interest in moral discernment, his use of images suggesting moral growth, and the relationship between the indicative and imperative. Thus, many of Matthew's and Paul's themes, concerns, and patterns of moral reasoning find similarities and counterparts in virtue theory.

While it stressed the possible similarities and links between virtue theory and the New Testament, this chapter did not argue that they are precisely equivalent. Indeed, this chapter highlighted three instances of where New Testament priorities would alter a virtue framework: Matthew's emphases on forgiveness and the centrality of Jesus, and Paul's emphasis on grace.

NOTES

1. In dealing with the Pauline material, I use only those letters where Paul's authorship is widely accepted: Romans, 1 & 2 Corinthians, Galatians, 1 Thessalonians, Philippians, Philemon. In appealing to the entire accepted Pauline corpus, I am following recent opinion that there is limited development within the letters. Cf. J. Christiaan Beker, *Paul the Apostle: The Triumph of God in Life and Thought* (Philadelphia: Fortress Press, 1980), pp. 32–33; Joseph A. Fitzmyer, "Pauline Theology," in *The New Jerome Biblical Commentary*, ed. Raymond Brown, Joseph Fitzmyer, and Roland Murphy (Englewood Cliffs: Prentice Hall, 1990), p. 1384; Roger Mohrlang, *Matthew and Paul: A Comparison of Ethical Perspectives* (New York: Cambridge University Press, 1984), p. 4.

2. I do not here deal extensively with the complicated hermeneutical issues. I do not argue for but assume the canon's authority and the usefulness of historical-critical and literary-critical readings of the text. I also do not discuss the criteria or precise nature of the continuity between Scripture's original meaning and its contemporary application. My use of Scripture in support of a virtue ethic does of course imply that virtue theory can be a meaningful and fitting contemporary appropriation of Scripture's moral import. See chapter 7 for further suggestions on the contemporary use of Scripture in ethics.

3. For example, Richard B. Gardner, *Matthew*, Believers Church Bible Commentary (Scottdale: Herald Press, 1991), pp. 90–98; Daniel J. Harrington, *The Gospel of Matthew*, Sacra Pagina Series (Collegeville: The Liturgical Press, 1991), 78–84. All Scripture quotations are from the New Revised Standard

Version Bible, copyright 1989, Division of Christian Education of the National Council of Churches of Christ in the United States of America.

This chapter does not attempt to discover or discuss the "historical Jesus." All references to Jesus are to the Matthean or Pauline Jesus.

4. Verhey refers to Matthew's version of the Beatitudes as calling for "certain character traits" and as constituting a "catalogue of virtues." Allen Verhey, *The Great Reversal: Ethics and the New Testament* (Grand Rapids: Wm. B. Eerdmans, 1984), p. 86; cf. Ulrich Luz, *Matthew 1–7: A Commentary*, trans. Wilhelm C. Linss (Minneapolis: Augsburg, 1989), p. 243.

5. For example, Harrington, *Gospel of Matthew*, pp. 87–91; Daniel Patte, *The Gospel According to Matthew: A Structural Commentary on Matthew's Faith* (Philadelphia: Fortress Press, 1987), pp. 78–79.

6. The regulations about retaliation (5:38–41) are illustrations of an attitude (desiring the welfare of one who would seek your harm), not just commands about specific actions. Cf. Ladd, *Theology of New Testament*, p. 129.

7. For example, the discussion of pious acts (alms, prayer, fasting) calls attention to the need for sincerity or purity of intention (6:1–8, 16–18).

8. For example, Gardner, *Matthew*, p. 275; Harrington, *Gospel of Matthew*, pp. 264, 266.

9. For example, Gardner, ibid., 333–37; John P. Meier, *The Vision of Matthew: Christ, Church, and Morality in the First Gospel* (New York: Paulist Press, 1979; reprint ed., New York: Crossroad, 1991), pp. 161, 164; Mohrlang, *Matthew and Paul*, p. 20.

10. Mohrlang, ibid., pp. 52, 114; Wolfgang Schrage, *The Ethics of the New Testament*, trans. David E. Green (Philadelphia: Fortress Press, 1988), pp. 43–45.

11. For example, George Eldon Ladd, *A Theology of the New Testament* (Grand Rapids: Wm B. Eerdmans, 1974), p. 130; Meier, *Vision of Matthew*, p. 101; Mohrlang, *Matthew and Paul*, pp. 52, 112.

12. "Compassion" may recall God's pity on Israel and point to Jesus' embodying or manifesting that same pity (Gardner, *Matthew*, pp. 167, 227). This does not alter Matthew's use of emotional terminology to depict the source or fountain of specific actions. Cf. Mark's depiction of Jesus, which portrays Jesus as operating from a fuller range of emotions (e.g., Mark 1:41; 7:34; 8:12; 10:14; 10:21).

13. Mohrlang, *Matthew and Paul*, pp. 113, 181n.49.

14. One need not be an ardent advocate of virtue theory to see a family resemblance between virtue theory and Matthew's concern with the "internal." George Ladd discusses the Sermon on the Mount as an "illustration" of "character" and "attitude," not as Law or legislation. Ladd's book shows little familiarity or interest in virtue theory; yet, when talking about Jesus' ethics, especially the Matthean texts, Ladd rejects legislative language in favor of words like character, attitude, and will. See: Ladd, *Theology of New Testament*, p. 129.

Thomas Ogletree's treatment of Matthew is similar. Although more familiar with and sympathetic to virtue theory, Ogletree also views obligation-dominant thinking as critical for Christian ethics. Yet Ogletree is so impressed with Matthew's focus on intentions, attitudes, and feelings that he views Matthew as expressing "in the language of law and commandment what might more appropriately be stated in the language of virtues" (Thomas W. Ogletree, *The Bible in Christian Ethics* [Philadelphia: Fortress Press, 1983], p. 111; also see, pp. 110–14; 196).

15. Cf. Luz, *Matthew 1–7*, pp. 346–47.

16. Jack Dean Kingsbury, "The Place, Structure, and Meaning of the Sermon on the Mount Within Matthew," *Interpretation* 41 (April 1987): 143.

17. Matt 19:21 (like 5:48) views perfection as the obligation of every Christian. "If you wish to be perfect" in verse 21 is the response to the question of what is still lacking (v. 20) to enter eternal life (v. 17; cf. v. 23). See Meier, *Vision of Matthew*, p. 140n.150; cf. Gardner, *Matthew*, pp. 294–95; Patte, *Gospel According to Matthew*, pp. 270–72.

18. Cf. Meier, *Vision of Matthew*, pp. 173–76.

19. Of course, Matthew would not use the language of "ideal." For Matthew the ethical norm is the "kingdom of heaven," God's eschatological rule that is encountered even now in the earthly and risen Jesus (e.g., 4:17). See, for example, Kingsbury, "Place, Structure, and Meaning," p. 143.

20. For example, Gardner, *Matthew*, pp. 162, 229; Kingsbury, ibid., and *Matthew as Story*, pp. 134–35, 144; Meier, *Vision of Matthew*, pp. 97–100; Ogletree, *The Bible in Christian Ethics*, pp. 95, 114.

21. Another biblical text that demonstrates a pronounced perfectionist thrust is the letter of James (e.g., 1:4; 3:2). James's perfectionism may come somewhat closer to a "brittle perfectionism" than does Matthew's.

22. A virtue ethic is also perfectionist in the sense of viewing as morally relevant every aspect of life and every voluntary human act. Although it is uncertain how Matthew's author would evaluate this sense of perfectionism, the intensity of the six "antitheses" (5:21–48) and Jesus' comments on the importance of speech (12:34–37; 15:10–11, 17–20) suggest a positive appraisal.

23. Cf. Luz, *Matthew 1–7*, pp. 224, 346; Schrage, *Ethics of New Testament*, p. 149.

24. Bonnie Thurston reads Matthew's call to be "perfect" as wholehearted discipleship. She suggests that this should not be understood as "a completed state of being," which is "an abstraction," but as following Jesus. "It is the person of Jesus whom we grow toward and follow in order to complete or mature ourselves. . . . It is the 'following after' which the rich young man found so difficult" ("Matthew 5:43–48," *Interpretation* 41 [April 1987]: 173). Although Thurston sees too much in specific verses, she offers a fair reading of Matthew's overall perfectionist thrust that bears obvious comparison with virtue theory.

25. For example, Jack Dean Kingsbury, *Matthew*, 2nd ed., Proclamation Commentaries (Philadelphia: Fortress Press, 1986), p. 83; Meier, *Vision of Matthew*, p. 73.

26. For example, Meier, ibid., pp. 45–51; cf. Wayne A. Meeks, *The Moral World of the First Christians* (Philadelphia: Westminster Press, 1986), p. 138.

27. Unlike the first century Jewish and Greek counterparts, Jesus' relationship to the disciples lacks a tone of engrossing study and scholarly exegesis. Moreover, unlike the student seeking a rabbi with whom to study, the disciples do not seek Jesus; he calls them (4:18–22; 9:9). In addition, discipleship in

134 Biblical Connections

Matthew is not a stage that ends when the disciple becomes a teacher or master. Jesus is always the Lord, and they are always the servants (10:24; 18:19–20; 24:35; 28:20; contrast Luke 6:40). See Eduard Lohse, *Theological Ethics of the New Testament*, trans. M. Eugene Boring (Minneapolis: Fortress Press, 1991), p. 48; Schrage, *Ethics of New Testament*, pp. 47–48; *Theological Dictionary of the New Testament*, 9 vols. trans. and ed. Geoffrey Bromiley (Grand Rapids: Wm. B. Eerdmans, 1964–1974), IV:444, 448–49, 455 (hereafter cited as *TDNT*).

Although not assumed in virtue theory's master/apprentice model, these aspects of Jesus' relationship with the disciples need not be seen as opposed to the virtue model. The virtue model neither demands engrossing study nor requires the student to initiate the relationship. And while the lifelong dependence on Jesus as master is unique, there is no reason to view it as negating the basic master/apprentice relationship.

28. The close association of the disciples and Jesus is highlighted in Matthew's use of the concept of "being with" (*meta* + genitive case) Jesus and the related idiom of Jesus' "being with" them (e.g., 18:20; 20:17–19; 26:18, 20, 36, 37–38, 40; 28:20). Through this language, Matthew limits the circle of those who are in close association with Jesus to his disciples and the church. See Jack Dean Kingsbury, *Matthew as Story*, 2nd ed. (Philadelphia: Fortress Press, 1988), p. 131; id., *Matthew*, pp. 83–85.

29. Cf. Lohse, *Theological Ethics*, p. 48; Mohrlang, *Matthew and Paul*, pp. 76–77, 90; *TDNT*, IV:441–42, 448–49.

30. For example, Kingsbury, *Matthew as Story*, pp. 139–140; Lohse, ibid., pp. 48–49.

31. A description of the master/disciple relationship in the Greek philosophical schools (e.g., those of Socrates and Aristotle) bears striking resemblance to Jesus and the disciples—including the importance of shared meals. Judaism's development of Rabbinic schools and their teacher/student or master/disciple relationship is apparently dependent, at least in part, on Hellenistic influences. Thus, there may be an indirect connection between the basic social practice familiar to Jesus and the practice of those who first articulated the importance to ethics of the master/apprentice relationship. Cf. *TDNT*, IV:417–40.

32. Matthew does not view this master/disciple relationship as limited to the earthly companions of Jesus. The church continues to share in this relationship, although obviously in a different way. This is seen when we combine the following three elements: (1) Matthew's efforts to foster the readers' identification with the disciples, (2) Matthew's use of the twelve, especially Peter, as a universal type for all disciples, and (3) Matthew's emphasis on Jesus' continuing presence within the church (18:18–20; 28:20).

On the first point, Matthew often cultivates either identity with or distance from the disciples depending on the attitude toward them expressed by Jesus or the narrator (Kingsbury, *Matthew as Story*, pp. 14–17). Matthew similarly fosters identification by referring to the disciples in familial terms (12:47–50; 18:35; 28:10) and as "little ones" (18:6, 10, 14) (Harrington, *Gospel of Matthew*, p. 19). On the second and third points, see, for example, Meeks, *The Moral World*, pp. 142–43; Meier, *Vision of Matthew*, pp. 97–100, 118–19; Schrage, *Ethics of New Testament*, p. 144. Examples of Peter as type for all disciples include the pericope of the walking on the water (14:22–33) and the call to take up one's cross (16:21–28).

33. Cf. Schrage, *Ethics of New Testament*, pp. 89–90.
34. For example, Harrington, *Gospel of Matthew*, pp. 246–72, especially p. 259; Meier, *Vision of Matthew*, pp. 106–35.
35. Harrington, ibid., p. 267.
36. For the following, cf. Gardner, *Matthew*, pp. 276–86; Harrington, *Gospel of Matthew*, pp. 263–72.
37. Cf. Patte, *Gospel According to Matthew*, pp. 253–54.
38. This point bears comparison with the role of rules in virtue theory. According to virtue theory, any community seeking a common good must set some standards. A group seeking a common end must identify, for example, the kinds of behavior that will exclude one from the group because that behavior impairs the group's movement toward the end.

Matthew's realization that some actions cannot be sustained, even within a church that is called to unlimited forgiveness, is similar. Matthew realizes that a community of limitless forgiveness still needs protection from unlimited offending. Thus Matthew, like virtue theory, recognizes that there must be some "fundamental ground rules of communal and social order" (Ogletree, *The Bible in Christian Ethics*, pp. 90, 199). The first Gospel is distinctive in that it outlines a process for deciding when one's sins surpass what the church community can tolerate. Instead of specific rules that determine when one is excluded from the community, Matthew outlines a process for determining when that line has been crossed. (Cf. Matthew's reluctance to anticipate divine judgment by separating the "weeds" from the "wheat" [13:24–30, 36–43].)

39. A focus on restoration/reconciliation is also clear from the context. The procedure's description is preceded by the parable of the lost sheep. This parable highlights both the concern devoted to reclaiming church members who have "strayed" and the joy that accompanies successful restoration. See Gardner, *Matthew*, p. 227. The procedure is then followed by both Peter's question concerning how often one should forgive (18:21–22) and the parable of the unforgiving servant (18:23–35). The emphasis in these stories is on forgiveness and mercy.
40. It is unclear whether the process is intended to cover all forms of sin or merely those committed against a fellow church member. "Against you" in verse 15 is absent from key manuscripts and may have been a scribal addition. If so, the offense was unspecified in the original text and the process covers all forms of sin. Cf. Gardner, *Matthew*, p. 281; Harrington, *Gospel of Matthew*, p. 268; Bruce M. Metzger, *A Textual Commentary on the Greek New Testament* (New York: United Bible Societies, 1975), p. 45.
41. Our moral interdependence is also seen in the warning not to put a "stumbling block" before "little ones" (18:6ff). This warning against causing others to sin recognizes that our mutual moral influence can be detrimental, not just positive.

Perhaps it is also significant in this regard that while the Matthean community had a group or groups that functioned as teachers, the first Gospel rejects titles such as "teacher," "rabbi," and "Father." Unlike the authoritative offices within Judaism, all members of the church are to serve each other, and all are "brothers." While this is a recognition of mutual dependence on God, it may also be a tacit recognition of our dependence on each other. See: 10:41; 13:52; 23:2–12; cf. Kingsbury, *Matthew*, pp. 103–5; id, *Matthew as Story*, pp. 156–58.

    42. A community context is particularly evident with regard to forgiveness. This section starts with Peter's question of how often one needs to forgive a "brother"—that is, a fellow member of the church (18:21; also see: 18:35). On the willingness to forgive, cf. 5:21–26; 6:12, 14–15. Since Jesus' command to become humble (18:3–4) is specifically addressed to the disciples (18:1), it also concerns the church community. Cf. the call to humility in the context of rejecting authoritative relationships within the church (23:8–12).

    43. Ogletree, *The Bible in Christian Ethics*, p. 121.

    44. Cf. Meier, *Vision of Matthew*, pp. 128–29.

    45. Cf. Ogletree, ibid., p. 127.

    46. Stanley Hauerwas and L. Gregory Jones, eds., *Why Narrative? Readings in Narrative Theology* (Grand Rapids: Wm. B. Eerdmans, 1989) is a useful anthology of theological and philosophical essays on narrative. The editors' opening essay (pp. 1–18) highlights different understandings of narrative and potential incompatibilities.

    47. MacIntyre, for example, views narrative as an important category for understanding the unity and connectedness of a human life and human action (*After Virtue*, pp. 204–25). In contrast, Nussbaum views narratives—especially certain forms of tragedy and fictional novels—as playing a vital role both in shaping character and in communicating things that elude standard forms of philosophical discourse. Nussbaum, *Fragility of Goodness*, pp. 378–94, "Flawed Crystals: James's The Golden Bowl and Literature as Moral Philosophy," *New Literary History* 15 (1983): 25–50, and "Narrative Emotions: Beckett's Genealogy of Love," in Hauerwas and Jones, *Why Narrative*, pp. 216–48.

While both MacIntyre and Nussbaum are using the term "narrative," it is less than obvious whether there is any connection between those uses.

    48. Kingsbury, *Matthew*, p. 92.

    49. Ibid., pp. 92–93.

    50. Cf. Mohrlang's discussion of *imitatio Christi* in Matthew (*Matthew and Paul*, pp. 76–77, 90).

    51. Kingsbury, *Matthew as Story*, pp. 10–28.

    52. Ibid., p. 14.

    53. Cf. Meier, *Vision of Matthew*, p. 180ff.

    54. Cf. Kingsbury, *Matthew as Story*, p. 111.

    55. For Matthew's use of various mechanisms to draw in and address the reader (e.g., historical present and imperative mood), see Kingsbury, ibid., pp. 36, 107–11; Patte, *Gospel According to Matthew*, p. 63.

    56. For example, Meeks, *Moral World of First Christians*, pp. 136–37; Mohrlang, *Matthew and Paul*, pp. 48–52, 68–70.

    57. Cf. Kingsbury, *Matthew as Story*, pp. 66–67; Mohrlang, *Matthew and Paul*, pp. 95, 107; Schrage, *Ethics of New Testament*, p. 148.

    58. Cf. Ulrich Luz, *Matthew 1–7*, pp. 215, 430; Schrage, *Ethics of New Testament*, pp. 79–81.

    59. Cf. Mohrlang's suggestion that the center or essence of the Sermon on

the Mount is not love but "righteousness," of which love is a crucial component (*Matthew and Paul*, pp. 98–99, 107).

60. Mohrlang, ibid., p. 21.

61. Cf. Mohrlang, ibid., pp. 96–98. Note also Mohrlang's acknowledgment that Matthew and Paul have somewhat different notions of love (p. 109).

62. It is striking that authors who assert the centrality of love are themselves unable to limit the discussion to the language of love. For example, Jack Kingsbury stresses the role of love in Matthew. Yet where Kingsbury emphasizes the centrality of love, he also talks about "greater righteousness," the role of law, humility before God, following Jesus' teachings, becoming servants of all, and models or examples provided by the first Gospel. In other words, despite claims about the crucial role of love, the language of love plays a minor role in Kingsbury's actual exposition of Matthew's ethics. See *Matthew*, pp. 85–93, especially pp. 92, 89.

63. When "law" is used by itself in Matthew, the reference is to the Pentateuch (the five books of Moses). Similarly, the expression "the law and the prophets" intends the entire Old Testament as it was known to Matthew's church. For example, Harrington, *Gospel of Matthew*, p. 91; Kingsbury, *Matthew*, pp. 85–86. In other words, when talking about the role of law in Matthew, we are talking about the Torah. And those who see Matthew's ethics primarily in terms of law view Matthew as advocating adherence to the Torah.

64. Texts like 7:12, 22:40, 23:23 and 24:20 show that Matthew's church followed the law as long as it did not conflict with Jesus' teaching and the requirements of love. Cf. Kingsbury, *Matthew*, p. 88; Luz, *Matthew 1–7*, p. 216.

65. As Patte notes, "the phrase 'fulfilling the law and the prophets' can have many connotations and thus by itself is quite ambiguous, as shown by the many proposals concerning its possible meanings" (*Gospel According to Matthew*, p. 71). Cf. Luz, *Matthew 1–7*, pp. 259–65; Mohrlan, *Matthew and Paul*, pp. 8–9, 16–17.

66. Kingsbury, *Matthew as Story*, p. 65.

67. Lohse, *Theological Ethics*, p. 70; Meier, *Vision of Matthew*, pp. 242–43; cf. Harrington, *Gospel of Matthew*, p. 86; Luz, *Matthew 1–7*, p. 285; Schrage, *Ethics of New Testament*, p. 60. It is significant that Jesus' sovereign "I say to you" in the antitheses repeats the phrase from 5:18, 20. The antitheses thus show the sense in which Jesus fulfills the law and the disciples are to exercise a "greater righteousness." Cf. Luz, *Matthew 1–7*, pp. 271, 279.

68. Cf. Luz, *Matthew 1–7*, pp. 285, 301–2, 317, 330, 344.

69. Cf. Gardner, *Matthew*, pp. 108–9; Kingsbury, *Matthew*, p. 87; Meier, *Vision of Matthew*, pp. 257–61; Schrage, *Ethics of New Testament*, pp. 60–61.

70. See Exod 20:7; 22:6–6; Lev 19:12; Num 30:3; 5:19–22; 30:17; Deut 23:22.

71. Exod 21:24; Lev 24:20; Deut 19:21.

72. Other possible abrogations of the law include the texts on divorce (5:31–32; 19:3–9) and defilement (15:10–11, 17–20).

73. For this and what follows, cf. Mohrlang, *Matthew and Paul*, pp. 19, 21, 25.

74. Cf. Luz, *Matthew 1–7*, p. 271; Mohrlang, ibid., pp. 24–25, 42–43, 47, 73–75.

75. Luz points out that the Lord's prayer is at the center of the Sermon on the Mount, and thus at the center of Matthew's first and longest ethical discourse (see *Matthew 1–7*, 367–90). Contra Willi Marxsen, *New Testament Foundations for Christian Ethics*, trans. O. C. Dean, Jr. (Minneapolis: Fortress Press, 1993), pp. 231–48. Marxsen sees nothing in Matthew except commands, demands, and the endless striving to earn God's approval.

76. Meeks, *Moral World of First Christians*, p. 140; cf. p. 142.

77. Luz, *Matthew 1–7*, p. 216; cf. pp. 328; 335. The remainder of this quote bears obvious comparison with virtue theory:

> He [Matthew] thinks of the Christian life most easily as a way which has the goal of perfection (5:20, 48) and whose direction and radicality are clearly marked by the individual commands, like tracers which are lighted by their goal. Matthew does not define what the definitive way is for the situation of each community and every Christian and especially not how far one is supposed to go on that way. He only says: as far as possible, in any case further than the scribes and Pharisees (5:20).

78. For example, Lisa Sowle Cahill, "The Ethical Implications of the Sermon on the Mount," *Interpretation* 41 (April 1987): 145–46, cf. pp. 147–49; Guelich, "Interpreting the Sermon," p. 129; Ladd, *Theology of New Testament*, pp. 128–29, cf. pp. 131–32; Richard Lischer, "The Sermon on the Mount as Radical Pastoral Care," *Interpretation* 41 (April 1987): 161, 163; Schrage, *Ethics of New Testament*, pp. 79–81. A. E. Harvey, *The Strenuous Commands: The Ethic of Jesus* (Philadelphia: Trinity Press International, 1990). Harvey views Jesus' use of legal forms and imperative declarations as teaching tools and challenging examples, not as strict rules of conduct.

79. Ogletree, *The Bible in Christian Ethics*, pp. 90, 114 respectively; cf. Kingsbury, *Matthew as Story*, pp. 132–33, and *Matthew*, p. 143.

80. This widespread agreement on Matthew's use of law language is particularly striking since there is little agreement among the cited authors as to Matthew's evaluation of the Mosaic law.

81. Although I believe that Matthew uses law language for various educative and descriptive purposes, there is no simple way to show this. It is the net effect of rules and commands throughout Matthew's narrative, not the result of a few specific verses. Luz's discussion of 7:12 (the "golden rule") is somewhat helpful (*Matthew 1–7*, pp. 428–31, especially p. 431).

The Sermon on the Mount is probably the most obvious example. The Sermon does not provide a comprehensive set of action-guiding rules or principles. Rather, through blessings, commands, and prayer, the Sermon paints images of faithful discipleship and God's approaching kingdom. See especially the hyperbolic commands at 5:29–30; 6:3, 6; 7:5.

82. Ogletree, *The Bible in Christian Ethics*, p. 196; cf. Patte, *Gospel According to Matthew*, pp. 73–74.

83. Cf. Patte, *Gospel According to Matthew*, pp. 73–74. The first Gospel's use of its sources also illustrates the need for discernment and wisdom in the appropriation of rules, laws, and commands. While scholars disagree on what changes Matthew makes to its sources, there is wide agreement that the first

Gospel's appropriation of those sources is informed by its author's context and various theological and ethical interests. Even Jesus' commands are not always conveyed or accepted without alteration. Those commands are interpreted in light of the needs, context, and interests of Matthew's community. In other words, Matthew's own appropriation of Jesus' commands illustrates the need for discretion and judgment in the interpretation/application of law language. Cf. Schrage, *Ethics of New Testament,* pp. 122–25; Lohse, *Theological Ethics,* pp. 29–30, 58–59.

84. Ogletree, ibid. I would argue that the action-guiding power of all deontological (and consequentialist) theories depends on a quality of skillful judgment that is akin to virtue theory's *phronesis.* However, unlike most modern ethical theories, the first Gospel never intimates that the application of rules is a linear or deductive process. Whatever the place of law language in Matthew, the first Gospel knows nothing of the supposed algorithmic principles of modern deontological theory. Cf. David Solomon, "Internal Objections to Virtue Ethics," in *Midwest Studies in Philosophy XIII Ethical Theory: Character and Virtue,* ed. Peter A. French, Theodore E. Uehling, Jr., and Howard K. Wettstein (Notre Dame: University of Notre Dame Press, 1988), pp. 437–38.

85. For example, Luz, *Matthew 1–7,* pp. 383–84, 389; Schrage, *Ethics of New Testament,* pp. 37–38.

86. Meier, *Vision of Matthew,* pp. 209, 245.

87. The first Gospel is filled with allusion, typology, and titles concerning Jesus. See, for example, Meier, ibid., pp. 52–68, 109, 116–19; Kingsbury, *Matthew,* pp. 33–65.

88. Cf. 16:18–19; 28:20. If Peter's walking on water (14:25–33) is a metaphor for the church, then we again see the church's dependence on Christ. Peter obeys Jesus' command and shares Jesus' power, but Peter remains dependent and ultimately needs Jesus to save him (Gardner, *Matthew,* pp. 228–29; Meier, ibid., pp. 98–100).

89. Meier, ibid., pp. 177–78.

90. I am not claiming that Paul's and Matthew's concerns and outlook are precisely the same in these areas. They are not. However, the differences are often subtle, and since our focus is on potential points of contact with virtue theory, these subtleties need not be explored here.

91. For example, Jerome Murphy-O'Connor, *Becoming Human Together: The Pastoral Anthropology of St. Paul* (Wilmington: Michael Glazier, 1982), pp. 83, 148–50; J. Paul Sampley, *Walking Between the Times: Paul's Moral Reasoning* (Minneapolis: Fortress Press, 1991), pp. 88–91. Daniel Patte, *Paul's Faith and the Power of the Gospel: A Structural Introduction to the Pauline Letters* (Philadelphia: Fortress Press, 1982), pp. 131–47, 171–75, 302–4 is helpful in calling attention to Paul's use of types and imitation, but he misconstrues their use.

92. See Robert F. O'Toole, *Who Is a Christian? A Study in Pauline Ethics* (Collegeville: The Liturgical Press, 1990), pp. 67–70, for suggestions on the emphases of these imitation texts.

93. Cf. Beker, *Paul The Apostle,* p. 248.

94. Paul is hardly unique in appealing to Jesus as model or example. In addition to the synoptics, see, for example, 1 Pet 2:21; 3:18; 4:1.

95. On virtue and vice lists in Paul, see Lohse, *Theological Ethics,* pp.

82–88; Murphy-O'Connor, *Becoming Human Together*, pp. 132–35; O'Toole, *Who Is a Christian?*, pp. 111–15.

96. Cf. Mohrlang, *Matthew and Paul*, pp. 104, 119–20.

97. Cf. O'Toole, *Who Is a Christian?*, p. 84. O'Toole is helpful in outlining several qualities, actions, and stances that Paul views as belonging to the Christian life (pp. 84–106).

98. O'Toole, ibid., pp. 29, 48, 65.

99. For example, E. Earle Ellis, *Pauline Theology: Ministry and Society* (Grand Rapids: Wm. B. Eerdmans, 1989), pp. 8–10, 42, 45–47; Murphy-O'Connor, *Becoming Human Together*, pp. 178–80.

"Body" language is one of several corporate images in the Pauline letters (cf. Beker, *Paul the Apostle*, pp. 307–8). This corporate dimension is often evident in Paul's use of "in Christ" or "with Christ," the various appeals to "baptism," the references to the community as a temple of God, and the idea of Christ as the new "Adam." See, for example, Beker, ibid., pp. 272–75; Ellis, ibid., pp. 8, 10, 42; Murphy-O'Connor, ibid., pp. 184–85; Sampley, *Walking Between the Times*, pp. 38–42.

100. Richard Dillon has suggested to me that we see here a substantial difference from virtue theory: as the above examples suggest, the corporate side of Paul's ethic is often aimed at building up the church, not at individual perfection subsidized by social connections. Dillon is largely right in his reading of Paul, but mistaken about the nature of virtue theory. As I noted in chapter two, virtue theory is not just concerned with individual perfection but also views various social relationships as intrinsic to the human good, as ends we seek for their own sake. Thus, Paul's emphasis on building up the church fits well with virtue theory's social or communal dimension. In both cases it makes good sense to seek the church's well-being even when there is no individual gain.

These comments must be balanced, however, with my discussion of Paul's real concern for individual moral responsibility and improvement. Moreover, as Sampley points out, Paul's commitment to community may be explained in part "by the ways the fellowship serves and assists the individual. . . . Community is the nurturing context within which the individual is expected to live" (*Walking Between the Times*, p. 43).

101. For the following, cf. Murphy-O'Connor, *Becoming Human Together*, pp. 159–60, 209–10; O'Toole, *Who Is a Christian*, pp. 44–49, 61.

102. I assume here that the conflict between "weak" and "strong" reflects a situation in the Roman church and is not simply a reworking of 1 Cor 8–10. An introduction to the debate concerning these texts and the occasion for Romans is found in Karl P. Donfried, ed., *The Romans Debate: Revised and Expanded Edition* (Peabody: Hendrickson, 1991).

103. Murphy-O'Connor underestimates the value of individuals in Paul's moral vision (see *Becoming Human Together*, pp. 102, 181–82). For a more balanced account, see for example, Sampley, *Walking Between the Times*, pp. 37, 42–47, 51, 55, 64–66, 70, 118–19.

104. E. P. Sanders, *Paul and Palestinian Judaism: A Comparison of Patterns of Religion* (Minneapolis: Fortress Press, 1977), p. 446.

105. Cf. Beker, *Paul the Apostle*, pp. 306–22.

106. The most obvious reason for this difference is their different understandings of the law's continuing role. Matthew tends to stress continuity with the Mosaic law—for example, the theme of prophetic fulfillment (2:5f, 17f, 23; 3:3; 4:14f; 8:17) and the affirmation of law (5:19). Paul sees the law, which has been co-opted by the powers of sin and death (1 Cor 15:56; cf. Rom 8:2–4), as coming to an end in Christ (e.g., Rom 10:4; Gal 3:13). Cf. Mohrlang, *Matthew and Paul*, pp. 27–34.

The different emphases on discernment may also stem from their different genres—that is, the situational and occasion-driven nature of Paul's letters readily lend themselves to an emphasis on discernment (see references in text).

107. For example, O'Toole, *Who Is a Christian?*, pp. 37–39; Sampley, *Walking Between the Times*, pp. 54, 63–64. The term "conscience" is also related to critical judgment of oneself and one's actions (e.g., Rom 2:15; 9:1; 13:5; 1 Cor 8:7, 10, 12). Joseph A. Fitzmyer, "Pauline Theology," p. 1414; Schrage, *Ethics of New Testament*, pp. 195–196.

108. For example, Murphy-O'Connor, *Becoming Human Together*, pp. 201–2; O'Toole, ibid., pp. 62; 121; Sampley, ibid., pp. 98–99.

109. Cf. Lohse, *Theological Ethics*, pp. 91–93.

110. See Beker, *Paul the Apostle*, p. 321; Ellis, *Pauline Theology*, pp. 35–39; Schrage, *Ethics of New Testament*, p. 198.

111. On the limited role of rules or maxims in Paul, cf. Sampley, *Walking Between the Times*, pp. 95–99.

112. A situational ethic is ruled out, for instance, by the norm and example of Christ (e.g., Rom 8:29) or the importance of "building up" fellow church members (e.g., 1 Cor 10:23; 14:4). On the singular direction yet concrete specificity of Paul's ethics, cf. Schrage, *Ethics of New Testament*, pp. 187–94.

113. For example, Fitzmyer, "Pauline Theology," p. 1401; Ladd, *Theology of New Testament*, pp. 519–21.

114. For example, O'Toole, *Who Is a Christian?*, pp. 17–18, 55–57; *TDNT*, V: 944.

115. Murphy-O'Connor, *Becoming Human Together*, p. 35.

116. This point is particularly evident in Gal 5:16–25 where a virtue and vice list is sandwiched between two different terms for walking or living (vv. 16, 25).

117. For example, Jerome Murphy-O'Connor, "The First Letter to the Corinthians," p. 807, and Brendan Byrne, "The Letter to the Philippians," pp. 796–97, in *The New Jerome Bible Commentary*; Sampley, *Walking Between the Times*, p. 20.

118. See, for example, Fitzmyer, "Pauline Theology," p. 1401; and Jerome Murphy-O'Connor, "The Second Letter to the Corinthians," in *The New Jerome Biblical Commentary*, p. 820.

119. For example, C.E.B. Cranfield, *The Epistle to the Romans*, 2 vols. (Edinburgh: T. & T. Clark, 1975–1979), 2:605–11; Joseph A. Fitzmyer, "The Letter to the Romans," in *The New Jerome Biblical Commentary*, pp. 855, 862.

Rom 12:2 reflects Paul's assumption that grace and human responsibility go together. By using the passive imperative "be transformed," Paul simultaneously gives the Spirit credit for the transformation and underlines our responsibility in allowing it to occur. Cf. Phil 2:12–13: "work out your own salvation . . . for it is God at work in you."

120. For example, Beker, *Paul the Apostle*, pp. 218–20; O'Toole, *Who Is a Christian?*, p. 86; Sampley, *Walking Between the Times*, pp. 20–22. Beker rightly points out that "sin" is not part of Paul's various images of growth. Sin is not tolerated or bemoaned as necessary and only rarely applied to the Christian life. Sin "belongs to the 'no longer' of Christian life" (p. 219).

121. For example, Beker, *Paul the Apostle*, p. 255; Michael Parsons, "Being Precedes Act: Indicative and Imperative in Paul's Writing," *Evangelical Quarterly* 88(2): 114; Schrage, *Ethics of New Testament*, p. 171.

122. Romans 6 provides a clear example of Paul's free movement from declaration to exhortation. For other examples of similar language used in both the indicative and imperative, see 1 Cor 5:7 or compare Gal 3:27 with Rom 13:14.

123. For example, Lohse, *Theological Ethics*, pp. 108–9; Parsons, "Being Precedes Act," p. 111. Contrast, for example, Meinert H. Grumm, "The Gospel Call: Imperative in Romans," *The Expository Times* 93 (May 1982): 239–42. Grumm so emphasizes the indicative (God's gracious act) that it is as if no effort or striving (the imperative) is necessary on the believer's part.

Other examples of the close relationship between indicative and imperative are found at Rom 12:1–2 and Phil 2:12–13. In both texts, God's gracious activity and our efforts are mentioned in the same breath.

124. For example, Beker, *Paul the Apostle*, pp. 277–78; Ladd, *Theology of New Testament*, pp. 524–25; Lohse, ibid., pp. 109–10; Mohrlang, *Matthew and Paul*, p. 118.

125. For example, Beker, ibid., pp. 152–59, 189–92, 215, 363–65; Fitzmyer, "Pauline Theology," pp. 1392–94; Ladd, ibid., pp. 369–73; Sampley, *Walking Between the Times*, pp. 7–24.

126. Cf. Schrage, *Ethics of New Testament*, pp. 181–83.

127. Parsons ("Being Precedes Act," p. 127) is cautious about the phrase "being precedes act" because it does not express the Spirit's role in the indicative/imperative connection.

128. Contra Kilner, "A Pauline Approach to Ethical Decision-Making," p. 373.

129. Mohrlang, *Matthew and Paul*, p. 86; O'Toole, *Who Is a Christian?*, pp. 17–20.

130. For example, Paul J. Achtemeier, *Romans*, Interpretation (Louisville: John Knox Press, 1985), pp. 16–17, 193–94; Beker, *Paul the Apostle*, 189–92, 215–17; Fitzmyer, "Romans," pp. 847–54, 865; O'Toole, *Who Is a Christian?*, pp. 22, 29–31, 79.

131. For example, Beker, ibid., pp. 278–83; Ellis, *Pauline Theology*, pp. 34–36, 45; O'Toole, ibid., pp. 23–25; Schrage, *Ethics of New Testament*, pp. 177–78.

132. Cf. Mohrlang, *Matthew and Paul*, pp. 86–89.

133. For example, Achtemeier, *Romans*, p. 217; cf. Mohrlang, ibid., p. 59; Schrage, *Ethics of New Testament*, pp. 184–85.

134. Cf. Kilner, "A Pauline Approach to Ethical Decision-Making," p. 368; Mohrlang, *Matthew and Paul*, pp. 118, 123.

135. Beker, *Paul the Apostle*, pp. 182–89, 245–48; Cranfield, *Romans*, 1:67; Lohse, *Theological Ethics*, pp. 159, 162–63; O'Toole, *Who Is a Christian?*, p. 88.

6

Theological and Biblical Objections

I cannot anticipate every or even most possible objections to the Christian appropriation of virtue theory. What I can do is address several objections that are likely to arise or are already suggested by the literature.[1] I will respond, in particular, to the following objections: (1) virtue theory is too self-centered or narcissistic to be truly Christian; (2) virtue theory is aristocratic and thus conflicts with Christianity's egalitarian thrust and sense of justice; (3) virtue theory is "sectarian"—encouraging withdrawal from the larger society or some form of relativism; (4) other ethical theories better reflect a basic Christian moral outlook.

The fourth objection is the most general and stands behind many nonvirtue accounts of Christian ethics. Objections one through three are related to each other. In part, these objections are reactions to virtue theory's self-referential nature. That is, they are directed at anticipated results or consequences of the individual's or community's concern with the cultivation of virtue and character. Virtue theory's self-reference is seen as ending in an ethic that (1) is narcissistic, or (2) is incompatible with social justice, or (3) encourages withdrawal and insulates one from those who ideas and concerns are different.

Despite their connection, these objections are separate criticisms and are here treated as distinct objections. The criticisms come from different writers and focus on different areas. The first is more focused on the individual than are the second and third, and the type of social concern in the second is different from that in the third. The third, finally, adds an epistemological element that is absent from the first and second. In short, these objections are distinct and require separate responses.

NARCISSISM

This objection is variously phrased. For instance, Wolfgang Schrage suggests that since love is self-surrender:

It cannot be self-realization. . . . Love is not a means to self-fulfillment. The end and measure of all things is therefore not . . . one's own virtuous life, but the well-being of others.²

Edward Lohse similarly suggests:

> Early Christian ethical instruction has no interest in encouraging a view of ethics as the development of one's self-understanding or the unfolding of one's own self-realization, but wants to show how Christians can live and act in a way that brings praise and honor to God.³

Others worry that virtue ethics is "self-centered" or they object to considering one's own virtues as a component in ethical decision making.⁴ In each case, the basic objection is that virtue ethics is self-centered or self-regarding while a truly Christian ethic is focused outside the self.

This objection is serious. We must be wary of doing the right or seeking the good solely because it will make us better. Moreover, an ethic that focuses exclusively on the individual's acquisition of excellence can hardly claim Christian status.

The objection fails at several points, however. First, ethical theories concerned with "doing the right" or "bringing honor and praise to God" or "seeking the well-being of others" implicitly share concerns regarding the self that are made explicit in a virtue framework. That is, ethical theories that seek the right or God's honor or another's well-being presuppose that we have or will develop the desires, tendencies, dispositions, and skills necessary to that end. Thus, theories that purport to focus outside the self simply assume that which virtue ethics makes explicit: we are or we can become the kind of people whose focus is directed outside ourselves and who embody the corresponding tendencies, dispositions, and skills.

Consider, for example, the concern that we do the right simply because it is right. This concern assumes that we are the kind of people who seek the right even when the specific instance does not make us more balanced or better integrated. But this assumption is a concern for virtue: we wish to be a certain kind of people (people who do the right even when they do not benefit) and the specific virtues we seek are those required or assumed by the central focus on doing the right (for example, justice, benevolence, and a desire to do the right).

The problem is not that virtue ethics is self-regarding. The real problem is that most nonvirtue theories, including those focused on God or others, fail to acknowledge their dependence on virtue considerations. Even an ethic focused outside the self entails a concern for virtue.

Second, it is not entirely fair to claim, as Edward Lohse does, that Scripture is unconcerned with the realization or fulfillment of the self. For instance, Paul's image of the Christian life as a race (1 Cor 9:24–27; Phil 3:11–17) and his challenges to "strive" for "spiritual gifts" and "to excel" in those things that edify the church (1 Cor 14:1, 12) suggest something akin to such fulfillment.

The New Testament also makes the seemingly paradoxical claim that our fulfillment or actualization comes from giving ourselves to others, not from a relentless focus on ourselves. Jesus announces a kingdom in which the one who would be first must be last (Mark 10:31), must be humble (Matt 23:12), must be a servant of all (Mark 9:35). One who wishes to save his or her life must be willing to lose it (Matt 10:39; 16:25; Mark 8:35). One who wants "treasures in heaven" must learn to give freely and trust God instead of riches (Matt 6:20; Mark 10:21–25; Luke 12:33). And one who desires life must choose the narrow, less traveled gate (Matt 7:14).

These apparently "upside down" assertions are, nevertheless, assertions about human fulfillment.[5] They claim that fulfillment, life, wholeness, and salvation belong to those who reach out in loving service. Human desires for wholeness and well-being are thus affirmed. The claim, however, is that those desires are satisfied through other-regarding actions and attitudes, not in some form of egotism. The New Testament is concerned with the self's realization or fulfillment but claims that such fulfillment cannot be found in a self-centered vision.

This seemingly paradoxical claim makes sense within a teleological virtue ethic. As we observed in chapter 2, a thing's true function, purpose, or role, is that thing's *telos* or end. So if, as the New Testament implies, our created function or role involves reaching out to God and others in love, then that other-regarding posture is essential to our end or *telos*, and the important virtues are those characteristics that constitute or lead toward that end.

In other words, accounting for human fulfillment as being found in other-regarding behavior is akin to saying, for instance, that a watch's function is to keep time. As a role or function of a watch is to keep time, so the role or function of a human involves other-regarding characteristics and behavior. True human excellence, the true human good, includes loving service to God and others.

In short, Scripture is concerned with human fulfillment, but not in a way that could be deemed self-centered or narcissistic. Moreover, a virtue framework easily accommodates the New Testament's vision of human fulfillment as being found in other-regarding characteristics and behavior.

Third, we should not lose sight of the New Testament's continual call for us to become certain kinds of people. The Beatitudes, Jesus' summons to love and humility, Paul's use of virtue and vice lists, and even the parable of the sheep and the goats challenge us to become certain kinds of people with certain characteristics and attitudes.[6]

If we are to honor this challenge, some of our moral reflection must be self-referential. That is, moral reflection must include consideration of how differing institutions, relationships, habits, practices, and particular actions will help or hinder our progress toward becoming the kind of people envisioned by Scripture.[7]

Unless we assume that one simply *wills* to be a certain kind of person, attention to how we are influenced by specific relationships, policies, practices, and actions is essential. Failure to attend to these influences is a denial of our finite, historical, and embodied nature. We are not angels standing outside our actions, untouched by our beliefs, histories, relationships, desires, and personal characteristics. As part of God's natural, created order, we are shaped in profound ways by biological, social, and historical forces.[8] Thus, if we are to honor Scripture's call, we must attend to the ways these forces influence and shape us.

We must, in other words, allow for some self-reference in moral reflection and deliberation. An ethic that seeks to fulfill Scripture's call cannot be exclusively other-regarding but must allow some self-regarding reflection. How would we fulfill Scripture's call if such self-reference were disallowed in moral reflection and deliberation?

Fourth and finally, it is simply odd to accuse virtue theory of being inherently narcissistic or self-centered since we can imagine many virtues that would be intrinsically other-regarding.[9] Justice, courage, and generosity lose something essential if they are unconcerned with the well-being of others. More important, many virtues that would belong to an explicitly Christian adoption of virtue theory are predominantly other-regarding—for example, faith, love, justice, and hospitality. How can ethic with so many other-regarding virtues be viewed as narcissistic, self-centered, or overly introspective?

In summary, the objection that virtue ethics is self-centered or narcissistic fails at several points: (1) even an ethic focused outside the self presupposes a concern for virtue; (2) Scripture is concerned with human fulfillment, and a virtue framework easily accommodates Scripture's vision that such fulfillment is found in other-regarding characteristics and behavior; (3) an ethic that responds to Scripture's call to become a certain kind of person must allow for some level of self-regarding reflection; (4) the Christian adoption of a virtue framework would include many other-regarding virtues.

ARISTOCRATIC TENDENCIES

Thomas Ogletree gives voice to this concern. He suggests that virtue theory is "aristocratic rather than democratic in . . . tendency." He sees this tendency arising from virtue theory's emphasis on individuals realizing "in their own beings what it is possible for human beings to become." Ogletree suggests that this may result in "a certain tolerance for human misery, inequality, and servitude provided the possibility for the accomplishment of human excellence is present for the worthy."[10] Ogletree goes on to note:

> When some fare well and attain much, it is almost always at the expense of others, indeed, not infrequently by virtue of the domination and exploitation of those others. Excellence achieved at such a price is morally dubious at best. It takes on a morally negative cast insofar as it is a function of structural forms of social injustice.[11]

The question is whether an interest in the individual's pursuit of human excellence is compatible with social (i.e., distributive) justice. An appeal for the Christian adoption of virtue theory must address this question, especially given Scripture's obvious concern for justice.

The key to this question lies in one's understanding of human excellence, of the human good or *telos*. As noted in chapter two, the human good or *telos* and various virtues are communal in nature. But since the good is a communal, shared good, and since many virtues derive their intelligibility (their point and purpose) from the shared pursuit of that good, then to cut others off from that good or excellence is to cut oneself off from it. In other words, since the human good is a shared, communal good, I cannot fully realize my *telos*, my good or end, without you.[12]

A genuine conflict with social justice arises only when the human good is conceived exclusively in individual terms. But the theory discussed in chapter 2 views the human good or *telos* as both individual and communal. The good toward which we aim is a shared, social reality that includes and makes possible the individual's thriving and excelling. When the good or *telos* is so conceived, it makes little sense to suggest that I can attain my good at your expense. I can fully excel only if we can excel.[13]

This assertion would be even more evident in an explicitly Christian virtue ethic. A Christian appropriation of virtue theory would view true human excellence, the true human good, as involving loving service to God and others. The individual's *telos*, his or her created role or function, includes other-regarding characteristics and behavior. Thus, it is not possible for me to excel at your expense: activities of exploitation and domination are contrary to a Christian notion of human excellence.

Put simply, if love, justice, and benevolence are part of the human good or *telos*, then it is nonsensical to suggest that one can excel through unloving or unjust activity. From a Christian perspective, the "faring well" and "attaining much" that comes "at the expenses of others" is not true human excellence.[14] Indeed, an understanding of human excellence that is achievable at another's expense more closely resembles Nietzsche's "will to power" and "Übermensch" than the visions proposed by either neo-Aristotelians or Christianity.[15]

Nevertheless, it must be acknowledged that a biblically informed Christian virtue ethic would not understand the content and character of "justice" in precisely the same way as some contemporary neo-Aristotelians. For instance, Alasdair MacIntyre reads Aristotle as supporting a form of distributive justice based on "desert in relation to contributions to the common tasks of that community in pursuing shared goods."[16] In this understanding, justice is a matter of what one merits or is due from his or her contribution to the common human good.

It is difficult to make generalizations about the meaning of justice in Scripture, but it is probably fair to say that a biblically informed understanding of justice will have a different emphasis than that suggested by MacIntyre's appeal to "desert" or merit. Biblical justice is preoccupied with the needs of those who are poor, weak, disadvantaged, or oppressed (e.g., Deut 24:17; Ps 10:17–18; Isa 10:1–2; Jer 5:28; Luke 4:18–19).[17] Biblical justice is thus less concerned with individual merit or excellence than with individual powerlessness and need. It is focused on aiding those in distress, not on calculating desert. It is more interested in protecting the powerless and enabling everyone to contribute than in identifying what some already contribute. In a biblical context, need and powerlessness are the most basic criteria for the distribution of benefits. It is only after this priority is met that ability and desert can become criteria for justice.[18]

This is not to suggest that biblical justice is somehow incompatible with a virtue framework. MacIntyre's appeal to the notion of desert is part of his attempt to highlight the individualism inherent in modern theories of justice. MacIntyre argues that theories as different as those of John Rawls and Robert Nozick share the presupposition that society is "but a collection of strangers, each pursuing his or her own interests under minimal constraints."[19]

Rawls's theory of justice focuses on the equal distribution of life's necessities and liberties. Nozick argues that justice concerns the just acquisition of property. But, says MacIntyre, both Rawls and Nozick share a view

> which envisages entry into social life as—at least ideally—the voluntary act of at least potentially rational individuals with prior interests who have to ask the question "What kind of social contract with others is it reasonable for me to enter into?"[20]

In other words, both Rawls and Nozick presume that society is really made up of a bunch of individuals who have little in common and who need to protect their own interests. Since their theories are built on this assumption, both Rawls and Nozick eschew any "notion of persons initially *bound together* in their pursuit of a *common* good."[21]

By contrast, a virtue conception of justice insists that we see ourselves as members of a community whose good we seek together. Justice is grounded in community and is guided by a shared understanding of the common human good, which includes both the individual's and the community's good. A virtue understanding of justice thus requires a substantive conception of what constitutes a good community and requires people to see themselves as linked together in more than an incidental way.[22] Such requirements are clearly at odds with many contemporary theories of justice.

This contrast between modern theories' individualist focus and virtue theory's focus on the shared human good accounts for MacIntyre's appeal to the notion of desert. The idea that one deserves something only makes sense in a social setting in which common commitment to shared goods determines the appropriateness of claiming that someone deserves this or that. MacIntyre claims, for example, that in an Aristotelian framework prices and wages would be based on what one deserves in terms of one's labor and its contribution to the community's good.[23] This way of testing the justice of prices or wages is quite different from asking about what the market will bear. It is also premised on the kind of shared commitment to a common human good that many modern theories of justice implicitly or explicitly seek to avoid.

MacIntyre is right to suggest that this is a "more Aristotelian and Christian view of justice."[24] The biblical context for justice is covenant community. For Israel and then the early church, justice concerned the social relationships among those who had been made a people by being covenanted to God. Scripture grounds its appeals for justice in God's creating a people by delivering them from oppression (e.g., Exod 22:21; 23:9; Lev 19:33–34; Deut 10:17–19; 24:17–22). Justice is linked to the creation and preservation of a specific kind of community (e.g., Lev 25:35–36; Ps 107:31–43; cf. Matt 6:33). Justice also serves the notion of a good community by using the plight of the weak and needy as a test of the community's health (e.g., Ezek 22:7; Zech 7:8–12; James 2:1–12).

Scripture's appeals for justice are therefore predicated on the existence of a certain kind of community with a specific history and self-understanding. Scripture, unlike Rawls and Nozick but like virtue theory, sees justice as grounded in community and as guided by a shared notion of what constitutes that community's good—that is, as guided by a vision of covenant relationship. While the emphasis is different from that suggested by MacIntyre's appeal to desert, a biblically informed view of justice is likely more at home in a virtue framework than in those offered by Rawls and Nozick.[25]

Chapters 4 and 5 highlighted several examples of how Christian thought may fill out and alter a basic virtue framework. The biblical view of justice provides another example of a Christian modification of a virtue framework: a biblically informed vision fits within virtue theory's community-oriented framework but views justice as directed to meeting basic human needs, especially the needs of the powerless, disadvantaged, and oppressed. The calculation of desert or merit will be secondary.[26]

I have thus far argued that virtue theory is compatible with distributive justice and that a Christian understanding of justice is focused on need. Before proceeding to the next section, I must admit that Ogletree is partially correct in characterizing virtue theory as "aristocratic rather than democratic in ... tendency." This admission is not an endorsement of one or another form of public government. Rather, it is a recognition of virtue theory's assumption that at any given time or circumstance some people will embody various virtues more fully than other people. Thus, some people's tasks will resemble those of teachers and leaders, while others will be more like students, learners, and even disciples.[27]

In this sense, virtue theory is more aristocratic than democratic in tone or flavor. Virtue theory does not assume that everyone has equal insight into every situation or that everyone's voice should carry equal weight in every decision. While open to abuse, this view is not inherently unjust. The notion that different people have different levels of moral insight and fulfill different tasks and roles is no more unjust than the recognition that parents and children or teachers and students often have different levels of insight and fulfill different roles.[28]

In sum, within a virtue framework it is almost unthinkable that human excellence could be achieved through the exploitation or domination of others. This would be especially true of a Christian appropriation of virtue theory: "excellence" achieved through the domination of others is counterfeit excellence. From a Christian perspective, true excellence involves reaching out to others in love and incudes a sense of justice that is more preoccupied with need than merit. Finally, virtue theory's "aristocratic" tone is not incompatible with social justice but simply recognizes differences in roles, needs, and abilities.

SECTARIAN

An often heard but seldom spelled out objection to virtue theory is the charge that it is "sectarian."[29] Although the meaning of this charge is often unclear, I take it that the central conviction is that virtue theory entails (1) social irresponsibility and withdrawal or (2) historical or epistemological relativism.[30] The sectarian charge suggests that virtue theory requires disinterest in and isolation from the rest of society or adopts some form of relativism, isolating its own claims from public defense or challenge.

Social Irresponsibility and Withdrawal

The "sectarian" objection has several problems. To start, the suggestion of social irresponsibility or withdrawal must confront virtue theory's inherent social nature. As noted in each of the previous chapters, virtues are not acquired in isolation. We learn the meaning of the virtues and slowly begin to acquire them by observing and living with others. Furthermore, many virtues find their point and purpose in social connections. Virtues as diverse as hospitality, justice, courage, friendship, and love relate us to others and demand that we seek their welfare.[31] Virtue theory is necessarily social, and it is difficult to reconcile this with the suggestion of social irresponsibility or withdrawal.

Of course, the issue may not be that virtue theory is too individualistic or private, but too little concerned with those outside one's particular community, too little concerned with broader culture and society. This way of phrasing the issue builds on virtue theory's contention that initiation and progress in the moral life depends on participation in a community that provides us with the requisite language, habits, dispositions, and skills. Such communities require consensus on many beliefs and practices and are thus restrictive in some way.[32] The fear is that this focus on community leaves little room for interest and participation in larger society.

Virtue theory can be used in ways that show disinterest in those outside one's community. The human history of excluding others—especially women, children, the poor, and people of other races and nationalities—suggests that any ethical framework can be used to exclude others. However, a virtue framework is not inherently incompatible with concern for or participation in broader society.

The question of compatibility depends in part on a community's understanding of various virtues. For example, to whom is hospitality directed? Is it operative outside one's community or only inside the group? Similarly, is justice apportioned according to merit or need or another measure? And is justice due equally to those inside and outside the community or are there different portions of justice? Comparable questions can be asked about most other-regarding virtues, and the answers help decide the extent to which an appropriation of virtue theory is compatible with concern for broader society. In other words, the basic notions and framework of virtue theory are compatible with concern for and engagement in broader society, but the extent of that compatibility is determined in part by how each community understands specific virtues. Depending on how the virtues are understood, a virtue ethic may urge extensive involvement beyond one's own community.

It is also important to note that from a virtue perspective, this question is not an "either/or" issue. There is no reason an individual or community must either be concerned with and participate in wider society or be uninterested and withdraw.[33] The individual or community may refuse to participate in aspects of the larger culture that are incompatible with the community's understanding of the virtuous life. This refusal is not necessarily a total rejection of the larger society.

The realization that specific activities or institutions are incongruent with the virtues is not equivalent to rejection of larger society. Indeed, this realization, while denying larger society's right to abrogate the virtues, can be part of a commitment to appropriate engagement. It can mean discerning and selective participation in larger society. Granted, what constitutes "appropriate" and "selective" is defined by the community striving for virtue.[34] But the point remains that such engagement can be extensive, albeit discriminating.

The effect of these remarks for a specifically Christian virtue ethic is that such an ethic can foster as great or as little engagement with those outside our communities as our understanding of the virtuous life permits. While the specific level of engagement depends on the particular Christian community and its social, cultural, and political environment, a Christian virtue ethic will likely fall between uncritical participation and total nonparticipation. Total nonparticipation is resisted by the gospel's message of reaching out to others, including one's enemies, in love. Uncritical participation is also unlikely since the gospel is often at odds with the prevailing culture and can only view that culture as in need of transformation.[35] There is, in short, no reason to assume that virtue theory, especially a specifically Christian virtue ethic, will be unconcerned with or refuse to participate in broader society and culture. That participation will likely be selective and discerning, however.

Relativism

There is something odd about accusing virtue theory of relativism. An ethic concerned with virtues such as honesty, truthfulness, and practical wisdom is not compatible with a strong relativism. These virtues are by definition concerned with what is honest, true, and reasonable. It is, in other words, difficult to understand how a charge of relativism can be leveled at a theory that seeks to engender people who are honest, reasonable, and open to the truth.

This "oddity" does not, however, make the point strongly enough. Virtue theory's internal intelligibility is premised on an epistemological realism. A teleological virtue ethic includes the notion of a determinant human good or *telos* and deals with how we move from our current state to that end (see chapter 2). This basic structure is predicated on realism. For example, the contrast between our current state and our *telos* depends on an ability to ascertain our true nature and assess any discrepancy between that nature and our current state.

One can debate how completely the *telos* is or can be grasped. One can argue about the ways in which it is uncovered and discuss the encounters, skills, or learning that will assist or obstruct its discovery. But if virtue theory is coherent, one cannot debate whether the human good or *telos* is open to discovery and communication or whether our current state can be described and tested against the *telos*. Whatever form of realism is promoted, a teleological virtue ethic presupposes the ability to be world—or reality—guided. Without this assumption, virtue theory's basic structure becomes incoherent.[36]

Admittedly, it is possible that those making the charge of relativism do not mean to say that virtue theory believes the world to be unknowable, only that it tends not to take conversation with other viewpoints seriously.[37] If this lesser charge is the real complaint, then it probably rests on the confluence of virtue theory's need for communities of consensus and its notion that some (those who embody the relevant virtues) are better able than others (those who lack the relevant virtues) to make correct moral judgments. The charge also may concern the notion, widely held among writers on virtue, that moral convictions are always the convictions of some specific group and will reflect their history, language, practices, and beliefs.[38]

The complaint then is that these notions conjoin in insulating a community's convictions from those who differ. I have already mentioned virtue theory's "aristocratic" tone: the assumption that at any given time some people will more fully embody various virtues and have greater insight into a situation than others. If this "aristocratic" assumption is inflexibly combined with emphases on historical particularity and the need for community consensus to guide virtue's formation, then virtue theory seems to allow or even encourage dismissing outsiders' perspectives as lacking the education in virtue necessary for judging rightly. After all, they (those outside our community) do not belong to a group that inculcates the relevant virtues through the proper training, language, and practices. Thus, virtue theory appears to isolate convictions from challenge and encourage a practical, if not theoretical, relativism.

While this situation is conceivable with virtue theory, it is not necessary or even likely. The unwillingness or inability to hear others is not inherent in the theory. Although virtue ethics can be used to insulate us from those who differ, it can just as easily include openness to other communities, traditions, and viewpoints. The need for communities of consensus may limit this openness, but the ability to engage others in discussion on areas of common concern is readily built into a virtue framework.

There is, for instance, good reason to think that diverse communities can engage in constructive dialog about the nature and content of various virtues and the good life. It is difficult to imagine a community or culture that lacks concepts of truthfulness and courage, for example. While the precise nature of these concepts may differ, such notions are prerequisites for the functioning and survival of most (if not all) conceivable forms of human community. Thus, most (if not all) communities have a significant point of contact and potential common concern.[39]

Similarly, unless a community believes itself to have a complete and comprehensive understanding of the human *telos*, contact and communication with others is essential—they may have insight into the human good that we lack. The need for a more adequate understanding of the human good provides a powerful incentive for seeking out and engaging others in dialog.

We cannot decide in advance what revisions a community should be willing to make or what convictions its members should be willing to abandon. All that is required to avoid the charge of relativism is an indication that the community is not completely closed to other communities and their convictions. A partial openness to others fits easily with virtue theory's need to better understand the human good and the various virtues.

In summary, the assumptions, structure, and coherence of a teleological virtue ethic require some form of historical and epistemological realism. Moreover, virtue theory can include the openness necessary to avoid the charge of practical relativism.

OTHER ETHICAL THEORIES

Among the objections to the Christian appropriation of virtue theory is the contention that another theory better reflects a basic Christian moral outlook. We can safely assume this contention lies explicitly or implicitly behind many nonvirtue accounts of Christian ethics. After all, when one puts forward a Christian ethic, one usually contends or assumes that that ethic accounts for basic Christian convictions.[40]

We cannot rule out a priori that another ethical scheme will better reflect basic Christian concerns and modes of moral reasoning. Indeed, since I am not familiar with every moral theory propounded within Western society, and since I am conversant with only a few theories discussed in non-Western society, I am not absolutely certain that virtue theory is the most helpful moral theory available to Christians. I do contend, however, that a neo-Aristotelian virtue framework is more helpful and appropriate to Christian thought than other major, well-known theories discussed in contemporary Western society.

Chapters 4 and 5 scanned a portion of the rich vision of Christian moral reasoning that emerges from systematic theology and the New Testament. Those chapters suggested that Christian moral reasoning includes concern for personal growth and transformation, focuses on both individuals and community, acknowledges the vital role we play in each other's moral journeys, refers to rules and commands, derives guidance from Christ's life and teaching, depends on the skills of "discernment" and "testing," and is ever in need of mutual forgiveness and God's grace. Chapters 4 and 5 also suggested numerous potential links and similarities between these concerns and virtue theory.

It is less obvious that other well-known moral theories can accommodate these various concerns and modes of reasoning. Theories centered in rules or duty have trouble accounting for Paul's infrequent appeal to rules, his insistence on discernment or testing, and his image of life as a race. Similarly, theories focused on consequences struggle to account for Matthew's respect for the law or the centrality of Christ's life and teaching.[41] In other words, theories focused on deontological or consequentialist thinking are ill-suited to express the wealth of Christian concerns and the vital role of such things as virtues, discernment, role models, and personal moral growth.

Certainly, most interesting moral theories include various elements—for example, rules, duty, consequences, community, and virtues. There are few "pure" ethical theories. However, when worked out, most "mixed" theories assimilate the various elements to one or two notions.[42] Virtue is often conceived only as the willingness or motivation to do one's duty or the ability to determine suitable ends and the means for achieving those ends.[43] Similarly, concern for community is often reduced to concern for those to whom we have obligations or for whom we should be seeking maximum well-being or happiness. Thus, when compared to either neo-Aristotelian virtue theory or Christian Scripture and theology, most ethical theories provide only thin accounts of such concepts as virtue, community, and personal growth.[44]

Another related problem is that contemporary theories desire a high level of systematization and codifiable law-like generalizations. The enlightenment's legacy is a vision of ethics that seeks formal elegance and an almost geometric clarity. Whether the writer is Henry Sidgwick, Immanuel Kant, G.E. Moore, R.M. Hare, or John Rawls, ethical theory's goal involves impartiality, universality, systematization, and a deductive calculus.[45] This vision of ethical theory mistrusts the untidiness suggested by Christianity's many moral concerns and modes of reasoning.

In other words, the vision underlying most ethical theories since the enlightenment is at odds with the multifarious concerns and modes of reasoning reflected in Christian Scripture and theology. Most ethical theories aspire to high levels of generalization, systematization, and math-like calculus. This aspiration does not mesh with the messy complexity and "subjective" (that is, discerning or prudential) nature of morality suggested in Scripture and theology.

The problem is not solved by the various forms of "situation" or "contextual" ethics. Such theories are reductionist. They try to discern or intuit what should be done in a specific situation guided only by a single principle of morality like love or response to divine action.[46] They do not seriously attend to norms and guidelines, the development of personal dispositions or capacities, a vision of the human good, and so on. Situation or contextual ethics, like most ethical theories since the enlightenment, fail to treat seriously many aspects of the moral life.[47]

In short, most ethical theories are ill-equipped to express the rich variety and complexity of Christian convictions and modes of reasoning. Many theories also tend to absorb the various ethical elements into one or two notions and thus provide only thin accounts of virtue, community, personal growth, and the human good. Moreover, the vision of ethics underlying most theories since the enlightenment is antagonistic to the untidy and many-faceted vision arising from Christian Scripture and theology. This is in striking contrast to the numerous connections and parallels seen in chapters 4 and 5 between virtue theory and Christian convictions.

I do not wish to deny the existence of many intriguing ethical critiques and theories from which we can learn. There can be no such thing as a Christian virtue ethic that never needs alteration. The vision of the human good is always being altered or refined and different Christian traditions will develop somewhat different accounts of the virtuous life.[48] Thus, we need not deny that a Christian virtue ethic can learn from liberation theologies, feminist ethics, developments in bioethics, and other practical and intellectual explorations.[49] Such critiques and theories may, for instance, enhance our vision of the human good.

Yet, even those critiques and theories readily appropriated by writers in virtue lack the extended and multifarious moral vision offered by a virtue framework. John H. Yoder's work, for example, is often used by writers interested in virtue and narrative.[50] But Yoder's work evidences little actual interest in the acquisition of virtue or personal growth and sanctification. While Yoder's discussions of community, pacifism, and church-state relations are helpful, it is a mistake to read him (or liberation theology or feminist ethics) as providing the kind of expansive moral vision that could substitute for a virtue framework.

My doubts about nonvirtue theories also include those critiques and theories that bear a family resemblance to virtue theory. Charles E. Curran's "relationality-responsibility model" resembles and shares much with a virtue framework.[51] That model has limitations, however. For instance, it so thoroughly grounds morality on relationships of responsibility that it lacks the teleological vision suggested by sanctification, Christology, Paul's image of racing, and the norm of Christ in Matthew. The relationality-responsibility model is thus unable to express the idea that we are on a journey whose goal is Christ-likeness. Although providing a fuller vision than most, the relationality-responsibility model is ultimately unable to express the full wealth of theological and biblical concerns.

In summary, most nonvirtue moral theories are ill-equipped to express the full range of Christian concerns and modes of reasoning. Even those from which we must learn and those that resemble a virtue framework have limitations. Such theories either do not or cannot express various aspects of the moral vision arising from Christian Scripture and theology.[52]

I cannot rule out that another ethical scheme will better reflect a basic Christian moral outlook. Still, the numerous and varied links and similarities with theology and Scripture suggest that a neo-Aristotelian virtue framework is more appropriate to Christian thought than other well-known theories discussed in contemporary Western society.[53]

CONCLUSION

There are, undoubtedly, other possible objections to a Christian virtue ethic than those raised in this chapter. We have, however, addressed several criticisms. Virtue theory, especially an explicitly Christian appropriation of virtue theory, is too other-regarding to be viewed as self-centered or narcissistic, and self-regarding reflection is an essential aspect of our response to Scripture's call to become a certain sort of person.

We have also seen that virtue theory is not incompatible with social justice because true excellence involves reaching out to others in love and cannot be attained through exploitation. Nor will adherents of virtue ethics withdraw from or be disinterested in the larger world. Rather, virtue ethics can encourage extensive involvement beyond one's own community. Its engagement will be selective and discerning, but this is not a refusal to participate in the broader society and culture.

In response to the charge of relativism, we looked at virtue theory's dependency on historical and epistemological realism and the potential for dialog with others concerning assorted virtues and the human good. Finally to the suggestion that other theories better reflect a Christian moral outlook, we argued that nonvirtue theories are ill-equipped and even adverse to expressing the variety and complexity of convictions and modes of moral reasoning seen in Scripture and theology.

Though these responses will not satisfy every critic; they hopefully open the door to further exploration and debate about the relative merits of virtue theory for Christians.

NOTES

1. Since my contention is that virtue theory is suited or helpful for Christian ethics, this discussion is limited to objections that are more theological or biblical in character. I leave to the authors cited in chapter 2 those objections that tend toward the more philosophical end of the spectrum.
2. Wolfgang Schrage, *The Ethics of the New Testament*, trans. David E. Green (Philadelphia: Fortress Press, 1988), p. 79.
3. Eduard Lohse, *Theological Ethics of the New Testament*, trans. M. Eugene Boring (Minneapolis: Fortress Press, 1991), pp. 215–16.
4. For example, Oliver O'Donovan, *Resurrection and Moral Order: An Outline for Evangelical Ethics* (Grand Rapids: Wm. B. Eerdmans, 1986), pp. 211–25; cf. Gilbert C. Meilaender, *The Theory and Practice of Virtue* (Notre Dame: University of Notre Dame Press, 1984), pp. 36–40; David Solomon, "Internal

Objections to Virtue Ethics," in *Midwest Studies in Philosophy XIII Ethical Theory: Character and Virtue*, ed. Peter A. French, Theodore E. Uehling, Jr., and Howard K. Wettstein (Notre Dame: University of Notre Dame Press, 1988), pp. 431–32, 434–35 (hereafter cited as *Midwest Studies XIII*).

5. The admittedly eschatological tone of these assertions should not be read as referring exclusively to the end of the age. The Gospels depict the kingdom as future, but also as influencing the present. Jesus thus claims that the messianic prophecies of Isaiah 35:5–6 and 61:1–2 are being fulfilled in him (Matt 11:2–6; Luke 4:21). If Jesus casts out demons by God's Spirit, "then the kingdom of God has come to you" (Matt 12:28). The kingdom is like a treasure whose possession outranks all other goods (Matt 13:44–46), and it is something to seek here and now (e.g., Matt 6:33). Similarly, Jesus can say of Zacchaeus that "today salvation has come to this house" (Luke 19:9). These examples point to the Gospels' affirmation that the kingdom is not only future but also "among you" (Luke 17:21). Cf. George Eldon Ladd, *A Theology of the New Testament* (Grand Rapids: Wm. B. Eerdmans, 1974), pp. 65–77; Allen Verhey, *The Great Reversal: Ethics and the New Testament* (Grand Rapids: Wm. B. Eerdmans, 1984), pp. 16, 18, 22.

6. See chapter 5. Although calling us to become certain kinds of people, the New Testament does not describe in detail how to cultivate the relevant characteristics and attitudes. It provides some clues (e.g., prayer, Jesus' example, the role of discipleship, care and accountability within Christian community), but it does not reflect extensively on the cultivation of character. We must look outside Scripture for this.

7. If this claim seems overstated, consider how much pastoral activity is geared toward generating a kind of self-reference in parishioners. Through prayers, counseling, and sermons, we encourage parishioners to test whether their actions and practices help or impede them from becoming the kind of people portrayed in Scripture. This is preciously the type of self-reference required by virtue theory.

8. Cf. Hendrikus Berkhof, *Christian Faith: An Introduction to the Study of the Faith*, Revised ed. trans. Sierd Woudstra (Grand Rapids: Wm. B. Eerdmans, 1986), pp. 189–90; James Wm. McClendon, Jr., *Systematic Theology: Ethics* (Nashville: Abingdon Press, 1986), pp. 62–67, 78–109.

9. Cf. Solomon, "Internal Objections," pp. 434–35.

10. Thomas W. Ogletree, *The Use of the Bible in Christian Ethics* (Philadelphia: Fortress Press, 1983), p. 32.

11. Ibid., p. 33; cf. Sarah Conly, "Flourishing and the Failure of the Ethics of Virtue," in *Midwest Studies XIII*, pp. 92–93.

12. Cf. Alasdair MacIntyre, *After Virtue*, 2nd ed. (Notre Dame: University of Notre Dame Press, 1984), pp. 174, 220, 258, and *Whose Justice? Which Rationality?* (Notre Dame: University of Notre Dame Press, 1988), pp. 104, 111, 203.

13. Cf. Cardinal Joseph Bernardin, "Why Virtues Are Basic to the Common Good," *Origins* 23 (October 21, 1993): 337–41; G. Simon Harak, *Virtuous Passions: The Formation of Christian Character* (New York: Paulist Press, 1993), pp. 37–40; Daniel Mark Nelson, *The Priority of Prudence: Virtue and Natural Law in Thomas Aquinas and the Implications for Modern Ethics* (University Park: The

Pennsylvania State University Press, 1992), p. 83; Nancy Sherman, *The Fabric of Character: Aristotle's Theory of Virtue* (Oxford: Clarendon Press, 1989), pp. 25, 109–11, 132–33.

Admittedly, depending on how a community's limits are conceived, others can be excluded, dominated, and exploited. That is, oppression of those outside the community is not conceptually incompatible with every vision of a community's good. Indeed, oppression of those outside the community need not be seen as unjust or even "oppressive"—justice may be understood as due only those within the relevant community.

This possibility is not unique to virtue theory. Depending on how the community's limits are understood, almost any ethic and theory of justice can be used to exclude and dominate. The issue is not whether virtue theory is compatible with social justice—it is. The real issue concerns any ethic and involves the following kinds of questions: How are the community's limits and boundaries understood? How is this community to relate to those outside its boundaries? What is the basis for admission into this community? Answers to these kinds of questions help determine if those outside the community can be dominated and whether their domination is understood to be morally problematic.

14. To Ogletree's credit, he admits in a footnote that the conflict with justice is "more true of popular understandings of perfectionism than of its more careful philosophical articulations" (*Bible in Christian Ethics*, p. 45n.30).

15. Cf. MacIntyre, *After Virtue*, p. 258.

16. MacIntyre, *After Virtue*, p. 251. See also, ibid., pp. 192, 202, and *Whose Justice?*, pp. 104–7, 119.

17. See also Ps 72:2; 82; 146:5–10; Isa 1:17; Mal 5:28; Matt 25:31–46; Luke 1:47–55; 7:21–30.

18. For this and what follows, see, among others, *The Anchor Bible Dictionary*, 1992 ed., s.v. "Just, Justice," III:1127–29; *The Eerdmans Bible Dictionary*, 1987 ed., s.v. "Just, Justice," 613–14; *Harper's Bible Dictionary*, 1985 ed., s.v. "Justice," pp. 519–20; Robert M. Veatch, *The Foundations of Justice: Why the Retarded and the Rest of Us Have Claims to Equality* (New York: Oxford University Press, 1986), pp. 23–39; Perry B. Yoder, *Shalom: The Bible's Word for Salvation, Justice, and Peace* (Newton: Faith and Life Press, 1987), pp. 28–38. Cf. Donald E. Gowan, "Wealth and Poverty in the Old Testament: The Case of the Widow, the Orphan, and the Sojourner," *Interpretation* 41 (October 1987): 341–53.

19. MacIntyre, *After Virtue*, p. 251.

20. Ibid.

21. Robert B. Kruschwitz and Robert C. Roberts, eds., *The Virtues: Contemporary Essays on Moral Character* (Belmont: Wadsworth, 1987), p. 194.

22. MacIntyre, *After Virtue*, pp. 244, 250–51, and *Whose Justice?*, pp. 122–23.

23. MacIntyre, *Whose Justice?*, p. 112.

24. MacIntyre, *After Virtue*, p. 251.

25. That a biblically informed vision of justice is compatible with a virtue framework appears even more likely when one considers the vice of *pleonexia*. According to MacIntyre, *pleonexia* is a vice opposed to justice and is best

understood as "acquisitiveness, acting so as to have more as such" (*Whose Justice?*, p. 111). *Pleonexia* is thus the tendency to engage in the activity of acquiring more simply for the sake of acquiring more. MacIntyre rightly suggests that such acquisitiveness is viewed by modern society as an economic virtue (ibid., p. 112, and cf. *After Virtue*, p. 254). But a biblical perspective will concur with the Aristotelian claim that such acquisitiveness is a vice, not a virtue. Indeed, the Scriptural claim is actually stronger than the Aristotelian assertion, for the bible views acquisitiveness or greed as both a vice against justice and as a form of idolatry—for example, Ps 10:2–3; Prov 1:19; Mark 10:21–25; Luke 12:15–21; 16:13–15, 19–25; 19:8–9; Rom 15:26–27; Eph 5:3, 5; Col 3:5; James 2:2–7.

26. MacIntyre's reading of Aquinas provides a helpful qualification of his reading of Aristotle. Although still concerned with what one is due, MacIntyre sees Aquinas as including the ideas that every human owes certain things to all other humans and that ownership is limited by human need. MacIntyre, *Whose Justice?*, p. 199.

27. Cf. MacIntyre, *Whose Justice?*, pp. 105–6.

28. An adequate notion of justice will recognize different roles, needs, and abilities. Without this recognition, justice would require, for instance, that parents treat all children exactly alike. But the priority and preferential treatment parents give their own children is proper and necessary to good parenting. Also proper is the parent's realization that his or her own children must be handled according to each child's specific personality, character, failings, and aptitude. Parents do not treat all children exactly alike, and unless we regard such differences as inherently unjust, our notion of justice must allow for diverse roles, needs, and abilities.

29. For a fuller and somewhat different treatment of this issue, see Joseph J. Kotva, Jr., "Christian Virtue Ethics and the 'Sectarian Temptation,'" *Heythrop Journal* 35 (January 1994): 35–52.

30. James Gustafson, "The Sectarian Temptation: Reflections on Theology, the Church, and the University," *Proceedings of the Catholic Theological Society* 40 (1985): 83–94; Scott Holland, "The Problems and Prospects of a 'Sectarian Ethic': A Critique of the Hauerwas Reading of the Jesus Story," *The Conrad Grebel Review* 10 (Spring 1992): 162–67; David Hollenbach, *Justice, Peace, and Human Rights: American Catholic Social Ethics in a Pluralistic World* (New York: Crossroad, 1988), p. 79; Wilson D. Miscamble, "Sectarian Passivism?" *Theology Today* 44 (April 1987): 69–77; Paul Nelson, *Narrative and Morality: A Theological Inquiry* (University Park: The Pennsylvania State University Press, 1987), pp. 122–39. Cf. O'Donovan, *Resurrection and Moral Order*, pp. 221–22; Gilbert C. Meilaender, *Faith and Faithfulness: Basic Themes in Christian Ethics* (Notre Dame: University of Notre Dame Press, 1991), p. 11.

It is never completely clear whether the sectarian charge is being leveled at virtue theory or only at specific proponents of virtue theory. Moreover, this debate is carried out in such a heated fashion that it is hard to determine which ideas, concepts, and theories are actually at issue. The debate's ferociousness suggests that it is as much a clash of personalities as it is a debate about the merits and shortcomings of certain moral and theological ideas. However, for the sake of this discussion, I assume the sectarian charge is leveled mainly at virtue theory and centers on the issues of withdrawal and relativism.

31. For example, MacIntyre, *After Virtue*, pp. 156, 223, 229, 244–55; Gilbert C. Meilaender, *Friendship: A Study in Theological Ethics* (Notre Dame: University of Notre Dame Press, 1981); Martha C. Nussbaum, *The Fragility of Goodness: Luck and Ethics in Greek Tragedy and Philosophy* (New York: Cambridge University Press, 1986), pp. 350–52, 362–66.

32. Cf., for example, Alasdair MacIntyre, *Three Rival Versions of Moral Enquiry: Encyclopaedia, Genealogy, and Tradition* (Notre Dame: University of Notre Dame Press, 1990), pp. 17, 69–64; Gilbert Meilaender, "Virtue in Contemporary Religious Thought," in *Virtue—Public and Private*, ed. Richard John Neuhaus (Grand Rapids: Wm. B. Eerdmans, 1986), pp. 18, 29.

33. Cf. this and what follows with Stanley M. Hauerwas, *Christian Existence Today: Essays on Church, World and Living in Between* (Durham: The Labyrinth Press, 1988), pp. 11, 15–16, 84, 113–22, 183–85, and "Will the Real Sectarian Stand Up?" *Theology Today* 44 (April 1987): 87; Meilaender, *Faith and Faithfulness*, pp. x, 9, 12, 20, 32–33, 116, 133–38, 146–50.

34. From a virtue perspective, a community striving for virtue cannot simply let the "masses" or "larger society" (i.e., those outside one's community) determine "appropriate engagement." Unless those outside the community are regarded as virtuous, allowing them to determine "appropriate engagement" leaves this vital judgment to those who may lack the skills, dispositions, and traits needed to judge wisely.

35. A tension between Christian convictions and the prevailing culture is recognized by "nonsectarians" like H. Richard Niebuhr. The incongruity and tension between Christian concerns and the larger society's practices and beliefs are "what gives sense ... to the whole Niebuhrian theme of social transformation through Christ" (Charles Scriven, *The Transformation of Culture: Christian Social Ethics after H. Richard Niebuhr* [Scottdale: Herald Press, 1988], p. 60).

36. Cf. L. Gregory Jones, *Transformed Judgment: Toward a Trinitarian Account of the Moral Life* (Notre Dame: University of Notre Dame Press, 1990), p. 39; MacIntyre, *Three Rival Versions*, p. 200.

37. This reading of the relativist charge was suggested by an anonymous reader of a draft of my "Christian Virtue Ethics and the 'Sectarian Temptation.'"

38. For example, MacIntyre, *Whose Justice?*, pp. 1–11, 388–403; Stanley Hauerwas, with Richard Bondi and David Burrell, *Truthfulness and Tragedy: Further Investigations into Christian Ethics* (Notre Dame: University of Notre Dame Press, 1977), pp. 9–10; Stanley Hauerwas, *The Peaceable Kingdom: A Primer in Christian Ethics* (Notre Dame: University of Notre Dame Press, 1983), pp. 1, 35, 59–62, 69.

39. Cf. MacIntyre, *After Virtue*, pp. 191–93; Lee H. Yearley, "Recent Work on Virtue," *Religious Studies Review* 16 (January 1990): 2–3. See also MacIntyre, *Three Rival Versions*, pp. 5, 58–126, 170–205, 225–36, and *Whose Justice?*, pp. 326–88.

Stanley Hauerwas makes the case that Aquinas and Aristotle had very different understandings of the virtue "courage" ("The Difference of Virtue and the Difference it Makes: Courage Exemplified," *Modern Theology* 9 [July 1993]: 249–64). This reminds us that even virtues like courage and truthfulness are not universal in any straightforward sense. Individuals and communities can mean quite different, even incompatible things, by courage, truthfulness, and so on. Yet, Hauerwas's ability to compare Aquinas's and Aristotle's notions of courage indicates that both were recognizable as concepts of "courage." For all their differences, there is enough family resemblance or analogical similarity to allow for conversation and a point of common concern. Indeed, it is this family resemblance that makes so rewarding a book like Lee H. Yearley's *Mencius and Aquinas: Theories of Virtue and Conceptions of Courage* (Albany: State University of New York Press, 1990).

40. One explicit example is Philip L. Quinn's argument that Christian ethics "is, at bottom, not an ethics of virtue but an ethics of duty" ("Is Athens Revived Jerusalem Denied?" *Asbury Theological Journal* 45(1): 50).

41. Theories focusing on consequences or "proportionality" also confront the New Testament's virtual lack of consequence calculation. Without negating the need for or helpfulness of consequence calculation, the New Testament's omission of such calculation from its rich moral vision questions the sufficiency of a Christian ethic centered on consequences. Cf. Ogletree, *Bible in Christian Ethics*, pp. 204–5.

42. Cf. Ogletree, ibid., p. 31; William Spohn, "The Return of Virtue Ethics," *Theological Studies* 53 (March 1992): 64–65; Trianosky, "What Is Virtue Ethics all About?" *American Philosophical Quarterly* 27 (October 1990): 340.

43. Duty assimilates the virtues in William K. Frankena's work: "The function of the virtues ... is not to tell us what to do but to ensure that we will do it willingly in whatever situations we may face" (*Ethics*, 2nd ed. [Englewood Cliffs: Prentice-Hall, 1973], p. 67, and see pp. 62–70). Robert M. Veatch also sees virtues as "only instrumentally important for producing right conduct" ("The Danger of Virtue," *Journal of Medicine and Philosophy* 13 [November 1988]: 445. See also his "Against Virtue—A Deontological Critique of Virtue Theory in Medical Ethics" in *Virtue and Medicine: Explorations in the Character of Medicine*, ed. Earl E. Shelp [Dordrecht: D. Reidel, 1985], pp. 329–45). Cf. MacIntyre, *After Virtue*, pp. 232–33; Walter Schaller, "Are Virtues No More Than Dispositions to Obey Moral Rules?" *Philosophia* (July 1990): 195–207.

44. The "proportionalism" debate reduces morality to questions of commensurate or proportionate reason and focuses on decisions, deeds, and acts. Questions concerning virtues, moral growth, community interdependence, and the educative function of rules, etc., receive little attention. This limited vision comes in part from Peter Knauer's assertion that commensurate reason "provides the criterion for every moral judgment" ("The Hermeneutic Function of the Principle of Double Effect," in *Readings in Moral Theology No. 1: Moral Norms and Catholic Tradition*, ed. Charles E. Curran and Richard A. McCormick [New York: Paulist Press, 1979], p. 2).

Similarly, although resembling an emphasis on "testing" or "prudence," the discussions of "right reason" focus on decisions, deeds, and acts, but pay scant attention to such things as other virtues and the relationships necessary to becoming prudential. For example, Josef Fuchs, "Naturrecht oder naturalistischer Fehlschluß?" *Stimmen der Zeit* (Juni 1988): 407–23. This evaluation is not changed by discussions of the fundamental option, conscience, and the goodness/rightness distinction. These discussions are not chiefly concerned with the acquisition of virtues, the nature of our communities, or a vision of the human *telos*. Instead they concern whether one is open and striving toward God and whether decisions and actions are morally right. Again, for example, Josef Fuchs, *Christian Morality: The Word Becomes Flesh* (Washington: Georgetown University Press, 1987), pp. 19–49, 118–33.

45. Cf. Stanley G. Clarke and Evan Simpson, eds., *Anti-Theory in Ethics and Moral Conservatism* (Albany: State University of New York Press, 1989); Albert R. Jonsen and Stephen Toulmin, *The Abuse of Casuistry: A History of Moral Reasoning* (Berkeley: University of California Press, 1988), pp. 278–303.

46. *The Westminster Dictionary of Christian Ethics*, 1986, s.v. "Situation Ethics," by James F. Childress.

47. Cf. Nelson, *Priority of Prudence*, p. 139.

48. See chapters 2 and 3.

49. These critiques and theories must also learn from virtue ethics. For example, Daniel Putman argues that "virtue theory can help sort out some of the assumptions behind discussions of caring and relational ethics" ("Relational Ethics and Virtue Theory" *Metaphilosophy* 22[3]: 231). Indeed, Putman is largely correct, I think, in suggesting that the "analysis of caring and empathy is part of that [virtue] movement" (ibid., p. 238).

50. Yoder's work, for example, shows up repeatedly in the indexes of Hauerwas's *The Peaceable Kingdom* and McClendon's *Ethics*.

51. For example, *Directions in Fundamental Moral Theology* (Notre Dame: University of Notre Dame Press, 1985), pp. 12–14, 21–23, 63–97, 188–94, 226–35. Cf. H. Richard Niebuhr, *The Responsible Self: An Essay in Christian Moral Philosophy* (New York: Harper and Row, 1963). I use Curran as the example since Niebuhr died having only begun writing his ethics.

52. In pointing out that nonvirtue theories, even some very helpful ones, do not account for the entire Christian moral vision, I am not affirming a "comprehensive complementarily." See Edward L. Long, Jr., *Survey of Christian Ethics* (New York: Oxford University Press, 1967), p. 312; Ogletree, *The Bible in Christian Ethics*, p. 45n.31.

"Comprehensive complementarily" assumes that the various elements of ethical reflection are independent of each other—as if virtue-based reasoning simply needs to be put alongside or added to other elements like rules, duties, and the assessment of consequences. This approach fails to see that if one accepts virtue-based reasoning in any significant degree, then such things as rules and duties cannot be viewed as independent. Instead, rules, duties, consequences, and so on must be seen as deriving their function and intelligibility from a specific (virtue) context: character formation within communities directed by a vision of the human *telos*. We cannot, in other words, simply add virtue to these other approaches because in recognizing the significance of virtue we fundamentally alter how those other elements are understood. Cf. Stephen E. Fowl and L. Gregory Jones, *Reading in Communion: Scripture and Ethics in the Christian Life* (Grand Rapids: Wm. B. Eerdmans, 1991), pp. 9–12,

24–25. A similar but less severe problem can be seen in the "multi-perspectival perspective" suggested by David Clowney, "Virtues, Rules, and the Foundations of Ethics," *Philosophia* (July 1990): 49–68, especially p. 66.

53. For a contrasting position, see Tom L. Beauchamp, "What's So Special about the Virtues," in Shelp, *Virtue and Medicine*, pp. 307–27, especially p. 323. Beauchamp argues that the virtue tradition adds nothing that cannot be equally well captured by competing ethical systems.

7

Conclusion: An Appeal for a Christian Virtue Ethic

I have argued throughout this book that virtue theory is compatible with Christian convictions and modes of moral reasoning, and further, that Christian convictions are better expressed in a virtue framework than in the theories currently dominant in Western theology and philosophy. I have, in short, argued for a Christian virtue ethic.

I supported these claims by highlighting potential links and parallels between, on the one hand, virtue ethics and, on the other hand, Christian theology and Scripture. I noted, for example, that both sanctification and virtue theory stress lifelong, goal-oriented moral growth and the transformation of character. I also noted that Christology enhances our understanding of sanctification's goal: clues to the content and meaning of that goal are found in Jesus' life and way. My treatment of Christology went on to argue that virtue ethics can focus on Jesus' paradigmatic humanity by pointing to him as our true *telos*. By viewing Jesus' life, teaching, death, and resurrection as providing vital clues to our true nature and end, virtue theory can voice Jesus' centrality in a way that is difficult to express in other ethical schemes.

The parallels between theological anthropology and virtue theory involve human agency and community. Both theological anthropology and virtue theory view us as self-forming agents who are neither completely determined nor completely free. Both theological anthropology and virtue theory also view community as essential to the moral life.

My treatment of Matthew and Paul suggested that they, like virtue theory, are concerned with dispositions and attitudes. Matthew and Paul also work from ethical perspectives that parallel virtue theory's concern for the individual's moral improvement in the context of relationships and corporate activity. Matthew's and Paul's pointing to various people as worthy examples similarly agrees with virtue theory's claim that we gain moral insight by attending to how such examples handled situations similar or analogous to our own.

In addition, my treatment of Matthew discussed its perfectionist thrust and its use of rules and law language. Matthew's perfectionism resembles virtue theory's notion that the *telos*, as an ideal of human excellence, always calls us toward a fuller realization of the human good. Matthew's use of rules and law language fits with virtue theory's idea that rules and laws serve various pedagogical functions.

I also remarked on Paul's language of discernment and his images of "walking" and "racing." Paul's language of discernment parallels virtue theory's notion of practical wisdom or prudence. But his infrequent appeal to rules or principles or methods of moral calculation places him in tension with many nonvirtue theories. Paul's images of "walking" and "racing" suggest virtue theory's emphasis on continuity and growth in the moral life. This emphasis is in contrast to the focus of most contemporary theories on discrete acts and dilemmas.

The indicative/imperative relationship in Paul's letters also resembles virtue thinking. Both the indicative/imperative relationship and virtue theory assume a link between who one is and what one does, between "being" and "doing." The indicative/imperative relationship also shows that the need for moral encouragement and admonition arises from the fact that we are not yet what we are called to be. This tension is reflected in virtue theory's tripartite structure: in both virtue theory and Paul's letters, moral instruction (including precepts, injunctions, and prohibitions) stems from a concern for the transition from who we are to who we could become.

Besides looking at similarities and parallels, I underlined several areas in which a basic virtue framework needs to be adapted, altered, and filled out if it is to be thoroughly Christian. The sections on sanctification and Paul's letters emphasized the priority of God's grace. Any ethic claiming the designation "Christian" must recognize our dependence on God's initial and sustaining grace. I likewise suggested that a virtue framework must be modified to fit personal eschatology's hope in "life after death," Matthew's emphasis on forgiveness, and the centrality of Jesus seen in Christology and Matthew. Another modification of virtue theory was suggested in chapter six's discussion of justice: biblical justice concentrates on need, not merit.

These points illustrate the types of alteration virtue theory must undergo if it is to be fully Christian. There is, however, no inherent tension or opposition between these points and virtue ethics. My discussions of forgiveness and justice suggest that such emphases refine and develop (rather than oppose) virtue theory's understanding of a community's life and practice. The section on sanctification showed that we can affirm God's prevenient grace without negating the need for moral growth or our active role in that growth. The section on personal eschatology stressed that hope in "life after death" is hope that the journey toward our *telos* does not end in death but continues beyond the grave. And the discussion of Christology argued that a virtue framework is better able than most to express Christ's centrality.

Besides showing virtue theory's parallels with and ready adaptation to Christian convictions, I buttressed by argument by addressing several objections to a Christian virtue ethic. Virtue theory is variously viewed as inconsistent with an emphasis on God's grace, self-centered, incompatible with distributive justice, and "sectarian"—encouraging withdrawal from larger society or some kind of relativism. I insisted, however, that these objections misread virtue ethics.

My response to those objections included the following arguments: (1) Grace makes our effort and moral growth possible but does not eliminate the need for effort and growth. (2) Virtue theory is too other-regarding to be viewed as overly self-centered. (3) A proper understanding of human excellence shows virtue theory's compatibility with, even demand for, distributive justice. (4) Virtue theory does not necessarily encourage withdrawal from larger society. A virtue ethic can advocate extensive, although selective, involvement beyond one's own community. (5) Theoretical or practical relativism is incompatible with virtue theory's internal coherence.

I also addressed the objection that other theories are better equipped to express Christian convictions (see chapter 6). I argued that it is the nonvirtue theories that are ill-suited to the variety and complexity of Christian convictions and modes of moral reasoning. While virtue ethics has parallels and links to many aspects of Christian thought, nonvirtue accounts are inadequate for the rich moral vision suggested by theology and Scripture. In addition to chapter 6, the sections on Christology and Paul's notions of discernment and moral growth highlighted points where a virtue framework is better suited to Christian convictions than are the currently dominant nonvirtue theories.

In short, my argument rests on four major points. First, virtue theory has many similarities and parallels to Christian convictions and modes of moral reasoning. These similarities range from sanctification's emphasis on moral growth to the logic underlying the indicative/ imperative relationship in Paul. Second, where obvious parallels are lacking, virtue theory is readily adapted to Christian convictions. There is, for example, no tension between a basic virtue framework and an emphasis on forgiveness. Indeed, some Christian convictions, like

Christ's normative humanity, find especially fitting expression in a virtue framework. Third, the common objections to a Christian virtue ethic misread the consequences of virtue theory's interest in the cultivation of character. Virtue theory is not inconsistent with grace nor is it self-centered, incompatible with distributive justice, or "sectarian." Fourth, nonvirtue ethical theories are inadequate to Christian convictions. Jesus' normative humanity and Paul's images of "walking" and "racing" are just two examples of Christian concerns that are barely mentioned or excluded in most nonvirtue theories. Even when one or two Christian convictions receive appropriate expression, nonvirtue theories fail to attend to or express the full range and scope of convictions and modes of reasoning suggested by Scripture and theology.

If these points are even partially correct, then there is a sense in which we need or would benefit from a Christian virtue ethic. Why a Christian virtue ethic? The most basic and substantial reason is that Christian convictions and modes of reasoning are compatible with and expressible in a virtue framework. The failure of nonvirtue theories to treat adequately the full range of Christian convictions provides an added motive. Moreover, since the common objections to virtue theory are misdirected, there is no immediate obstacle to the Christian appropriation of a virtue framework. In short, Christians need virtue ethics because virtue theory promises a fitting forum for the expression of our convictions and modes of moral reasoning.

ADDITIONAL BENEFITS OF VIRTUE THEORY

My principal argument is complete. However, before concluding, I want to suggest additional potential benefits of the Christian adoption of a virtue framework. I want, in other words, to round out my central argument with some further suggestions about how we as Christians might benefit from, how our moral reflection might be enriched by, virtue theory's account of the moral life.

It must be emphasized that these are suggestions, not completely developed arguments. They are meant to provoke thought and stimulate imagination. They are a way of hinting at or pointing to constructive possibilities that lie outside this work's purview.

Resisting Reductionist Pressures

Adopting a virtue framework would allow us to develop a structured account of the moral life in which many Christian concerns and modes of reasoning find expression. One potential benefit of such a multi-faceted account is an ability to highlight and remind us of the extensive considerations, resources, and issues deserving our attention.

Most of us live somewhat fragmented lives that do not embody the entire range of Christian convictions. It is difficult to keep in view the many considerations, resources, and issues that belong to a Christian moral outlook. Various societal and academic tendencies compound this difficulty by encouraging a curtailed or restricted moral vision. Our society emphasizes individual choice and autonomy but virtually ignores community interdependence. Our society also views as mere personal preference our choices of such things as books, movies, schools, and friends—concealing the degree to which such "mundane" choices reflect and reinforce moral character. Many current textbooks on ethics focus on modes of moral calculation or on dilemmas and quandaries but leave out consideration of character development, role models, visions of the human good, and so on. Even certain readings of the Christian story encourage a restricted moral vision. For instance, Christians who place great stress on individual salvation sometimes slight consideration of community and distributive justice. Conversely, those who place great emphasis on justice can overlook the importance of the individual's moral growth.

There are, in other words, many tendencies and pressures to circumscribe our moral vision. My suggestion is that we will more readily keep the whole range of Christian concerns in focus if we have an ordered account of the moral life that integrates many Christian themes and concerns. I argued that a virtue framework promises just such an account.

Said differently, I propose that the type of moral account made possible by the Christian adoption of a virtue framework will help offset assorted reductionist pressures. Take, for example, some of the reductionist tendencies mentioned here. A virtue framework's dual focus on individual and community might facilitate our keeping both in view. A Christian virtue ethic could not slight consideration of community since a virtue framework always views the individual in assorted social relationships. Conversely, virtue theory's stress on the cultivation of character focuses attention on individual moral growth. Similarly, attention to everyday, "mundane" choices and actions is demanded by virtue theory's perfectionist thrust. And, as indicated in chapter 6 above, disregarding distributive justice would be incompatible with a Christian virtue ethic's understanding of human excellence.

In short, a virtue framework may help counter reductionist pressures by providing an integrated, multi-faceted account of the moral life. Such an account would make it more difficult to focus exclusively on individual choice or moral dilemmas, for example, since that account would give at least an equally visible role to the counterbalancing themes of community interdependence and character development.

Exploring Themes Absent from Scripture and Theology

A further potential advantage of virtue theory is its exploration of concerns and themes absent from or only implied in Christian practices, theology, and Scripture.

For example, the moral role of friendship is seldom mentioned in Christian ethics and receives scarce attention in theological, biblical, or liturgical reflection. Yet authors in virtue theory underscore the moral significance of different types of friendships. Indeed, it is difficult to talk about a shared human good and the forces integral to the cultivation of character without discussing the assorted relationships we group under the label "friendship." Thus, adopting a virtue framework could prompt us to explore the importance of these relationships. Attention to authors in virtue theory might similarly spur our exploration of narratives, luck, imagination, memory, socially defined roles, and so on.[1]

In other words, virtue theory's potential benefits go beyond accommodating and recalling Christian convictions. It can also supplement and expand our moral reflection. Although Scripture and theology are rich moral resources, they are not exhaustive. Virtue theory can enrich and enlarge our moral vision.

Informing Our Reading and Use of Scripture

In chapter 5 I used the connections and parallels between Scripture and virtue theory to appraise virtue theory without explicitly exploring the role or roles Scripture would play in a Christian virtue ethic. I want now to propose that the Christian adoption of a virtue framework would carry with it various promising ways of understanding Scripture's present and ongoing moral significance. Adopting a virtue framework will, I suggest, enhance our perception of the ways in which Scripture continues (or can continue) to function morally.

The following examples will perhaps clarify what I have in mind. Consider, for instance, the Bible's collections of rules and commands. In a virtue framework, there is no slavish adherence to rules, but neither are rules rejected as irrelevant. Instead, when looking from a virtue perspective we see the Bible's collections of rules as encapsulating the guidance and wisdom of some who went before us in the faith. The community can then use those rules as part of its discernment process—continually testing whether those rules shed light on the community's current situation. A virtue framework would also support appealing to biblical rules when one lacks the time or ability to make his or her own prudential judgments. A Christian virtue ethic may also probe the Bible's collections of rules for images of the human *telos*.

Similarly, virtue theory's need to picture the human good might appeal to various aspects of Scripture. Stories of the Exodus, Jesus' interaction with disciples and strangers, parables and apocalyptic images of the kingdom of God, for example, could help shape our understanding of the human good.

A virtue perspective might also view Scripture as useful in shaping our accounts of particular virtues. One example of this is the suggestion (see chapter 6) that biblical justice is centered on need. Scripture studies could be used similarly to explore the content of humility, peaceableness, hospitality, fidelity, courage, and other virtues.

A virtue framework might additionally encourage exploring the moral impact of Scripture's liturgical role. It makes sense in a virtue framework to suggest, for example, that Scripture's integral part in the weekly ritual plays a key role in shaping our moral outlook and character. Virtue theory's interest in shaping character would encourage exploration of such suggestions.

These potential uses of Scripture are only examples, but they hint at the possibilities inherent in working from a virtue perspective.[2] Virtue ethics opens noteworthy avenues for understanding and appropriating Scripture's present and ongoing moral significance. By looking from a virtue framework we see manifold ways in which the Bible continues (or may continue) to have profound moral significance.

In short, I suggest that working from a virtue perspective would advance our understanding of Scripture's roles in the moral life. That perspective would enable proposals like the following: the Bible provides guidance encapsulated in rules, provides images of the human *telos*, informs our understanding of particular virtues, and shapes our identities and characters through its use in weekly ritual.

Virtue Theory and Christian Convictions: Mutually Edifying

In pointing to ways in which Christians might benefit from virtue ethics, I do not wish to suggest a "one-way street." I hope that it is already clear that I expect a mutually edifying union of Christian convictions and virtue ethics. Virtue theory can voice and expand Christian moral reflection, but Christian convictions also correct, refine, develop and enhance virtue theory.

For example, Christian belief in God's reconciling and empowering grace can serve as a corrective to virtue theory's potential for "works righteousness," grim determination, and even despair. Virtue theory calls us to endless moral progress. Without a sense of grace, this call could elicit the stern striving that robs life of its joy and readily falls victim to despair. It is easy to anguish over the slight moral progress we sometimes make. It is easy to despair at our backsliding and failure.

The Christian response to this is grace and forgiveness. We are not alone. God goes with us and before us, forgiving our failures and empowering us. God likewise calls our communities to forgive, restore, and empower. Virtue theory enjoins endless progress. The Christian faith reminds us that any progress is itself a gift of God and that we may always fall back on God's grace.[3]

Christian convictions could also be instrumental in filling out the virtue notion of a human *telos*. Philosophical accounts of the *telos* are often so general that they offer little moral guidance. A conspicuous example of this is MacIntrye's (admittedly provisional) definition of the human good in *After Virtue*: "the good life for man is the life spent in seeking for the good life for man, and the virtues necessary for the seeking are those which will enable us to understand what more and what else the good life for man is."[4]

While intriguing, this kind of definition does not provide an adequate picture of the human good. Virtue theory's tripartite structure depends on an at least partially determinate image of the human *telos*. Philosophical accounts often provide only the barest sketch of that end.[5]

Although professional philosophers often remain silent on the shape and content of the human *telos*, Christianity has many resources for developing fuller images of the human end. I suggested earlier that Christology and assorted dimensions of Scripture are such resources. In addition, areas of theological exploration as diverse as anthropology, creation, and revelation provide fertile ground for developing and refining pictures of the human *telos*. These theological categories include consideration of the kind of creatures we are, the roles and purposes for which we were created, and our relationship to ultimate reality. Such reflections can furnish rich, textured images of the human good. Our liturgical practices might provide a similarly prolific source for images of the human end. Prayer, confession, Scripture reading, homilies, and the like, assume and promote powerful images of who we are and where we should be headed.

I am not suggesting that one "Christian" image of the human end would emerge or that Christians would fully comprehend that end. Different Christian traditions will develop somewhat different pictures of the human good. We must also heed MacIntyre's reminder that our understanding of the *telos* will change and develop during our journey.[6] We would, in addition, be foolish to neglect the potential insights derived from philosophy, science, poetry, and other religious traditions.

The point is simply that Christians possess many resources for refining, filling out, and picturing the human good. Christian Scripture, theology, and practice can add substance, depth, and texture to the virtue notion of a human *telos*.

I look forward, then to a mutually edifying union of Christian convictions and virtue theory. This book's central argument is that virtue theory is compatible with and remarkably capable of expressing Christian convictions. Virtue theory may offer various additional benefits: countering reductionist pressures, stretching our moral reflection beyond what is obvious in Scripture and theology, and advancing our understanding of Scripture's present and ongoing moral roles.

Christian convictions will not leave virtue ethics unaltered, however. Christian convictions will correct, refine, and develop a basic virtue framework. An explicitly Christian virtue ethic must include, for example, the centrality of Jesus (chapters 4 and 5), an emphasis on forgiveness (chapter 5), and an understanding of justice that focuses first on need, and then on desert (chapter 6). In addition, a Christian understanding of grace can correct virtue theory's tendency toward a grim determination or works righteousness, and Christian convictions and practices can add content to the virtue notion of a human *telos*.

A virtue framework can voice and expand Christian moral reflection. Christian theology, Scripture, and practice can correct, refine, and develop a virtue framework. This combination is, I suggest, mutually edifying.

CONCLUSION

Soon after starting this project I talked about it with a good friend who is a Presbyterian minister. His initial response to it was, "There's nothing new here." This abrupt and seemingly harsh statement caught me off guard. After further discussion, I discovered that my friend's comment was not a challenge to this project's value. His comment was instead directed at what he took to be the obvious similarity between the Christian moral life and a neo-Aristotelian, teleological virtue ethic.

It seemed to him that Christianity presumes that the moral life is a journey toward becoming a certain kind of person within a certain kind of community. It seemed natural to him to focus on character and virtue, granting dilemmas only a secondary or ad hoc status in moral reflection. Similarly obvious to him were things like the need for moral growth and transformation, the importance of role models and mentors, and the helpful but limited nature of rules.

For my friend, the connections and compatibility between Christianity and virtue theory are obvious. This is not true for most. Many doubt that compatibility. Many fail to see compelling similarities or connections. This book tried to make the compatibility and connections more apparent. Indeed, I went as far as to claim that we need a Christian virtue ethic.

Nonvirtue accounts have thus far failed to do justice to the rich moral vision suggested in our theology and Scripture. Virtue theory, on the other hand, provides an ethical structure eminently suited to our convictions and modes of moral reasoning. Virtue theory has many similarities and parallels with Christian moral thought. It is also readily molded to and notably capable of expressing Christian convictions. And, as I suggested above, a virtue framework may expand and enrich our moral reflection in various ways.

There is then a sense in which we as Christians need virtue ethics: virtue theory offers an ethical framework notably suited to Christian convictions, modes of reasoning, and ongoing moral reflection.

NOTES

1. Current work on friendship is cited in chapter 1. The current work on luck and narrative is mentioned in chapters 2 and 4 respectively. Stanley Hauerwas offers some intriguing suggestions on memory and imagination—for example, Stanley Hauerwas, *Against the Nations: War and Survival in a Liberal*

Society (New York: Winston Press, 1985), pp. 51–90; cf. Craig Dykstra, *Vision and Character: A Christian Educator's Alternative to Kohlberg* (New York: Paulist Press, 1981), pp. 63–88. On role specific behavior, see Alasdair MacIntyre, *After Virtue*, 2nd ed. (Notre Dame: University of Notre Dame Press, 1984), pp. 59, 128–29; cf. James D. Wallace, "Ethics and the Craft Analogy," pp. 230–31 and David B. Wong, "On Flourishing and Finding One's Identity in Community," p. 331 in *Midwest Studies in Philosophy Volume XIII Ethical Theory: Character and Virtue*, ed. Peter A. French, Theodore E. Uehling, Jr., and Howard K. Wettstein (Notre Dame: University of Notre Dame Press, 1988), cited hereafter as *Midwest Studies XIII*.

2. Works that begin to explore the above mentioned uses of Scripture include Bruce C. Birch and Larry L. Rasmussen, *Bible and Ethics in the Christian Life*, revised and expanded edition (Minneapolis: Augsburg Fortress, 1989); Stanley Hauerwas, *A Community of Character: Toward a Constructive Christian Social Ethic* (Notre Dame: University of Notre Dame Press, 1981), pp. 53–71; Stephen E. Fowl and L. Gregory Jones, *Reading in Communion: Scripture and Ethics in Christian Life* (Grand Rapids: Wm. B. Eerdmans, 1991); Joseph J. Kotva, Jr., "Scripture, Ethics, and the Local Church: Homosexuality as a Case Study," *Conrad Grebel Review* 7 (Winter 1989): 41–61, and cf. my "Welcoming the Mentally Handicapped: A Case Study in Christian Character," *Restoration Quarterly* 34 (Fourth Quarter 1992): 223–37.

3. Cf. Hendrikus Berkhof, *Christian Faith: An Introduction to the Study of the Faith*, Revised ed. trans. Sierd Woudstra (Grand Rapids: Wm. B. Eerdmans, 1986), pp. 477–78.

Christian eschatology adds a similar note of hope to virtue theory's striving. Christian eschatology involves our clinging to God's promise that the kingdom will one day come and that our own journeys will not be without meaning. These are vital hopes for an ethic that otherwise offers death as the culmination and final word on our moral progress.

4. MacIntyre, *After Virtue*, p. 219.

5. Cf. Sarah Conly, "Flourishing and the Ethics of Virtue," in *Midwest Studies XIII*, pp. 88–93. Conly rejects virtue theory as offering accounts of the *telos* that are either arbitrary and ad hoc or "too broad to serve as a foundation for a theory of virtue and vice" (p. 90). Similar concerns are raised by Robert M. Veatch, "Against Virtue—A Deontological Critique of Virtue Theory in Medical Ethics" in *Virtue and Medicine: Explorations in the Character of Medicine*, ed. Earl E. Shelp (Dordrecht: D. Reidel, 1985), pp. 331–33 and R. Jay Wallace, "Virtue, Reason, and Principle," *Canadian Journal of Philosophy* 21 (December 1991): 469–70.

6. MacIntyre, *After Virtue*, p. 219. See also Stanley Hauerwas, "The Virtues of Happiness," *Asbury Theological Journal* 45(1): 21–24; Nancy Sherman, *The Fabric of Character: Aristotle's Theory of Virtue* (Oxford: Clarendon Press, 1989), pp. 9–11, 43–44, 84–94.

Index

agency. *See* human agency
Alderman, Harold, 56
anthropology. *See* theological anthropology
Aquinas, St. Thomas, 1, 44n.34, 162n.26, 163–64n.39
Archimedean point, 55–56, 58
Aristotle, 1, 27, 44n.34, 143n.31, 148, 162n.26, 163–64n.39

Beatitudes, 104, 132n.4, 146
Beauchamp, Tom L., 166n.53
Berkhof, Hendrikus, 72, 74–75, 77–78, 81–85, 88–89, 93n.1, 94n.8, 95nn. 26, and 27, 97nn. 50, and 56, 100n.98
bias, 70–71
Bondi, Richard, 62n.11
Buddhism, 56–57, 66nn. 41, and 42

Carney, Frederick S., 51
Cessario, Romanus, 53, 64n.26
character. *See* virtues
Christian tradition, 1, 48–49, 56, 58–61, 64n.27, 66n.42, 67–68nn. 47, 48, and 70. *See also* religious traditions
Christ-likeness, 72–74, 76, 78, 86, 95n.26, 100n.98, 120, 125, 158
Christology, 60, 69–70, 78–90, 93, 93n.2, 97nn. 57, and 58, 100n.98, 169, 175; as compatible with virtue ethics, 80–81, 85–86, 89–90, 93, 93n.2, 167, 169; nonvirtue theories inadequate to, 86–89, 167, 170
church, 50, 60, 85, 92, 99, 109–10, 115, 119–22, 124, 127, 134nn. 28, and 32, 135nn. 38, 39, 40, and 41, 136n.42, 137nn. 63, and 64, 139n.88, 140n.100, 141n.112
church discipline, 109, 135n.38
community 21, 34, 36, 64n.26, 90, 92, 108, 123, 129, 135–36n.41, 136n.42, 138n.77, 140nn. 99, and 100, 149, 152, 154–56, 160n.6, 161n.13, 163n.34, 176. *See also* church; friendship; Matthew's ethics, as individual and corporate; Paul's ethics, as individual and corporate; role models; *telos*, as individual and corporate
comprehensive complementarily, 165n.52
consequences: role of, 34, 45n.57
consequentialism, 26, 32–33, 45n.54, 66n.36, 139n.84, 156–57, 164n.40, 165n.52. *See also* virtue ethics, relationship to other theories
Conze, Edward, 66n.41
courage, 9, 11, 20–21, 45n.52, 146, 152, 155, 164n.39, 173
craft analogy, 18–20, 80
Curran, Charles E., 158

179

death, 76–78, 94n.6, 97n.54, 127, 129, 141n.106, 169
denominations, 59–60, 67–68n.47, 70–71, 79. *See also* ecumenicism
deontology, 32, 34, 46n.70, 63nn. 14, and 16, 66n.36, 116–18, 139n.84, 156–57, 164n.43
dilemmas, 31, 124, 171–72, 176. *See also* quandaries
Dillon, Richard, 140n.100
discernment, 31–37. *See also* Matthew's ethics, discernment in; Paul's ethics, discernment in; prudence
discipleship, 80–81, 89, 98n.72, 100n.100, 107, 112, 114, 117, 133–34n.27, 134nn. 28, 31, and 32, 137n.67, 138n.80, 151, 160n.6
Donahue, James A., 63n.16
Dunne, Joseph, 71
Dyck, Arthur J., 63n.14

ecumenicism, 2, 59–61. *See also* denominations
emotions, 10–12, 23–24, 26, 104–6, 120–21, 132n.12
epistemology, 57–58, 143, 153–55, 159. *See also* relativism
Erickson, Millard J., 72–73, 75, 77–78, 94n.8, 94–95n.19, 95n.26, 96n.36
eschatology, 126–28, 160n.50, 177n.3; personal component of, 71, 76–78, 94n.6, 96–97n.50, 97nn. 54, and 56, 102n.110, 168–69

feminist ethics, 10, 101n.101, 158, 165n.49
Finger, Thomas N., 96n.44, 101n.102

forgiveness, 61, 74, 109–10, 168, 174–75. *See also* Matthew's ethics, forgiveness in
Fowl, Stephen E., 67n.44
Frankena, William K., 48, 51, 164n.43
freedom, 72–73, 82, 84 86, 90–91, 93
friendship, 6, 10–12, 21, 23, 28–29, 33–34, 36, 39, 41n.17, 63n.17, 152, 172, 176n.1
Fuchs, Josef, 164–5n.44
functional concepts, 17–18, 40–41n.8, 41n.9, 145
fundamental option, 165n.44

Gadamer, Hans-Georg, 58
Gospel of Matthew. *See* Matthew's ethics
grace, 74–76, 91, 127–30, 141n.119, 168–70, 174
Grumm, Meinert H., 142n.123

Harvey, A. E., 138n.78
Hauerwas, Stanley, 44n.42, 50–52, 62n.12, 70–71, 94n.10, 136n.46, 163–64n.39, 176n.1
Herms, Eilert, 63n.16
Hick, John, 56
Himes, Michael J., 14n.13
historical consciousness, 8–10, 14n.13
human agency, 26–29, 38, 44n.37, 90–91, 146. *See also* moral luck
human good. *See* telos
humility, 109–10
Hunter, James Davison, 14n.11

incarnation, 79, 83–84, 86
intellect, 23–24, 26, 28, 80
internal qualities, 104–6, 120–21. *See also* emotions; Matthew's ethics,

internal qualities (*continued*)
  role of internal qualities in; Paul's ethics, role of internal qualities in Islam, 55–57, 64n.27, 66n.42, 67n.43

Jesus Christ: as embodiment of human *telos*, 69, 78, 80, 81, 83–90, 93, 97n.57, 100–101n.99, 101nn. 100, and 101, 119, 167; historical encounter with, 79, 84–86; historical investigation of, 82, 85–86, 99nn. 86, and 88, 132n.3; as irrelevant for ethics, 87, 99–100n.96, 100nn. 97, 99, and 100; resurrection as validation of, 84. *See also* Christology
Johnson, Elizabeth A., 97n.58, 101n.101
Jones, L. Gregory, 50, 67n.44, 136n.46
justice, 21, 23, 33–34, 45n.52, 88, 114, 143–44, 146, 147–50, 152, 159, 161nn. 13, and 25, 162n.28, 168–71, 175

Kingsbury, Jack, 111–12, 137n.62
Knauer, Peter, 164n.44
Kraus, Norman C., 79–81, 87–89, 98n.71, 100n.98
Krieg, Robert A., 97n.58
Küng, Hans, 100n.100

Ladd, George, 132n.14
law. *See* Matthew's ethics, law in; Paul's ethics, law in; rules
liturgy, 173, 175
Lohse, Edward, 144–45
Louden, Robert B., 45n.48
love, 21, 72–73, 78, 80, 82–84, 87–88, 91–93, 120–21, 125, 129–30, 143–46, 148, 151–52, 157, 159; of enemies, 104, 113–14, 153. *See also* Matthew's ethics, love in
love of enemies, 104, 113–14, 153
luck. *See* moral luck
Luz, Ulrich, 117, 138nn. 75, and 77

McClendon, James Wm., 52, 54, 63–64n.20, 64n.21, 65n.30
MacIntyre, Alasdair, 7, 17, 40n.3, 43n.33, 54–55, 58, 64n.27, 65nn. 32, and 34, 98n.71, 136n.47, 148–50, 161n.25, 162n.26, 174
Macquarrie, John, 73, 75, 78, 94n.8, 95nn. 22, and 23, 95n.26, 97nn. 50, 54, and 56
Marxsen, Willi, 138n.75
master/apprentice relationship, 80–81, 89, 107–8, 119, 134nn. 27, 31, and 32, 151
Matthew's ethics, 103; antitheses in, 104, 115–16, 133n.22, 137n.67; as compatible with virtue ethics, 105–8, 110–11, 113, 116, 131, 132n.14, 138n.77, 167–68; depiction of character traits in, 111–12; discernment in, 117–18, 138–39n.83, 139n.84; eschatological warnings in, 113–14; forgiveness in, 109–10, 118–19, 135nn. 38, and 39, 136n.42, 168; as individual and corporate, 108–10, 135nn. 38, 39, 40, and 41, 136n.42; Jesus as norm in, 111, 115–16, 118–19, 133n.19, 137n.64, 139n.88, 156; law in, 113–18, 137nn. 63, 64, 67, and 72, 138nn. 77, 78, 80, 81, and 83, 139n.84, 141n.106, 156, 168; literary devices in, 110–13, 134n.32, 136n.55; love in, 103, 113–14, 118, 137nn. 62, and 64;

Matthew's ethics (*continued*)
  master/apprentice relationship in, 107–8, 119, 134nn. 27, 31, and 32; as perfectionist, 106–7, 133nn. 17, 22, and 24, 138n.77, 167–68; role of internal qualities in, 104–6, 132n.12, 167; as shaping the reader, 112–13, 136n.55
Meeks, Wayne, 116
Meilaender, Gilbert C., 49
Moltmann, Jürgen, 100n.99
moral deliberation. *See* prudence; discernment
moral growth, 24, 27–29, 43n.26, 45n.52, 74, 76, 81, 91, 93, 95n.19, 96n.36, 109, 124–25, 152, 169, 171, 174. *See also* virtues, how acquired
moral luck, 29–30, 39

narcissism. *See* virtue ethics, as narcissistic
narrative ethics, 110–11, 136nn. 46, and 47, 172
Nelson, Daniel Mark, 40n.3
Nelson, Paul, 65n.34
neo-Aristotelian, 13n.4, 148
Niebuhr, H. Richard, 163n.35, 165n.51
Niebuhr, Reinhold, 100n.97
Nozick, Robert, 149–50
Nussbaum, Martha, 18, 27, 29, 35, 40n.3, 43n.33, 117, 136n.47

Ogletree, Thomas W., 109–10, 117, 132n.14, 147, 150, 161n.14

Patte, Daniel, 137n.65, 139n.91
Paul's ethics, 53, 103, 131n.1; as compatible with virtue ethics, 123–29, 131, 140n.100, 167–68; discernment in, 122–24, 141nn. 106, and 107, 156, 168–69; eschatology in, 126–28; grace in, 127–30, 141n.119; the indicative and imperative in, 126–28, 142nn. 122, 123, and 127, 168; as individual and corporate, 121–23, 129, 140nn. 99, and 100; law in, 127, 129–30, 141n.106; moral growth in, 53, 124–26, 168; role models in, 119–20, 139n.94; role of internal qualities in, 120–21, 127, 167; rules in, 123–24, 141n.111, 156; similarities to Matthew's ethics, 119–23, 139n.90
Phillips, Derek, 7
Pinckaers, Servais, 42–43n.25
Pincoffs, Edmund L., 36, 43–44n.33, 44n.34, 117
Placher, William, 56, 67nn. 45, and 46
pleonexia, 161–62n.25
Porter, Jean, 63n.16
practical wisdom. *See* prudence
prayer, 6, 96n.44, 116, 118, 132n.6, 138nn. 75, and 81, 175
predestination, 75, 96n.36
proportionalism, 164nn. 41, and 44
prudence, 9, 31–37, 39, 45n.52, 118, 122–24, 138–39n.83, 139n.84, 141nn. 106, and 107, 164–65n.44, 168
purgatory, 97n.54

quandaries, 5, 171. *See also* dilemmas
Quinn, Philip L., 48, 164n.40

Ramsey, Paul, 100n.97
Rawls, John, 149–50, 157

relationships, 21–22, 33, 39, 45n.52, 90, 92, 108, 123–24, 134n.28, 146. *See also* friendship; community
relativism, 57–58, 65–66n.36, 143, 153–55, 159, 169
religious convictions: priority of 1, 57–59, 66–67n.42
religious traditions, 55–57, 59, 64n.27, 65nn. 32, and 36. *See also* Christian tradition
Roberts, Robert C., 43n.33
role models, 6, 21, 29, 36–37, 39, 46n.72, 107, 111, 113, 119, 139n.94, 176. *See also* master/apprentice relationship
Rorty, Amelie O., 43n.33
rules: limits of, 8, 32, 35, 46n.70, 88–89, 165n.52, 176; role of, 34–36, 95n.19, 116–17, 135n.38, 138n.77, 156, 173

Sachs, John R., 101n.102
sanctification, 60, 69–78, 94n.6, 124–25; as compatible with virtue ethics, 50, 73–74, 76, 78, 93, 96n.44, 167; as dependent on grace, 74–76; other terms for, 94n.9; as teleological, 72–74, 76–78, 93, 94n.10; as unfinished, 76–78, 96–97n.50, 97n.54
Schillebeeckx, Edward, 85–86, 88–89, 99nn. 86, 88, 89, 94, and 95
Schrage, Wolfgang, 143–44
sectarianism, 59, 143, 151–53, 162–63n.30, 166n.35, 170
self-reference, 143–47, 159, 160n.7
Sermon on Mount, 104, 106, 132n.14, 136–37n.59, 138nn. 75, and 81
Sherman, Nancy, 32, 40n.3, 43n.33
Singh, Nripinder, 55

sin, 90–91, 95n.26, 109, 127–29, 135nn. 38, 40, and 41, 141n.106, 142n.120
situational ethics, 141n.112, 157
Stocker, Michael, 10–11
Stout, Jeffrey, 14n.11, 67n.45

Taylor, Richard, 49
telos, 17–20, 37–39, 40n.3, 59, 69, 72, 76, 78, 80, 85, 87, 89, 93, 95n.26, 98n.71, 100n.101, 145, 147–48, 154–55, 164n.44, 169; as active, 20, 22; content of, 20–23, 38, 42n.20, 174, 177n.5; as individual and corporate, 21–22, 34, 41n.17, 92, 102n.110, 108, 140n.100, 147–50, 152; relationship of rules to, 36–37, 173; role of virtues in, 20–23, 25–26
theological anthropology, 69, 90–93; compatible with virtue ethics, 90–93, 157
Thurston, Bonnie, 133n.24
Torah, 116, 118, 137n.63
truth claims, 55, 57–59
truth-telling, 65–66n. 36, 155

universals, 65–66n.36

Veatch, Robert M., 164n.43
Verhey, Allen, 132n.4
virtue ethics, 5, 16–39; additional benefits of, 170–76; as aristocratic, 147, 150–51, 154; as compatible with Christian convictions, 1–3, 48–61, 64n.27, 67n.44, 68n.48, 143, 150–51, 153, 156–59, 161–62n.25, 167–70, 174; confusion about, 16; consequences in, 34, 45n.57; as

virtue ethics (*continued*)
  narcissistic, 49, 143–47, 159, 169; neo-Aristotelian, 2, 16; objections to, 76, 143–59, 169; as perfectionist, 37–39, 46n.73, 106; reformulation of, 2–3, 60–61, 69, 74, 76, 78, 91, 93, 104, 118–19, 129–31, 150, 157–58, 168, 174–75; relationship to other theories, 5, 7–8, 10–13, 21, 30–34, 39, 45n.54, 46n.70, 54–55, 63n.14, 65n.30, 123–24, 144, 149, 156–58, 165n.52, 169, 171; as relativistic, 151, 153–55, 159, 169; renewed interest in, 5–13; as resisting reductionist pressures, 10–13, 170–72; as response to historical consciousness, 8–10; as response to moral decline, 6–8; rules in, 34–36, 46n.70, 135n.38, 173; as sectarian 162–63n.30, 169–70; teleological structure of, 2, 17–20, 38, 145, 154; as tradition-neutral, 55–56, 65n.34; tripartite structure of, 17, 19–20, 38, 128–29, 168, 174. *See also* Christology, as compatible with; Matthew's ethics, as compatible with; Paul's ethics, as compatible with; sanctification, as compatible with; theological anthropology, as compatible with; virtues

virtues: how acquired, 6, 9, 11, 24, 27–29, 30, 35, 107–8, 152, 154, 160n.6; infused, 64n.26; instrumental value of, 25–26, 43n.29; list of, 43n.33; nature of, 23–26, 38, 42–43n.25, 152, 173; priority of, 30–31; role in discernment, 33, 151, 154, 163n.34; satisfaction in, 25–26; as ends in themselves, 25–26, 43n.29. *See also* prudence; *telos*, role of virtues in

Wadell, Paul, 63n.17
Walker, Margaret Urban, 44n.42
Wallace, James D., 43n.33
will, 146. *See also* emotions
worthy examples. *See* role models; master/apprentice relationship

Yoder, John H., 99–100n.96, 158